THE SECURITY OF SELF

THE SECURITY OF SELF

A Human-Centric Approach to Cybersecurity

Edited by Emily B. Laidlaw and Florian Martin-Bariteau

University of Ottawa Press
2025

Les Presses de l'Université d'Ottawa / University of Ottawa Press (PUO-UOP) is North America's flagship bilingual university press, affiliated to one of Canada's top research universities. PUO-UOP enriches the intellectual and cultural discourse of our increasingly knowledge-based and globalized world with peer-reviewed, award-winning books.

www.Press.uOttawa.ca

Library and Archives Canada Cataloguing in Publication

Title: The security of self : a human-centric approach to cybersecurity / edited by Emily B. Laidlaw and Florian Martin-Bariteau.
Names: Laidlaw, Emily B., editor | Martin-Bariteau, Florian, 1987- editor
Series: Law, technology, and media.
Description: Series statement: Law, technology, and media | Includes bibliographical references.
Identifiers: Canadiana (print) 20250270234 | Canadiana (ebook) 20250270439 | ISBN 9780776645605 (softcover) | ISBN 9780776645612 (hardcover) | ISBN 9780776645629 (EPUB) | ISBN 9780776645636 (PDF)
Subjects: LCSH: Computer security. | LCSH: Behavioral cybersecurity. | LCSH: Computer security—Psychological aspects. | LCSH: Microcomputers—Access control.
Classification: LCC QA76.9.A25 S43 2025 | DDC 005.8—dc23

Legal Deposit: Fourth Quarter 2025
Library and Archives Canada

© Emily B. Laidlaw and Florian Martin-Bariteau 2025
All rights reserved.
Creative Commons Open Access Licence
Attribution-Non-Commercial-Share Alike 4.0 International (CC BY-NC-ND 4.0)
By virtue of this licence you are free to:
Share — copy and redistribute the material in any medium or format.
Attribution — You must give appropriate credit, provide a link to the license, and indicate if changes were made. You may do so in any reasonable manner, but not in any way that suggests the licensor endorses you or your use.
Non-Commercial — You may not use the material for commercial purposes.
No Derivatives — If you remix, transform, or build upon the material, you may not distribute the modified material.
No additional restrictions — You may not apply legal terms or technological measures that legally restrict others from doing anything the license permits.

Production Team

Copy editing	Tanina Drvar
Proofreading	Lauren McClellan
Typesetting	Édiscript enr.
Cover design	Benoit Deneault

Cover image
Marie-France Larocque, *Watching Me*, acrylic, 2022

We gratefully acknowledge the Social Sciences and Humanities Research Council of Canada, Canada Research Chairs Program and University of Ottawa Research Chairs Program.

PUO-UOP gratefully acknowledges the funding support of the University of Ottawa, the Government of Canada, the Canada Council for the Arts, the Ontario Arts Council and the Government of Ontario.

About the Cover Art

Watching Me, acrylic, 2022

This piece represents the fear of the unknown engendered by a constantly changing society. Social media, like the eye in the web, invades us and spies on us. The city no longer has any secrets. Human beings no longer have any secrets. Marie-France Larocque (née Carisse), originally from Ottawa, has been painting since a young age. She discovered abstract art during the COVID-19 pandemic, following the death of her father. Her art escapes into colour and experiments with different materials and finishes. She paints under the name CarisseArt, inspired by her father's name, Arthur. Her greatest pleasure is to let her imagination run wild and then discover what her work reveals through the eyes of others—a lucid abstraction, as she describes it. Her social media profile is at: https://facebook.com/carisseartpp/.

Table of Contents

CHAPTER 11

List of Figures

Acknowledgements

The idea for this volume grew in an organic manner within the vibrant Canadian technology and cybersecurity policy community. Through a series of conversations and advocacy, and long conversations between the editors and with the authors in the margins of convening across Canada, it became apparent that Canada's cybersecurity policy was broken and an exercise of reframing may be needed.

In June 2023, we convened a group of Canadian thought leaders from various disciplines to join us in a workshop hosted at the University of Concordia to discuss the idea and lay the foundation of what became this collection. We are extremely grateful to the colleagues who accepted to join us on this adventure—and to adapt and revise their manuscripts as the Canadian policy context kept changing, up to the prorogation and the call for an election in the winter of 2025. We would also like to thank the many peer reviewers who undertook to provide thoughtful reviews within relatively tight time frames. We are deeply indebted to all of them for their perseverance and for their commitment to this project.

We are greatly appreciative as well for the excellent copy-editing work of Valerie Lennox (J.D. '25) at the University of Calgary Faculty of Law and her remarkable attention to detail. Support for the workshop, the copy-editing work as well as the cost of editing and publishing this manuscript under an open access licence was made possible thanks to the financial support of the Social Sciences and Humanities Research

Council of Canada (SSHRC) through the Human-Centric Cybersecurity Partnership, the Canada Research Chair in Cybersecurity Law, and the University of Ottawa Research Chair in Technology and Society.

Finally, our warm thanks to the teams at the University of Ottawa Press. Their enthusiastic response to our project proposal is very much appreciated. As always, it has been a pleasure to work with them.

We hope that you will enjoy this book and that you will find it to be a thoughtful reflection on some of the policy issues and challenges that face us in the near future.

Conceptualizing Security of Self

Emily B. Laidlaw
and Florian Martin-Bariteau

*C*ybersecurity is a powerful term that draws political and policy
attention, as well as legal and financial risk. The assumption
is that we all know what we are referring to when the term "cybersecurity" is used. However, there is no single accepted definition
of cybersecurity. Indeed, there are over four hundred definitions of
cybersecurity (Deibert, 2018, p. 411), and the term is often left unde-
fined in legislation and by government and industry bodies (see, for
example, Bill C-51). Typically, cybersecurity has been conceived narrowly as protecting the "confidentiality, integrity, and availability of
data," usually in the context of national security or to protect corporate assets. The result is that many of the individual and collective
ways that humans are put at risk have been unexamined, or under-
researched, from a cybersecurity perspective. Indeed, until 2023, the
ISO/IEC 27032 standard for cybersecurity was only about the "pres-
ervation of confidentiality, integrity and availability of information"
(International Standards Organization [ISO], 2012). The new version
reframes it as the "safeguarding of people, society, organizations and
nations from cyber risks" in the sense of "keep[ing] cyber risk at a tol-
erable level" (ISO, 2023). Yet, the standard of care is still centred on the
security of information (ISO, 2020)—and people are only considered
through their interaction with information systems.

We contend that the cybersecurity lens is a powerful one,
and opens the door to different ways of conceiving of rights and

responsibilities in law and policy that are important. This volume takes the view that from a practical and normative standpoint, a broad, human-centric approach to cybersecurity is crucial. It does not seek to solve the question of what cybersecurity is by adding another definition to the list. Rather, it endeavours to move beyond the definitional, and advance the field of *human-centric cybersecurity* through interdisciplinary examination of the various "human" factors that comprise the cybersecurity experience.

This collection offers a new approach to human-centric cybersecurity: the *security of self*. It invites a paradigm shift where cybersecurity's core purpose is to protect people—and society—from harm, and where empowering individual and collective rights is central to our experiences of a secure cyber environment. In this reframing, humans are a feature, not a bug, of the cyber environment. The focus then shifts from centring the conversation on infrastructure or organizations to understanding human thinking and behavioural patterns (Grobler et al., 2021, p. 2) and centring policies around them. States, organizations, and infrastructure are, of course, still protected, but from a bottom-up approach that builds on securing the self.

The Many Faces of Cybersecurity

The dominant narrative of cybersecurity is that it concerns national security or organizational risk. When examined from a national security perspective, the primary need is a secure state, while humans are secondary, or a byproduct of securing the cyber environment (Liaropoulos, 2015). The assumption is that if critical infrastructure is protected, for example, then so are humans. This is a crucial—arguably foundational—dimension of cybersecurity, but it is incomplete. Most important for our purposes, it sets the narrative of cybersecurity in a one-dimensional direction that militarizes Internet governance (Shackelford, 2014).

The idea that human rights or self-empowerment might be central to developing security is not a point of emphasis—it is rather ignored—within a national security-centric framework. In the face of a national security risk, humans are seen either as a threat to be stopped, or as potential victims to be saved from some impending doom. Under current frameworks and approaches to cybersecurity, it appears complex—if not impossible—to understand people in any other role.

Similarly, cybersecurity can also be conceptualized in terms of organizational and operational risk. This approach focuses on the trade and commercial dimensions of securing data that are collected, used, and disclosed by an organization. It is an environment where economic imperatives dominate, and users are protected as part of facilitating commercial transactions. Cybersecurity is a financial, legal, and reputational cost to companies. Protecting "users" — not people — is therefore treated as a compliance cost, skating past the ways that technology is integrated into every facet of our lives and identities.

The narrative is beginning to change thanks to an increase of legal obligations related to data protection, consumer protection, and commercial and technical unfair practices harming people. For example, in the European Union, data protection is a fundamental right (*Charter of Fundamental Rights*, 2012, s. 7) and foundational to the *General Data Protection Regulation* (GDPR). However, this approach is not present in most other legal frameworks — and even the GDPR is mostly a compliance framework. In the United States, the Federal Trade Commission investigates data security matters relying on a century-old provision that prohibits unfair and deceptive practices (*Federal Trade Commission Act*, 1914, s. 5). In Canada, the *Personal Information Protection and Electronic Documents Act* (PIPEDA) protects consumer privacy through corporate accountability and consent mechanisms. To date, the most meaningful enforcement decision came from the Competition Bureau levying the *Competition Act* to fine Facebook for unfair marketing practices due to false and misleading claims in their privacy policies (*Facebook Inc.* — Registered Consent Agreement, 2020). Such frameworks miss a much-needed fundamental rights foundation. This could have changed with the reform proposed in Bill C-27 (2022) in the previous Parliament. However, the Bill that died on the Order Paper in January 2025, was still falling short of enshrined data protection as fundamental rights, and the reformed framework would have remained a compliance mechanism for commercial organizations.

Most legal frameworks still frame cybersecurity as a compliance exercise. Flowing from the above conceptualizations, the solutions tend to be technical and policy-based in nature with a focus on industry standards and incident response mechanisms. If the focus tends to be on system aspects to defend against bad actors, current challenges of the digital context require a move away from such an approach toward a broader perspective on cybersecurity that would shift attention to the people, who they are, and how they might be protected.

The "human factor" in cybersecurity is often seen as a vulnerability that must be fixed to protect society. Humans are treated as the weakest link, contributing to a pervasive and counterproductive culture of victim-blaming at best, which ignores the various potential misuses of such systems and harm-facilitating design choices.

Since the Internet's commercialization in the early 1990s, a vision of the Internet as a separate domain from the physical world necessitating different rules and practices has been promoted (Krishnamurthy et al., 2021). While this concept of the Internet's exceptionalism was always controversial, the concept of the otherness of technology left an indelible mark. This characterization is at odds with the experience of technology for many and the changing view of security in general.

Human-centric cybersecurity has emerged as a critical and more complete accounting of cybersecurity. This approach aims to centre the needs, preferences, practices, and biases of human users in cybersecurity practices and policies. It takes a holistic approach to cybersecurity and positions it as a social practice with humans at the centre as the objects of security (Klein & Hossain, 2020, p. 6). This shift is subtle but critical.

Human-centric cybersecurity offers a broadened view of security, one that aligns with evolving approaches in security studies, that shifts from threats to the state, to human security, to protect individuals from a variety of threats to their well-being, such as climate change, poverty, and social groups (Krishnamurthy et al., 2021).

By positioning humans at the centre as the objects of security, a broader framework emerges, although one on which there is not yet consensus.

The *security of self* approach seeks to dig deeper into how to breathe life into a human-centred approach to cybersecurity, reframing conversations and enabling a holistic approach to solutions. It is best understood as an addition to the human-centric cybersecurity narrative, one that helps centre it and make it actionable.

At its core, there is both an outward-looking and inward-looking dimension to this approach to cybersecurity. Looking outward, the focus is on taming threats to our security; looking inward, it is on managing our vulnerabilities (Grobler et al., 2021, p. 2). Ron Deibert attaches a human rights framework to human-centric cybersecurity. The analytical driver is not national security, but rather international human rights and humanitarian law (Deibert, 2018, pp. 412–414). In this way, cybersecurity is as much about technical security as it is about protecting freedom of expression and thought, privacy and freedom of association, and ensuring that there are mechanisms to enforce such rights (pp. 416–420).

Human rights, too, have external and internal dimensions, protecting individuals and groups from harm and enabling enjoyment of rights. Grounding cybersecurity in the needs and rights of individuals, security of self is best viewed as a tripartite framework: 1) protecting against threats to security and human rights; 2) understanding human behaviour and protecting the vulnerable; and 3) enabling protection of rights. In a Canadian context, this means protecting the underlying values of the *Charter of Rights and Freedoms* (1982) of "dignity, equality, liberty, respect for the autonomy of the person, and the enhancement of democracy" (*Health Services and Support v British Columbia*, 2007, para. 81).

Consider the ways that security of self can be compromised. When we think of protecting children from "sextortion," it is often framed as online abuse rather than a matter of cybersecurity. As Benjamin Wittes argues, whether hacking a teenager's camera or sextorting them through social media and private messaging, it is the same attack vector as stealing a company's financial data. This is a group we should be particularly concerned about, as children and teenagers often have lax security standards, are prolifically online, and are developmentally vulnerable (Wittes et al., 2016; Bradshaw & Vaillancourt, 2024). Changing the lens enables different questions to be asked. What security measures are to be implemented to protect children from luring for the purpose of committing a criminal offence? Why is the default design feature that cameras are to be uncovered?

In a similar vein, why do algorithms push content, such as self-harm and eating disorder content, that are known vulnerabilities of the young? Should there be guardrails on social media's use of rewards and punishments, such as likes, notifications, popularity metrics, and endless scrolling, in order to influence our behaviour and maximize time spent on their sites (5rights Foundation, 2023)? A traditional approach narrowly focuses on security of data, misleading advertising, user choice, or similar concerns. However, through the lens of the security of self, the window of threats widens, and forces the analysis of the particular vulnerabilities being exploited, the necessary steps to protect users, and who bears responsibility. For example, social media design raises questions about mind hacking and the right to freedom of thought and opinion (Laidlaw, 2024). Platform power raises questions about appropriate accountability frameworks of information gatekeepers (Laidlaw, 2015, 2023), a question that takes on even more urgency as the same platforms of power become artificial intelligence (AI) gatekeepers. Various jurisdictions are now legislating that safety be retrofitted into social media design, such as Europe's *Digital Services Act*, the United Kingdom's *Online Safety Act,* and Canada's short-lived Bill C-63 (2024). We suggest that a permissive regulatory environment, coupled with a narrow view of cybersecurity, contributed to an approach to safety that missed the core threats for so long.

Through the lens of security of self, the cybersecurity narrative then pivots, as well as technical and policy design choices. What if smart home devices were designed to meet the security needs of vulnerable people, and not to enhance corporate surveillance and interconnectivity? What if virtual reality (VR) and extended reality (XR) devices, universes, and platforms were designed to empower individual expression, and not amplify harmful "click-bait" content and engagements and other manipulative practices? What if people were empowered with technical and policy tools to protect themselves from the always-developing algorithmic surveillance society? What if AI and other security systems were designed and assessed from a community perspective? What if we allowed citizens and researchers to actually unveil the inner workings of socio-technical systems? What if we built policy frameworks around victims and community support? This book invites policy-makers, developers, designers, and deployers to reverse course.

The focus on vulnerabilities of people, and not technologies, pivots us to a rights-based discussion. The conversation is then centred on the vulnerabilities of particular groups, and the ways that technology can either facilitate rights protection or undermine it. Consider intimate partner and gender-based violence, and the particular threats posed to these groups by Amazon Ring or Apple AirTag, which have been used as tools of surveillance and abuse against women and other vulnerable people. Safety features have been retroactively fitted into the product to mitigate unintended harmful uses—following investigations and press reports harming their reputations—rather than implemented at the initial design phase. The same goes for the

ways journalists and elected officials are increasingly targets of surveillance. Pegasus spyware, for example, was found on several journalists' and activists' phones, including that of murdered journalist
Jamal Khashoggi's wife (Forbidden Stories, n.d.). Zero-day vulnerabilities and back doors are exploited by states—and often sustained
at the request of the national security community—but they endanger
people and communities (Perlroth, 2021).

Disinformation is another area where narratives matter.
Information manipulation is by no means a new phenomenon.
Propaganda, rumours, and reputation annihilation have always been
weapons of manipulation by malicious actors, from state-sponsored
campaigns to corporate actions and individual vendettas. Technology
has simply made this practice more affordable, global, and precise
(Bradshaw, 2020). Whether it is state-backed election interference,
creating fake accounts to harass and label journalists as enemies of
the state, the spread of false health information during health crises,
or the use of generative AI to create intimate images of high school
classmates, the falsity can be viewed as a "digital infection" (Smith,
2021, p. 182). Disinformation has similar dynamics to traditional
cybersecurity, but it weaponizes the entire information ecosystem
and Internet infrastructure. A traditional cybersecurity approach
tends to only be concerned with disinformation when it crosses a
threshold to become a threat to national security and democracy
more broadly, or privacy compliance more specifically. This misses
the complex dynamic at play. The cybersecurity risk lies in the day-
to-day ways that these technologies, and individuals, are exploited.
Security of self can be protected by examining the broad nature of
these threats, including threats to human rights and dignity, vulnerabilities of certain individuals and communities, and broader frameworks to protect the integrity of our systems as well as individual
and collective rights (Laidlaw, 2022).

As technology evolves and all aspects of our lives and citizenry
are now digital (Dubois & Martin-Bariteau, 2020a, 2020b), the risks
to our security of self are amplified. Internet of Things (IoT) devices
crowd our homes and bodies, spaces where we tend to feel our most
intimate and unguarded, and make the cybersecurity problem more
diffuse. Generative AI, with all its potential, can be weaponized to
inflict harm, hallucinate false answers convincingly, and build datasets to train its models on bias, personal information, and toxicity.
VR—and XR—can immerse users in an environment so realistic and

"boundary-less" that it can hijack the mind. All these technologies are opportunities for improved productivity, human connection, healing, and entertainment, among other things. They are, in short, significant, which is why an approach that places humans at the centre should be the framework for their safe development and use.

We are still at the beginning of understanding human-centric cybersecurity, and these examples only begin to scratch the surface. This book advances the field by unpacking various dimensions of human-centric cybersecurity from different disciplinary perspectives. We framed it as *security of self* because of the individual and collective ways that humans are at risk, and the need for solutions that not only protect us from harm but also empower us to thrive. A holistic approach is therefore necessary, and this requires different disciplines to figure out how they can fit together coherently (Jacob et al., 2020, p. 62).

To that end, this book is structured into two overlapping parts. In Part I, authors unpack specific risks to *security of self* through a series of case studies highlighting the need to recast cybersecurity narratives and policies. In Part II, authors examine gaps that must be filled to better protect the security of self, whether from a technical or policy perspective, as well as the practices of researchers and victims to shed light on harmful behaviours and support their victims.

The Need for New Cybersecurity Narratives

In Chapter 1, **Jane Bailey, Jacquelyn Burkell,** and **Kristen Thomasen** examine whose security is at stake. As they identify, we must understand that the security risk is not just the inherent vulnerability of technology. Rather, technology itself can be the source of individual and systemic harm. They examine Amazon Ring and its vulnerability to hacking, as well as its facilitation of interpersonal and state policing. They argue that human safety should be at the centre of these technologies, requiring that cases that have traditionally been relegated to the "edge" instead be front and centre in risk analysis and mitigation.

The lack of human-centricity in "smart" appliances appears to be a core concern for the *security of self*. In Chapter 2, **Matthew Bush** and **Atefeh Mashatan** examine technical solutions and state-of-the-art cybersecurity approaches for smart homes. Highlighting the disconnect between user needs and the technological landscape, they draw attention to the need to better understand the user in the design of the connected home. At the moment, vendor-specific complex settings and poor design lead consumers to compromise security for functionality, forcing non-expert consumers to make decisions about settings and uses without an understanding or an explanation of the security risks of these decisions. Such design practices leave them in a perpetual and unknown state of vulnerability.

The increase of connected homes and lives is born out of the supposition that, all too often, digitization and connection are assumed to be positive. However, the security of self is also put at risk by the information that is spread at a time of increased connectivity of users through social media platforms, mobile devices, and other technological tools. Dark patterns and targeted information manipulations are often discussed as key risks to digital safety. However, an underexplored risk is the way that certain technologies facilitate mind manipulation. In Chapter 3, **Jordan Loewen-Colón, Sharday Mosurinjohn,** and **Amarnath Amarasingam** examine VR and its facilitation of consciousness hacking. VR can improve moods, body dysmorphia, and learning, but can also be exploited to shape realities in other ways, to induce dissociative states, manipulate memories, and pressure extremist ideologies. The risks range from the mundane to the existential, and the authors advocate for stronger safeguards to mitigate VR misuse.

Information manipulation should also be considered a cybersecurity threat when coordinated on a larger scale. While usually ignored or understood as a political or democratic threat, in Chapter 4, disinformation and information manipulation are reframed as a cybersecurity threat by **Jonathon W. Penney**. While information manipulation has recently been acknowledged as a key threat to democracy by the Canadian Cybersecurity Centre (2023), this approach is largely missing from the cybersecurity literature, and dominant paradigms appear largely inadequate to address the risk. The proposed reframing offers a policy approach centred on user protection and safety, which integrates psychological and behavioural factors, as well as the human costs of information manipulation. Indeed, beyond the threats to democracy, information manipulation and coordinated online campaigns on social media can impede the safety of users, both online and offline.

Social media platforms are also at the centre of Chapter 5, in which **Chris Tenove** and **Heidi Tworek** explore how those socio-technical systems can be a vector for technology-facilitated insecurity, especially for public figures. Through a case study of online abuse of health communicators during the COVID-19 pandemic, they demonstrate why online abuse is a cybersecurity issue, linking online and offline risks that should be central to cybersecurity policies and studies. They argue for greater protection and support for victims of online abuse, public figures, and other users alike.

The Path Toward Security of Self

In the realm of technology-facilitated harms, the increasing deployment of AI systems is another area that has been documented as the source of potential harms for users. In Chapter 6, **Sébastien Gambs** explores how recent advances in the field of security and privacy of machine learning could be leveraged to empower users and deliver technical solutions to enhance security of self. He highlights that beyond technical solutions, individuals need to be protected by strong legal frameworks that allow and mandate such practices.

Even though privacy and data security are often presented as the core of cybersecurity policies, the protection of individuals appears as an afterthought in practice. Most data protection laws in Canada are relatively toothless, lacking incentives for organizations to change their practices and failing to protect individuals. In 2022, Bill C-27 proposed to introduce a right of action that could equip victims with a tool to hold organizations and developers accountable. In Chapter 7, **Teresa Scassa** explores how the reform meshed with evolving class action jurisprudence, and whether it could satisfy the goals of compensation and behaviour modification to better safeguard the security of self.

Since the *Bletchley Declaration* on AI (2023), we can see a shift toward AI safety, but the narrative is still techno-centric, looking at risk management and system security. In Chapter 8, **Fenwick McKelvey, Nick Gertler,** and **Alex Megelas** argue that well-designed, community-based algorithmic impact assessments could be a key tool to encourage a human-centric approach to AI safety and provide users with necessary information about such systems. Such community-based practices would reduce the risk of harm and empower users in their security.

However, the ability to understand the technology at stake is a key element of cybersecurity hygiene, from evidence gathering to claiming legal remedies and holding organizations accountable for their technological impact assessments. Yet, such an understanding is increasingly complicated by layered legal protections that, in protecting industry interests, impede the security of self and user empowerment. In Chapter 9, **Adam Molnar** highlights public interest researchers—academics, activists, journalists, and civil society organizations—as key actors to generate independent insights and investigations that are not imbued by state or industry interests. Through the study of independent academic researchers, he sheds light on the increasing risks born by those researchers as they seek to unveil design choices and surveillance frameworks harming the public. In the quest for a *security of self* approach, it is essential to also ensure the self-security of those investigating the risks.

A *security of self* approach to cybersecurity also needs to consider the user. As noted by Bush and Mashatan in Chapter 2, it is essential to support user agency—but forward-thinking policy should empower victims of online harms. The increasing use of digital platforms and devices has led to an increase in online crimes, notably online scams and fraud. Yet, online crimes are under-reported—especially for some types of crimes where victims could be shamed, or for marginalized communities that have lost trust in the state's ability to protect them (Council of Canadian Academies, 2023).

Two case studies look at how victims can leverage online forums, and the need to support victims networks. In Chapter 10, **Pascale-Marie Cantin, Fyscillia Ream**, and **Benoît Dupont** examine the mutual help practices adopted by victims of romance fraud in the aftermath of their experiences. Victims use online discussion forums to tell their stories, seek assistance, expose criminals, and raise awareness about their modus operandi. Victims also support each other and facilitate connection with communities and professional support. In Chapter 11, **Fyscillia Ream, Akim Laniel-Lanani**, and **Benoît Dupont** explore the behaviours of digital vigilantism where victims organize to expose fraudsters, seek retribution, and inform and raise awareness of online fraud. They also highlight some of the risks of such practices and the need to provide better support to victims of online crimes in Canada.

A New Policy Approach for the Digital Context

Cybersecurity is a powerful term that needs a new understanding to empower our societies—and ourselves—to thrive in the digital context. Our collection proposes an approach that centres on the lived experiences of people and their flourishing in society, and which governs infrastructure in response.

The Security of Self is a manifesto for a holistic and collaborative approach to cybersecurity that involves technology companies, security researchers, policy-makers, civil society, and users. Cybersecurity is a shared responsibility that must be rooted in human-centric principles. As such, cybersecurity strategies and policies need to go beyond their traditional national security focus and include people and communities at their core. This mindset grounds the cybersecurity agenda in the needs and rights of individuals. It also calls for cybersecurity strategies and policies to consider the diversity of individual risks and harms in the digital context, and include, for example, support for victim networks as discussed in the final chapters.

The previous Canadian parliament discussed many policy reforms, from privacy and AI governance (Bill C-27), to national cybersecurity (Bill C-26), to age restriction (Bill S-210), to online harms (Bill C-63), and to security of the electoral process (Bill C-65). These bills died on the Order Paper when Parliament was prorogued in January 2025. Regardless of what may be re-introduced, the digital policy issues the bills aimed to tackle, and that are discussed in this collection, will continue to be of pressing concern to governments for many years to come.

These essays call on policy-makers — at all levels of government — to act to protect Canadians by recentring their digital policy compass on the security of self. It will require more than just a few bills. It calls on a whole-of-government and a whole-of-society approach.

The lessons and recommendations from this collection are key resources to support such holistic policy approaches that move away from mere infrastructure and industry compliance to refocus on the lived experience of Canadians. Ultimately, we believe this volume can act as a compass for the next government to finally deliver on a comprehensive strategy to protect the security of self.

References

5Rights Foundation. (2023). *Disrupted childhood: The cost of persuasive design.* https://5rightsfoundation.com/wp-content/uploads/2024/08/5rights_DisruptedChildhood_G.pdf

Bill C-63, *An Act to enact the Online Harms Act, to amend the Criminal Code, the Canadian Human Rights Act and An Act respecting the mandatory reporting of Internet child pornography by persons who provide an Internet service and to make consequential and related amendments to other Acts*, 44th Parliament, 1st Session, 2024. https://www.parl.ca/DocumentViewer/en/44-1/bill/C-63/first-reading

Bill C-27, *An Act to enact the Consumer Privacy Protection Act, the Personal Information and Data Protection Tribunal Act and the Artificial Intelligence and Data Act and to make consequential and related amendments to other Acts (Digital Charter Implementation Act)*, 44th Parliament, 1st Session, 2021. https://www.parl.ca/legisinfo/en/bill/44-1/c-27

Bill C-51, *An Act to enact the Security of Canada Information Sharing Act and the Secure Air Travel Act, to amend the Criminal Code, the Canadian Security Intelligence Service Act and the Immigration and Refugee Protection Act and to make related and consequential amendments to other Acts (Anti-terrorism Act)*, 41st Parliament, 2nd Session, 2015 (assented 18 June 2015; SC 2015, c. 20). https://www.parl.ca/legisinfo/en/bill/42-1/c-51

The Bletchley Declaration by Countries Attending the AI Safety Summit, 1 November 2023. Government of the United Kingdom, https://www.gov.uk/government/publications/ai-safety-summit-2023-the-bletchley-declaration/the-bletchley-declaration-by-countries-attending-the-ai-safety-summit-1–2-november-2023

Bradshaw, S., Bailey, H., & Howard, P. N. (2020). *Industrialized disinformation 2020: global inventory of organized social media manipulation* [Working Paper 2021.1]. Computational Propaganda Research Project.

Bradshaw, S. & Vaillancourt, T. (2024). *Freedom of thought, social media and the teen brain*. Centre for International Governance Innovation. https://www.cigionline.org/publications/freedom-of-thought-social-media-and-the-teen-brain/

Canadian Charter of Rights and Freedoms, Part 1 of the *Constitution Act*, 1982, being Schedule B to the *Canada Act 1982* (UK), 1982, c 11.

Charter of Fundamental Rights of the European Union, 2012, Official Journal of the European Union, 26 October 2012, C326/391.

Council of Canadian Academies. (2023). *Vulnerable connections. The expert panel on public safety in the digital age*. Council of Canadian Academies. https://cca-reports.ca/reports/public-safety-in-the-digital-age/

Deibert, R. J. (2018). Toward a human-centric approach to cybersecurity. *Ethics & International Affairs, 32*(4), 411–424.

Dubois, E. & Martin-Bariteau, F. (2020a). Citizens and their political institutions in a digital context. In W. H. Dutton (Ed.), *A Research agenda for digital politics* (pp. 202–212). Edward Elgar.

Dubois, E. & Martin-Bariteau, F. (2020b). Citizenship in a digital context. In E. Dubois & F. Martin-Bariteau (Eds.), *Connected Canada: A research and policy agenda for digital citizenship* (pp. 1–20). University of Ottawa Press.

Facebook, Inc.—Registered Consent Agreement (19 May 2020), CT-2020-004. Competition Tribunal. https://decisions.ct-tc.gc.ca/ct-tc/cdo/en/item/471812/index.do

Federal Trade Commission Act, 1914, 15 USC § 45.

Forbidden Stories (n.d.). *The Pegasus project.* https://forbiddenstories.org/case/the-pegasus-project/

International Standard Organization. (2012). *Information technology—Security techniques—Guidelines for cybersecurity* (ISO/IEC Standard No 27032:2012). https://www.iso.org/obp/ui/en/#iso:std:iso-iec:27032:ed-1:v1:en

International Standard Organization. (2020). *Information technology—Cybersecurity—Overview and concepts* (ISO/IEC Standard No TS 27100:2020). https://www.iso.org/obp/ui/en/#iso:std:iso-iec:ts:27100:ed-1:v1:en

International Standard Organization. (2023). *Cybersecurity—Guidelines for Internet security* (ISO/IEC Standard No 27032:2023). https://www.iso.org/obp/ui/en/#iso:std:iso-iec:27032:ed-2:v1:en

General Data Protection Regulation 2016/679. *Regulation (EU) 2016/679 of the European Parliament and of the Council of 27 April 2016 on the protection of natural persons with regard to the processing of personal data and on the free movement of such data, and repealing Directive 95/46/EC (General Data Protection Regulation)* [GDPR], Official Journal of the European Union, 4 May 2016, L 119/1.

Grobler, M., Gaire, R., & Nepal, S. (2021). User, usage and usability: Redefining human centric cyber security. *Frontiers in Big Data,* 4(1), 583723. https://doi.org/10.3389/fdata.2021.583723

Health Services and Support—Facilities Subsector Bargaining Assn. v. British Columbia, 2007 SCC 27.

Jacob, J., Peters, M., & Yang, T. A. (2020). Interdisciplinary cybersecurity: Rethinking the approach and the process. In K. R. Choo, T. H. Morris, & G. L. Peterson (Eds.), *National Cyber Summit (NCS) research track* (pp. 61–74). Springer International Publishing. http://dx.doi.org/10.1007/978-3-030-31239-8_6

Klein, J., & Hossain, K. (2020). Conceptualising human-centric cyber security in the arctic in light of digitalisation and climate change. *Arctic Review on Law and Politics,* 11, 1–18. https://doi.org/10.23865/arctic.v11.1936

Krishnamurthy, V., Schmidt, D., & Lehr, A. (2021). Cybersecurity and human rights: Understanding the connection. In J. Andrew & F. Bernard (Eds.), *Human rights responsibilities in the digital age: States, companies, and individuals* (pp. 22–26). Bloomsbury Publishing.

Laidlaw, E. (2015). *Regulating speech in cyberspace: Gatekeepers, human rights and corporate responsibilities.* Cambridge University Press.

Laidlaw, E. (2022). *Mis- dis- and mal-information and the convoy: An examination of the role and responsibilities of social media.* Public Order Emergency Commission.

Laidlaw, E. (2023). The challenge designing intermediary liability laws. *Canadian Journal of Law and Technology, 21*(1), 67–97.

Liaropoulos, A. (2015). A human-centric approach to cybersecurity: Securing the human in the era of cyberphobia. *Journal of Information Warfare, 14*(4), 15–24.

Online Safety Act, 2023 c. 50.

Perlroth, N. (2021). *This is how they tell me the world ends: The cyberweapons arms race.* Bloomsbury Publishing.

Personal Information Protection and Electronic Documents Act (PIPEDA), SC 2000, c. 5.

Regulation (EU) 2022/2065 of the European Parliament and of the Council of 19 October 2022 on a Single Market For Digital Services and amending Directive 2000/31/EC (Digital Services Act).

Shackelford, S. (2014). *Managing cyber attacks in international law, business, and relations: In search of cyber peace.* Cambridge University Press. https://doi.org/10.1017/CBO9781139021838

Smith, T. (2021). The infodemic as a threat to cybersecurity. *The International Journal of Intelligence, Security, and Public Affairs, 23*(3), 180–196. https://doi.org/10.1080/23800992.2021.1969140

Wittes, B., Poplin, C., Jurecic, Q., & Spera, C. (2016). *Sextortion: Cybersecurity, teenagers, and remote sexual assault.* Brookings Institute. https://www.brookings.edu/articles/sextortion-cybersecurity-teenagers-and-remote-sexual-assault/

PART I

REFRAMING CYBERSECURITY NARRATIVES

CHAPTER 1

Whose Security Are We Talking About Anyway? The Case of Amazon Ring

Jane Bailey, Jacquelyn Burkell,
and Kristen Thomasen

Abstract

Conceptions of "cybersecurity" often focus on the protection of digital assets, including from human-related risks. Critical technology scholars and feminist scholars studying oppression-based violence, however, emphasize that even those technologies designed to offer protection can actually cause harm, particularly to members of groups who are most at risk of negative effects due to social or political marginalization. In this chapter, we emphasize the security risks for (some) humans that arise from technology—and specifically from technology that is positioned as *promoting* security. We use the example of Amazon Ring, one of many integrated and Internet-connected home surveillance systems. The system centres around a doorbell camera that feeds information to an operator through a cell phone app. Operators can add other home surveillance devices, too. Although Ring is marketed as a security system, it offers little in the way of actual protection and can instead expose users and others to new forms of individual and systemic violence. Such monitoring systems provide no active protection against violence, serving at best as passive observational tools that could, for example, warn that a dangerous intruder is at the door without the capacity for actual intervention. Moreover, Ring enables various forms of violence: through the traditional cybersecurity scenario of malicious hacking; through internal corporate structures that facilitate unwanted third-party access to information recorded by the system; through an abusable system that can be co-opted, for example, by a violent intimate partner, to surveil the person supposedly protected by the system; and through the establishment of a surveillance infrastructure that predictably creates vulnerability to systemic and epistemic violence for those who are captured in the surveillance records. In order to protect against these and other harms potentially caused by home surveillance and security technologies, we require a risk assessment process that includes a focus on the potential negative consequences of the technology, and that centres the perspectives of marginalized groups who are disproportionately at risk of negative impacts. To this end, we offer four recommendations: first, we cannot assume that technologies are positive or even neutral in their impact on individual or collective human safety and security; second, technology design and deployment decisions must focus on individual and collective *human* safety, with particular attention to the potential for violence arising from the technology itself; third, we must resist the unthinking resort to techno-solutionist responses to complex human problems; and fourth, a broader holistic strategy that includes regulating technology corporations and their use of data is needed to address the possibility of system harms.

The focus of this volume is a re-imagination of cybersecurity, specifically to bring *human* security into the conversation. The concept of cybersecurity originates in the protection of digital assets (e.g., databases, computers) from digitally mediated threats (e.g., system hacking) as these relate to national (Diebert, 2018) and corporate (Li & Liu, 2021) interests. To the extent that people entered these early discussions, they were positioned as security risks for digital systems (Bowen et al., 2011; Ghafir et al., 2018), either *directly*, such as hackers, or *indirectly*, such as individuals becoming targets of social engineering efforts to release security-related information such as passwords (Hatfield, 2018). With the issues framed this way, proposed responses tend to focus on digital security "solutions" and security training (Pattabiraman et al., 2017). Like other forms of techno-solutionism (Morozov, 2013), such technological "solutions" may not only be inapt for resolving complex human problems; they can also create new problems that actually jeopardize the safety of members of marginalized communities (Strohmayer et al., 2022) by, among other things, defining security risks from the perspective of dominant group members. Human-centric cybersecurity, by contrast, identifies the protection of human rights and civil society as the ultimate purpose of efforts to protect digital assets (Diebert, 2018). Even in these discussions, however, the central preoccupation is with risks to digital infrastructure (Slupska & Tanszer, 2021)—admittedly insofar as those implicate *human* security and human rights (Diebert, 2018)—and the focus of cybersecurity systems and processes is to protect that digital infrastructure.

Missing from these discussions is a critical insight: Technology is not simply and only vulnerable to attacks, it creates and facilitates individual and systemic violence (Strohmayer et al., 2022) undermining human rights and civil society. In other words, where human security is concerned, technology is as much to be protected against as it is to be protected. This issue is highlighted in cybersecurity ethics (Nissenbaum, 2005; Formosa et al., 2021), and particularly in feminist approaches to cybersecurity (Strohmayer et al., 2022). Formosa et al. (2021) present a "principalist" framework for cybersecurity that places human well-being firmly at the centre of cybersecurity discussions, making it clear that cybersecurity, even as it protects digital systems and assets against threats, cannot come at the expense of human safety and security. Strohmayer et al. (2022) apply a "feminist and justice-oriented lens to technology creation and testing" (p. 61), and call for a "paradigm shift" to focus on human safety in the design and implementation of digital systems. They focus particularly on technology-facilitated violence (TFV) enabled and perpetrated via digital technologies and recognize individual, structural, and systemic harms (Dilts et al., 2012) that can be caused or mediated by these forms of technology.[1] The feminist perspective demands an entirely different positioning of human security—not ignored, and not a side effect of digital security, but rather as something that is potentially at risk from TFV. That perspective also demands recognition of the fact that the risk of harm from many forms of TFV is unevenly borne by members of communities already marginalized by racism, sexism, homophobia, transphobia, ableism, and other oppressions and their

---

1.   TFV can encompass a wide variety of technologies, each of which may raise different kinds of safety and security concerns for different populations. Since our focus is on literature and examples involving digital technologies, our use of the term TFV in this chapter is confined to digital technologies.

intersections, with a growing amount of feminist work focusing on gender-based TFV (GBTFV) (e.g., Strohmayer et al., 2022; Bailey & Burkell, 2021).

TFV presents a particular challenge when technologies are deployed to protect or ensure security of systems or of people. In this chapter, an example of a specific security technology—Amazon Ring—is explored to highlight the individual, structural, and systemic security risks that are produced from or facilitated by this technology. We situate this analysis in a discussion of individual and systemic TFV (Bailey & Burkell, 2021; Bailey et al., 2021; Dunn, 2021) and an analysis of feminist approaches to cybersecurity that identify TFV as a central cybersecurity concern (Slupska & Tanszer, 2021; Strohmayer et al., 2022). We argue that TFV's effects, including individual, systemic, and societal violence, must be key considerations in the design of security technologies.

1.1. Technology-Facilitated Violence as a Matter of Cybersecurity

Technology is often positioned as *vulnerable* to security threats, and also as part of the solution to security (including cybersecurity) issues. Discussions of TFV, by contrast, focus on the harms that can be caused or facilitated by technology, including the wide range of digital information communication tools—for example, cell phones, apps, Internet websites, and artificial intelligence (AI) (Bailey & Dunn, 2023)—and technological surveillance "solutions" to security issues. Violence, in this chapter and other contexts, refers to the continuum of violence originating in feminist anti-violence work, which encompasses not just physical, but also sexual, emotional, and psychological harms, and includes harassment and coercive control (Bailey & Dunn, 2023). Furthermore, drawing on the intersectional feminist scholarship of Crenshaw (1991), Jiwani (2006), Hill Collins (2017), and other Black and women of colour writers, we conceive of violence not just in terms of acts perpetrated by and on individuals, but also those that have systemic and structural impact (Bailey & Burkell, 2021) including exclusion and silencing (Fricker, 2007). This comprehensive definition of violence is adopted to ensure that the individual and collective effects of harmful technological practices are visible as forms of violence that demand redress (Bailey & Burkell, 2021). It is also particularly well suited to account for oppression-based forms of TFV, such as GBTFV, which is the focus of our Amazon Ring analysis.

Online forms of TFV targeting individuals are widespread, with 60 percent of the 18,149 respondents of the 2022 international survey by the Centre for International Governance Innovation (CIGI) in eighteen countries reporting having experienced at least one of thirteen forms of online harm, ranging from physical threats to blackmail, to being monitored or spied on, to being impersonated online, to non-consensual use of intimate images, to harassment based on marginalizing factors such as race and gender (Dunn et al., 2023, pp. 5, 12). Equally widespread are the effects on individuals of systemic and structural violence in the digital environment. CIGI's report reaffirms prior research results demonstrating TFV patterns that reflect, repeat, and reinforce pre-existing oppressions, noting an "unhealthy digital environment" in which "women and LGBTQ+ people suffer disproportionately" and people are often targeted because they are members of marginalized communities (Dunn et al., 2023, p. 2). Such attacks prevent members of targeted communities from "participating freely, safely and authentically" (Dunn et al., 2023, p. 2) in the digital milieu, occasioning negative effects on, among other things, physical safety, mental health, personal reputation, close relationships, employment and business opportunities, the desire to live, and sexual autonomy and freedom (Dunn et al., 2023, pp. 2, 34, 41). Many of these harms can also be understood as violations of security of the person, which under national and international human rights norms includes both bodily and psychological integrity.[2] Digital technologies can also undermine free and safe participation in physical public spaces (Thomasen, 2022, pp. 142–169).

However, it is not only individually perpetrated acts that negatively affect bodily and psychological integrity in the digital milieu. Digital technologies themselves have been shown to repeat and sometimes exacerbate forms of exclusion and disproportionate targeting of members of marginalized communities, thus exposing those communities to a range of structurally violent acts from disproportionate privacy violations including, enhanced monitoring and surveillance, to discriminatory algorithmic sorting that negatively affects access to

---

2. For example, s. 7 of the Canadian *Charter of Rights and Freedoms* (1982), which protects "life, liberty and security of the person" has been interpreted to include the right to bodily privacy, bodily health, and "psychological integrity" (*Blencoe v BC [Human Rights Commission]*, 2000), while the South African *Bill of Rights* (Constitution of the Republic of South Africa, 1996) defines freedom and security of the person to include the right to "be free from all forms of violence from either public or private sources," as well as the right to "bodily and psychological integrity" (ss. 12[1] and 12[2]).

resources such as credit, job opportunities, and information (Bailey & Burkell, 2021, pp. 6–7). These technologies can, for example, increase social fragmentation by disseminating and amplifying harmful online content (Denham et al., 2021; Haunschild et al., 2022; Morales, 2023), or increase the likelihood of incarceration by subjecting members of minority populations to increased monitoring by police (Byfield, 2019). These outcomes can in turn lead to negative self-perceptions and other physical and psychological consequences as experienced by targets of in-person social exclusion (Fricker, 2007; Wesselmann et al., 2016).

In the specific context of oppression-based TFV, burgeoning feminist and justice-oriented scholarship argues that the current focus on external threats to *systems* reflects the privileged male perspective that dominates technology industries, including in relation to cyber-security (Slupska & Tanczer, 2021). This traditional focus obfuscates threats to *people* that are internally initiated by others known to them, such as when intimate partners activate GPS systems in their partners' phones to monitor their movements (Parsons et al., 2019). The traditional focus precludes design decisions that could minimize threats of TFV by known actors, especially those which are common or predictable based on existing research on intimate partner and gender-based violence (Slupska & Tanczer, 2021). As Slupska's 2019 analysis of home security system threat assessments demonstrated, these technologies are often not designed to be resistant to some of the most significant threats of (ab)use in the domestic and intimate partner violence context. Moreover, Slupska (2019, p. 85) noted that in situations where domestic violence was considered in the threat assessment, the consideration was "dismissive and displace[d] the responsibility of protection onto the potential targets of abuse" by failing to recognize the lived experience of women victimized by domestic violence. Women in this situation are most at risk from the people they know and trust, including partners who may set up and control their access to technology entirely. In other situations, where women initially have control over information such as their passwords, their trust in their partner can lead them to share such information, which can then be used to violent ends, including remotely accessing technologies to monitor women targeted and even to "gaslight" them by changing the temperature or music in the home (Slupska, 2019, pp. 88–89).[3]

---

3.   *Gaslighting* is a coercive control tactic that can form part of intimate partner violence where "a partner repeatedly undermines and distorts their partner's reality by denying facts, the situation around them, or their partner's feelings and

Critical technology scholars working on the issue of oppression-based violence have also identified the ways in which a lack of attention to power relationships can lead to threat assessments and cybersecurity decision-making that harms the very audience meant to be protected (Strohmayer et al., 2022, p. 63). For example, algorithmic content moderation techniques on YouTube under-detected instances of content harmful to child viewers while also demonetizing LGBTQ+-driven channels by indexing peer support and stigma combating strategies as "sexually suggestive content." The consequences in each case for those ostensibly protected are negative: the creation of a false sense of security for children and caregivers who believe the YouTube algorithms protect against exposure to harmful content and the removal of supportive online content and environments for marginalized LGBTQ+ community members (Strohmayer et al., 2022, p. 63).

Outcomes such as these have resulted in calls for new technical strategies relating to cybersecurity and threat assessments, such as the inclusion of members of marginalized communities in threat assessment processes (Slupska & Tanczer, 2021) and transitioning from security toward safety in the design, development, and adaptation of pervasive technologies (Strohmayer et al., 2022, p. 68). Strohmayer et al. (2022) advocate for a focus on designing trustworthy[4] technologies and designing with abusability in mind, guided by three core feminist tenets relating to safety:[5]

---

needs. It can cause a survivor to question themselves and become unable to trust their own perceptions and judgements" (Western, n.d.).

4. Strohmayer et al. (pp. 65–66) work with an understanding of "trust" as "the exposure of oneself to a situation where the outcome is uncertain." They recommend three design strategies for technologists. First, introduce "design friction" by building in a pause for users to consider more deeply whether they trust a technology. Second, allow for dynamism in trust that recognizes that an individual's trust in systems may shift over time and that technologies must earn the trust of users by, for example, not asking for too much information too soon. Third, question the methods of trust by recognizing that use of a system may reflect more about necessity than choice or trust in that system, for example by creating innovative alternatives for helping people abused by a system that do not necessitate provision of further information.

5. Strohmayer et al. (pp. 66–67) recognize that information security practitioners often focus on how a product or system can be abused and recommend an expanded understanding of threats in light of "complex privacy and security practices inherent to social relationships." This will assist in moving beyond the traditional tendency to focus solely on external bad actors. Keeping "abusability" in mind allows developers to focus on mitigating how a wide range of

1) centring the experiences of those who are usually wrongly ignored as "edge cases" (even though, in the context of oppression-based threats, they should in fact be the focus of concern);

2) centring safety and unsafety throughout the design, development, and deployment lifecycles of pervasive technologies by engaging deeply with "abusability" and "trust"; and

3) engaging deeply with socio-technical aspects that relate to pervasive technologies (p. 68).

They suggest that working through these lenses will allow technologists to "fully take into consideration holistic safety of people," including those disproportionately at risk of oppression-based targeting, and shift the focus from designing out unsafety toward active engagement "with the very real risk that the technologies we build can and will be used for harm instead" (p. 68).

With these analyses in mind, a home-monitoring device—Amazon Ring—will be examined as a case study. Like the critical technology scholars referred to above, our focus will be on questions about who might be targeted by security threats, as well as who might benefit from them. Included in the latter category are technology corporations whose devices are marketed as protection but who at the same time engage in their own forms of TFV due to their interests in data collection for profiling purposes, and public actors such as law enforcement agencies with an interest in accessing privately collected data for their own profiling purposes. In both cases, it is noted that members of marginalized communities are particularly at risk of being targeted.

1.2. Internet-Connected Home "Security" Systems

Home monitoring devices have existed for a long time, but they have recently become more sophisticated. Many systems are now

---

"malicious actors might hijack or weaponize the system for harmful activity." Doing so will require taking into account oppression-based threats grounded in race, age, gender, and other axes of oppression to enhance recognition of predictable abuses, including in testing safety concerns and threat modelling based on lived experiences of harm grounded in various axes of marginalization. Finally, developers should "develop responsive systems" that not only consider abusability at the design stage, but also provide accessible avenues for reporting abuse created in consultation with trusted support services (e.g., domestic violence shelters and sexual violence counsellors).

Internet-connected and networked within the home architecture, and some connect with social networks beyond the home. There are several home surveillance systems commercially available for personal use. In this chapter we focus on one popular example of an integrated home surveillance system known as Ring, which is manufactured by Ring LLC, a corporation owned by Amazon.

Ring is in widespread use across Canada and the United States. The system centres around a doorbell camera and can include other devices like child monitors, camera-equipped motion sensor lights, and even an in-home drone, which record video and sound and send push notifications to the operator through a smart phone app.

Ring is marketed and sold as a security system, and sometimes specifically as a protective mechanism against violence. In conjunction with this marketing, in the United States, Ring LLC has entered into a range of partnerships with law enforcement and other agencies, both to distribute Ring devices to community members and to encourage or require users to share video and other data directly with law enforcement (e.g., Harwell, 2019; Kelley & Guariglia, 2022; Guo, 2021). While these partnerships have not developed yet in Canada, law enforcement has considered the possibility in at least one Canadian city—Windsor, Ontario (CBC News, 2022).

Claims that Ring and other similar systems reduce law-breaking have not been confirmed with evidence (Farivar, 2020; Guo, 2021; So, 2023). Nevertheless, framing Ring as a security system has promoted the system as a means of protection against violence. For instance, while Ring LLC does not overtly state that its cameras will prevent intimate partner violence, the company entered into a number of high-profile partnerships in the United States where free Ring cameras have been distributed to survivors of intimate partner violence as a means of providing security and protection from harm. Partnerships have included the YWCA, Women Against Abuse, and the National Network to End Domestic Violence (NNEDV), which has characterized the surveillance system as a means to provide more safety to survivors (NNEDV, 2022). Police agencies have cited expectations that the cameras will help survivors to "feel safe" in their residences, as well as capture evidence that can be used to aid prosecutions (Guo, 2021).

Critiques of some of these partnerships note that survivors were not adequately consulted, and that the Ring system necessarily relies on a policing response that could further harm the victim, including by their possible arrest (Guo, 2021). Feminist and justice-oriented scholars emphasize that in the context of family violence the abuser might obtain control over the system, facilitating pervasive surveillance and control of the entryway to the home and potentially additional inner spaces, thus enabling GBTFV (Slupska, 2019; Slupska & Tanczer, 2021). The framing of Ring as a survivor-operated security measure places the expectation on the target of potential violence to manage their own security through the system—which is meant to make such management easier through automation of notifications (Slupska, 2019). While the security system is positioned as a means of prevention, in an actual incident of violence it serves only as a passive tool of observation that cannot intervene to prevent harm (Koskela, 2000). Furthermore, Ring has been critiqued for its appeal to fear as a means of marketing (Benton, 2019), fanning a culture of distrust rather than strengthening neighbourhood relationships that could actually assist in contexts of interpersonal and intimate partner violence.

Ring has experienced several high-profile cybersecurity breaches in the time it has been marketed by Amazon. Ring's child monitors have been subject to hacking incidents, raising privacy and security concerns within the home, and prompting class action suits for negligence and invasion of privacy (e.g., *Orange v Ring*, 2019). Ring LLC attributed these security weaknesses to customers reusing their passwords (Quinton & Budington, 2019). These incidents highlight traditional cybersecurity concerns relating to external threats. While these security weaknesses are certainly concerning, particularly when the system is adopted to provide security, there is also significance in the opacity that Ring's use as a security tool brings to other concerns around oppression-based TFV.

Recently, the US Federal Trade Commission charged Ring LLC with failing to prevent unauthorized third-party access to the footage collected by its devices. The allegations include that a Ring LLC employee accessed thousands of video recordings from at least eighty-one female customers. Some impugned footage was taken from private spaces in the home including bedrooms and bathrooms (Federal Trade Commission, 2023). This example highlights Slupska and Tanczer's (2021) observation that technology can create the possibility for internally initiated threats against people and stronger external security measures would not address or prevent third-party malicious attacks. In this case, users of the security system are rendered vulnerable by Ring's own internal capabilities and structure.

Any online home surveillance system can be hacked by malicious outsiders, and many systems can create opportunities for abuse from within the home or within the commercial relationship between the user and the provider of the security service. But there is an additional layer of concern here, exemplified by Ring's appeal to community and law enforcement networks. Systems like Ring also enable or enhance systemic insecurity and epistemic violence through, for example, the criminalization of public existence, the othering of those captured on film, and the appeal to interpersonal and state policing (Gilliard, 2021; Browne, 2015).[6]

By virtue of creating video "evidence" of suspected crime or suspicious people, the surveillance system encourages interpersonal and state policing, even for instances that are not criminal or harmful (Gilliard, 2020). For example, neighbours might share videos of someone in their neighbourhood they deem suspicious, which might prompt a call to police simply by virtue of a person's appearance and mere presence (Haskins, 2019). This carceral response to video footage is increased through the fear-based marketing noted above, and the purported safety features of the system, like automatic push notifications and online neighbourhood social networks (Guariglia, 2019). It seems to further play into cultural tropes of the "home as a castle" that can be justifiably protected from outsiders (Thomasen, 2022, pp. 130–140), potentially motivating violence and vigilantism, as has already occurred in the United States when a Ring push notification of someone approaching a home led to a violent attack (McDaniel, 2022). This kind of response is prone to being especially harmful to communities and individuals who already disproportionately experience profiling, interpersonal surveillance, and othering (Ahmed, 2000).

Furthermore, Amazon previously indicated interest in associating Ring with Rekognition (Biddle, 2019), its facial recognition technology (FRT). This would allow homeowners to be notified if specific persons of interest appeared in their video footage. It would also automate and streamline the search through hours of footage, whether by homeowners, law enforcement, and/or Amazon. It is unclear whether the FRT program will proceed with Ring. However, if it does, the

---

6.   "Othering" is a process that "involves zeroing in on a difference [between people] and using that difference to dismantle a sense of similarity or connectedness between people" and paves the way toward discrimination, exclusion, and violence (Curle, 2020).

well-documented systemic biases of FRT systems will be translated into the surveillance infrastructure already established by Ring (Buolamwini & Gebru, 2018; Selinger & Hartzog, 2019). Invariably, such a surveillance network leads to insecurity for, and compromises the safety of, those under the gaze of the cameras, as well as those who might purport to rely on them (Calacci et al., 2022).

Ring has been characterized as a mechanism for protection from violence, yet the design and operation of the system enable TFV on various levels: through the traditional cybersecurity scenario of malicious hacking, through internal corporate structures allowing unwanted third party access, through an abusable system that can be employed to surveil an intimate partner, and through the establishment of a surveillance infrastructure that predictably creates the possibility for extensive systemic and epistemic violence. Caution should be used with a cybersecurity approach to a system like Ring that fails to see beyond the first or second risk, that is incapable of addressing TFV, and risks "security washing" (i.e., lending approval to) a system that permits broad instances of TFV. In the final section of the chapter, we outline some steps forward, guided by the feminist and justice-oriented approaches to cybersecurity outlined above and our examination of the various layers of TFV risk created by a system like Ring, with a focus on oppression-based risk.

1.3. Toward Harm-Centric Security Approaches

Slupska (2019, p. 84) defines cybersecurity as "best understood as the set of protocols, technologies, and practices designed to protect against threats mediated by technology." Risk assessment at the design stage is a key component of protection against such threats. Traditional risk assessment focuses on external threats to the security of systems, rather than on threats to people arising from the system (Slupska & Tanczer, 2021). Increasingly, as highlighted here and elsewhere in this collection, critical technology scholars are calling for a more human-centric approach, one that "encompasses not just the protection of information, machines, or networks, but also of the humans that use them" (Slupska, 2019, p. 84, citing von Solms & van Kierkerk, 2013); an approach that is grounded in the reality that humans from marginalized groups are disproportionately at risk. These same critical analyses highlight that technological systems, including cybersecurity systems, create or facilitate risks even as, or if, they protect against them, emphasizing that these risks include potential harm to individuals as well as systemic harms that exacerbate existing biases and inequalities experienced by members of marginalized groups (Strohmayer et al., 2022).

In light of these concerns, we offer four recommendations and calls for action. First, it cannot and should not be presumed that proposed technologies, including security technologies, are positive or even neutral in their impact on individual or collective human safety and security.

Second, the design and deployment of technologies, including cybersecurity technologies, must focus on *human* safety, with particular attention to the potential for systemic and individual violence arising from the technology itself and the disproportionate impact on members of marginalized groups. In this regard, we echo Strohmayer et al.'s (2022) call for impact analyses centred on the experiences of marginalized groups and individuals who are typically ignored as "edge cases." The impact of technology will be different for different individuals and different groups; thus we note that attention must be paid to the possibility that technological systems can be (ab)used by trusted others or outsiders, including government agencies, and turned against those they are supposedly designed to protect.

Third, we must resist unthinking resort to techno-solutionist responses to complex human problems even when they arise in a technological context (Morosz, 2013). Where technologies can be meaningfully deployed to enhance safety and security, those technologies must be effective, and not simply there to provide an illusion or expectation of particular outcomes. Further, care must be taken to ensure that the availability of a technological response does not shift the responsibility for security and safety on to those who are at risk, while removing responsibility from other responsible actors.

Fourth, a broader holistic strategy is needed to address the possibility of system harms. That strategy should include regulating technology corporations and their use of data, restricting state access to collected data, proactively monitoring for and penalizing discriminatory outcomes, and funding research, public discourse and engagement, and educational and policy initiatives aimed at addressing the underlying systemic drivers that disproportionately expose marginalized communities to violence in the first place.

Acknowledgements

Thank you to SSHRC for funding The eQuality Project, a seven-year research initiative of which this chapter forms a part. Thanks also to Avery Chisholm for research support.

References

Ahmed, S. (2000). *Strange encounters: Embodied others in post-coloniality.* Routledge.

Bailey, J., & Burkell, J. (2021). Tech-facilitated violence: Thinking structurally and intersectionally. *Journal of Gender-Based Violence, 5*(3), 531–542. https://doig.org/ 10.1332/239868021X16286662118554

Bailey, J., Burkell, J., Dunn, S., Gosse, C., & Steeves, V. (2021). AI and technology-facilitated violence and abuse. In F. Martin-Bariteau & T. Scassa (Eds.), *Artificial intelligence and the law in Canada* (pp. 229–246). LexisNexis Canada.

Bailey, J., & Dunn, S. Recurring themes in tech-facilitated violence over time: The more things change, the more they stay the same. In K. Summerer & G. M. Caletti (Eds.), *Criminalising intimate image abuse: A comparative perspective* (pp. 40–59). Oxford University Press.

Benton, J. (2019, May 1). The doorbell company that's selling fear. *The Atlantic.* https://www.theatlantic.com/ideas/archive/2019/05/amazon-owned-ring-wants-report-crime-news/588394/

Biddle, S. (2019, November 26). *Amazon's Ring planned neighbourhood "watch lists" built on facial recognition.* The Intercept. https://theintercept.com/2019/11/26/amazon-ring-home-security-facial-recognition/

Blencoe v. British Columbia (Human Rights Commission), [2000] 2 SCR 307.

Bowen, B. M., Devarajan, R., & Stolfo, S. (2011, November 1). Measuring the human factor of cyber security. In *2011 IEEE International Conference on Technologies for Homeland Security* (pp. 230–235), Waltham, MA, United States. https://doi.org/10.1109/THS.2011.6107876

Browne, S. (2015). *Dark matters: On the surveillance of blackness.* Duke University Press. https://doi.org/10.1215/9780822375302

Buolamwini, J., & Gebru, T. (2018, February 23–24). Gender shades: Intersectional accuracy disparities in commercial gender classification. In S. A. Friedler & C. Wilson (Eds.), *Conference on fairness, accountability and transparency: Proceedings of Machine Learning Research New York University* (pp. 77–91). PMLR. https://proceedings.mlr.press/v81/buolamwini18a/buolamwini18a.pdf

Byfield, N. P. (2019). Race science and surveillance: Police as the new race scientists. *Social Identities: Journal for the Study of Race, Nation and Culture, 25*(1), 91–106. https://doi.org/10.1080/13504630.2017.1418599

Deibert, R. J. (2018). Toward a human-centric approach to cybersecurity. *Ethics & International Affairs, 32*(4), 411–424. https://doi.org/10.1017/s0892679418000618

Dilts, A., Winter, Y., Biebricher, T., Johnson, E. V., Vázquez-Arroyo, A. Y., & Cocks, J. (2012). Revisiting Johan Galtung's concept of structural violence. *New Political Science, 34*(2), e191–e227. https://doi.org/10.1080/07393148.2012.676396

Calacci, D., Shen, J. J., & Pentland, A. (2022). The cop in your neighbor's doorbell: Amazon Ring and the spread of participatory mass surveillance. *Proceedings of the ACM on Human-Computer Interaction, 6*(1) 1–47. https://doi.org/10.1145/3555125

Canadian Charter of Rights and Freedoms, Part 1 of the *Constitution Act,* 1982, Schedule B to the *Canada Act 1982* (UK), 1982, c. 11.

CBC News (2020, January 23) *Windsor partnership with Amazon Ring doorbell could do more harm than good, experts say.* https://www.cbc.ca/news/canada/windsor/windsor-amazon-ring-partnership-could-do-harm-experts-say-1.5437144

Crenshaw, K. (1991). Mapping the margins: Intersectionality, identity politics, and violence against women of color. *Stanford Law Review, 43*(6), 1241–1299. https://doi.org/10.2307/1229039

Constitution of the Republic of South Africa, 1996, Chapter 2: Bill of Rights, s. 12. https://www.gov.za/documents/constitution/chapter-2-bill-rights

Curle, C. (2020). *Us vs them: The process of othering.* Canadian Human Rights Museum. https://humanrights.ca/story/us-vs-them-process-othering

Denham, J., Hirschler, S., & Spokes, M. (2019). The reification of structural violence in video games. *Crime, Media, Culture: An International Journal, 17*(1), 85–103. https://doi.org/ 10.1177/1741659019881040

Diebert, R. (2018). Toward a human-centric approach to cybersecurity. *Ethics & International Affairs, 32*(4), 411–424. https://doi.org/10.1017/S0892679418000618

Dunn, S. (2021). Is it actually violence? Framing technology-facilitated abuse as violence. In J. Bailey, A. Flynn, & N. Henry (Eds.), *The Emerald international handbook of technology-facilitated violence and abuse* (pp. 25–45). Emerald Publishing Limited. https://doi.org/10.1108/978-1-83982-848-520211002

Dunn, S., Vaillancourt, T., & Brittain, H. (2023). *Supporting safer digital spaces.* Centre for International Governance. https://www.cigionline.org/activities/supporting-safer-internet/

Farivar, C. (2020, February 15). *Cute videos, but little evidence: Police say Amazon Ring isn't much of a crime fighter.* NBC News. https://www.nbcnews.com/news/all/cute-videos-little-evidence-police-say-amazon-ring-isn-t-n1136026

Federal Trade Commission (2023, May 31). *FTC says Ring employees illegally surveilled customers, failed to stop hackers from taking control of users' cameras* [Press Release]. https://www.ftc.gov/news-events/news/press-releases/

2023/05/ftc-says-ring-employees-illegally-surveilled-customers-failed-stop-hackers-taking-control-users

Formosa, P., Wilson, M., & Richards, D. (2021). A principlist framework for cybersecurity ethics. *Computers & Security, 109*, 102382. https://doi.org/10.1016j.cose.2021.102382

Fricker, M. (2007). *Epistemic injustice: Power and the ethics of knowing*. Oxford University Press. https://doi.org/10.1093/acprof:oso/9780198237907.001.0001

Ghafir, I., Saleem, J., Hammoudeh, M., Faour, H., Prenosil, V., Jaf, S., Jabbar, S., & Baker, T. (2018). Security threats to critical infrastructure: the human factor. *The Journal of Supercomputing, 74*, 4986–5002. https://doi.org/10.1007/s11227-018-2337-2

Gilliard, C. (2020, January 9). *Caught in the spotlight*. Urban Omnibus. https://urbanomnibus.net/2020/01/caught-in-the-spotlight/

Gilliard, C. (2021, November 14). A black woman invented home security. Why did it go so wrong? *Wired*. https://www.wired.com/story/black-inventor-home-security-system-surveillance/

Guariglia, M. (2019, August 8). *Amazon's Ring is a perfect storm of privacy threats*. Electronic Frontier Foundation. https://www.eff.org/deeplinks/2019/08/amazons-ring-perfect-storm-privacy-threats

Guo, E. (2021, September 20). *How Amazon Ring uses domestic violence to market doorbell cameras*. MIT Technology Review. https://www.technologyreview.com/2021/09/20/1035945/amazon-ring-domestic-violence/

Harwell, D. (2019, August 28). Ring, the doorbell-camera firm, has partnered with 400 police forces, extending surveillance concerns. *The Washington Post*. https://www.washingtonpost.com/technology/2019/08/28/doorbell-camera-firm-ring-has-partnered-with-police-forces-extending-surveillance-reach/

Hatfield, J. M. (2018). Social engineering in cybersecurity: The evolution of a concept. *Computers & Security, 73*(1), 102–113. https://doi.org/10.1016/j.cose.2017.10.008

Haunschild, J., Kaufhold, M. A., & Reuter, C. (2022). Cultural violence and fragmentation on social media: Interventions and countermeasures by humans and social bots. In M. D. Cavelty & A. Wenger (Eds.), *Cyber security politics* (pp. 48–63). Routledge. https://doi.org/10.4324/9781003110224

Hill Collins, P. (2017). On violence, intersectionality and transversal politics. *Ethnic and Racial Studies, 40*(9): 1460–1473. https://doi.org/10.1080/0141 9870.2017.1317827

Jiwani, Y. (2006). *Discourses of denial: Mediations of race, gender and violence*. University of British Columbia Press.

John Baker Orange v Ring LLC and Amazon.com Inc. Statement of Claim, 28 USC § 1332 (2019). https://documentcloud.org/documents/6593079-JOHN-BAKER-ORANGE-v-RING-LLC-and-AMAZON-COM-INC.html.

Kelley, J. & Guariglia, M. (2022, July 15). *Ring reveal they give videos to police without user consent or a warrant.* Electronic Frontier Foundation. https://www.eff.org/deeplinks/2022/07/ring-reveals-they-give-videos -police-without-user-consent-or-warrant

Koskela, H. (2000). "The gaze without eyes": Video surveillance and the changing nature of urban space. *Progress in Human Geography, 24*(2), 243–265. https://doi.org/10.1191/030913200668791096

Li, Y., & Liu, Q. (2021). A comprehensive review study of cyber-attacks and cyber security: Emerging trends and recent developments. *Energy Reports, 7*(1), 8176–8186. https://doi.org/10.1016/j.egyr.2021.08.126

McDaniel, J. (2022). They got a Ring doorbell alert, then they opened fire on a bystander, police say. *The Washington Post.* https://www.washington-post.com/nation/2022/10/19/ring-doorbell-camera-shooting-florida/

Morales, E. (2023). Ecologies of violence on social media: An exploration of practices, contexts, and grammars of online harm. *Social Media + Society, 9*(3). http://dx.doi.org/10.1177/20563051231196882

Morozov, E. (2013). *To save everything, click here: The folly of technological solutionism.* Public Affairs.

National Network to End Domestic Violence. (2022, November 14). *Ring collaborates with the National Network to End Domestic Violence (NNEDV) to support survivors nationwide.* https://nnedv.org/latest_update/ring-col-laborates-with-the-national-network-to-end-domestic-violence-nnedv-to-support-survivors-nationwide/

Nissenbaum, H. (2005). Where computer security meets national security. *Ethics and Information Technology, 7*, 61–73. https://doi.org/10.1007/s10676-005-4582-3

Parsons, C., Molnar, A., Dalek, J., Knockel, J., Kenyon, M., Haselton, B., Khoo, C., & Deibert, R. (2019). *The predator in your pocket: a multidisciplinary assessment of the stalkerware application industry.* The Citizen Lab. https://citizenlab.ca/2019/06/the-predator-in-your-pocket-a-multidisciplinary-assessment-of-the-stalkerware-application-industry/

Pattabiraman, A., Srinivasan, S., Swaminathan, K., & Gupta, M. (2018). Fortifying corporate human wall: A literature review of security awareness and training. In M. Gupta, R. Sharman, J. Walp, & P. Mulgund (Eds.), *Information technology risk management and compliance in modern organizations* (pp. 142–175). IGI Global. http://dx.doi.org/10.4018/978-1-5225-2604-9.ch006

Quinton, C., & Budington, B. (2019, December 19). *Ring throws customers under the bus after data breach.* Electronic Frontier Foundation. https://www.eff.org/deeplinks/2019/12/ring-throws-customers-under-bus-after-data-breach

Selinger, E., & Woodrow H. (2019). The inconsentability of facial surveillance. *Loyola Law Review 66*, 101–122. https://scholarship.law.bu.edu/cgi/view-content.cgi?article=4053&context=faculty_scholarship

Slupska, J. (2019). Safe at home: Towards a feminist critique of cyber-security. *St. Anthony's International Review, 15*(1), 83–100. https://papers.ssrn.com/sol3/Delivery.cfm/SSRN_ID3429851_code3517815.pdf?abstractid=3429851&mirid=1

Slupska, J., & Tanczer, L. M. (2021). Threat modeling intimate partner violence: Tech abuse as a cybersecurity challenge in the Internet of Things. In J. Bailey, A. Flynn, & N. Henry (Eds.), *The Emerald international handbook of technology-facilitated violence and abuse* (pp. 663–688). Emerald Publishing Limited. https://doi.org/10.1108/978-1-83982-848-520211049

So, A. (2023, July 9). Why we don't recommend ring cameras. *Wired.* https://www.wired.com/story/why-we-do-not-recommend-ring/

Strohmayer, A., Bellini, R., & Slupska, J. (2022). Safety as a grand challenge in pervasive computing: Using feminist epistemologies to shift the paradigm from security to safety. *IEEE Pervasive Computing, 21*(3), 61–69. https://doi.org/10.1109/mprv.2022.3182222

Thomasen, K. (2022) *Private law & public space: The Canadian privacy torts in an era of personal remote-surveillance technology* [Thesis]. University of Ottawa, https://ruor.uottawa.ca/handle/10393/43746

Von Solms, R., & Van Niekerk, J. (2013). From information security to cyber security. *Computers & Security, 38*(1), 97–102. https://doi.org/10.1016/j.cose.2013.04.004

Wesselmann, E. D., Grzybowski, M. R., Steakley-Freeman, D. M., DeSouza, E. R., Nezlek, J. B., & Williams, K. D. (2016). Social exclusion in everyday life. In P. Rivera & J. Eck (Eds.), *Social exclusion: Psychological approaches to understanding and reducing its impact* (pp. 3–23). Springer International Publishing/Springer Nature. https://psycnet.apa.org/doi/10.1007/978-3-319-33033-4_1

Western Centre for Research and Education on Violence Against Women & Children. (n.d.) *Gaslighting in intimate relationships: A Form of coercive control you need to know more about.* https://gbvlearningnetwork.ca/our-work/backgrounders/gaslighting_in_intimate_relationships/Gaslighting-in-Intimate-Relationships.pdf

CHAPTER 2

Bringing Security Home: The Need for a Human-Centric Approach to Securing Smart Homes

Matthew Bush and Atefeh Mashatan

Abstract

In this chapter, the pressing issue of cybersecurity in smart home systems is discussed, with current approaches examined and substantial gaps identified. Attention is drawn to the emerging concept of human-centric cybersecurity as a solution to the shortcomings of traditional organizational approaches to securing smart environments. A deeper understanding of the intricate relationships between individuals and the technological ecosystems found within smart homes is advocated. This perspective is reflective of the concept of security of self that prioritizes the protection of individuals within personal digital ecosystems. Through this lens, an exploration of existing technical solutions and state-of-the-art approaches to smart home cybersecurity and privacy is undertaken, providing a brief insight into the gaps between human-centric needs and the current cybersecurity landscape. The over-reliance on vendor-specific solutions is critiqued, highlighting the inconsistencies and diverse competencies among various vendors. This environment leaves non-expert consumers with complex choices to make and often results in poorly configured systems with increased vulnerabilities. The discussion also encompasses the topic of user agency over data, emphasizing the need for a transparent system in which individuals can maintain substantial control and oversight over their information without requiring intricate configuration. The need for clear directives on data accessibility and the assurance of privacy without compromising the security and functionality of smart home systems is affirmed. The conclusion calls for a collaborative approach involving tech companies, policy-makers, and users, advocating for a shared responsibility model rooted in human-centric principles. The imperative for ongoing education to empower users is underscored, as is fostering a proactive stance on cybersecurity that merges robust default security features with user-friendly functionality. Applying and expanding upon these recommendations will enable leveraging the advantages of smart technologies while still providing adequate cybersecurity that is attuned to the needs of smart home users.

The purpose of cybersecurity is to ensure the confidentiality, integrity, and availability of information systems. Traditionally championed by national security agencies and financial institutions, its importance is now rising in the household. This necessity extends beyond high-stakes corporate and governmental spheres, affecting kitchens, living rooms, and bedrooms. While a breach at a national security agency or financial institution can affect millions, compromised homes represent a far more personal violation of these sanctuaries for security and privacy. In the physical world, houses have walls, doors, and locks. However, the digital world very often lacks these sorts of barriers. Individuals increasingly use devices that transmit massive amounts of sensitive data about their daily lives. These unique and personal dimensions are simply not addressed in typical enterprise cybersecurity approaches. Smart homes require a human-centric approach to cybersecurity that accounts for the needs of a diverse range of people and digital environments. At home, people are the most intimate versions of themselves. To ensure the security of self, a human-centric approach must protect users even when their guards are down.

Smart homes, part of the broader Internet of Things (IoT), are quickly becoming integral to daily life. Smart homes can encompass utilities from simple smart lighting to advanced home security with IoT cameras and sensors. While enhancing convenience, these technologies introduce a number of new security risks including unauthorized access and confidentiality threats stemming from system heterogeneity, resource limitations, and lack of standardization (Lin & Bergmann, 2016, p. 4). Growing interconnectedness and rising cyber-crime amplify these concerns. Compromised cyber-physical systems have even been used to facilitate real-world crimes as serious as home invasions (Blythe & Johnson, 2021, p. 21). Attacks on smart home systems not only threaten user data, but have wide-ranging impacts in the real world.

With rising cyber risks at home, the traditional specialized focus of cybersecurity in national and organizational realms appears increasingly inadequate. Governmental and organizational priorities continue to shape cybersecurity investment and development, with most consumers lacking the resources to attract the attention of experts. This means that most cybersecurity products are intended to protect critical infrastructure and sensitive information with a clear distinction between the organization and the external malicious actor. Notable foundations of today's information security standards can be traced back to efforts like the US Department of Defense Computer Security Center's Rainbow Series published in the 1980s and 1990s (National Institute of Standards and Technology, 2024). While national security remains a core focus, it often neglects the individuals these institutions aim to serve, leaving many people unknowingly exposed to risks in their own homes. There is a clear need for a different cyber-security paradigm that focuses on regular people.

A human-centric approach to cybersecurity focuses on the human experience and prioritizes protection from a user-driven perspective. This contrasts with traditional methods, which have different objectives and requirements. Individual influence in cybersecurity remains minimal compared to the resources driving monolithic organizational approaches. Despite its growing importance, the human-centric approach is still underdeveloped and often overlooked.

Despite this, the idea of human-centric security is not new. In fact, the United Nations Development Programme's Human Development Report (1994) concluded that "The concept of security has for too long been interpreted narrowly: as security of territory from external aggression, or as protection of national interests in foreign policy or as global security from the threat of nuclear holocaust [...] Forgotten were the legitimate concerns of ordinary people who sought security in their daily lives" (p. 22).

While this was an admission that the security of self should be a priority, these ideas were not given adequate attention in the international arena. The Government of Canada has been one of very few vocal governments in endorsing the concept of human-centric security, in its broader sense supporting initiatives such as the Human-Centric Cybersecurity Partnership (HC2P). HC2P is a trans-disciplinary group of researchers from academia, government, and industry that address broad socio-technological issues with human-centred solutions (HC2P, 2022). Even still, such efforts remain relatively recent developments.

Currently, little is known regarding user efficacy gaps and their impact on cybersecurity behaviour with smart home devices. Research on human elements in IoT cybersecurity is still an emerging field. While several studies address risk management and other key IoT cybersecurity considerations (e.g., Kim, 2017; Lu & Da Xu, 2018; Abbass et al., 2018, 2019; Choo et al., 2021), few focus on challenges on the user side. Smith et al. (2021) argue that understanding user concerns is a crucial step to developing IoT cybersecurity policies because users are the most affected group.

The knowledge gap in this domain is even more striking in smart home systems, where research on user behaviour is also scarce. Marikyan et al. (2019) note that users have mixed perceptions of smart home security. A survey of IoT users shows they tend to prioritize ease of use and comfort more than security (Grobelna et al., 2018). While not specific to smart homes, cybersecurity efficacy is closely linked to individual habits and behaviour (Hong & Furnell, 2021). Moreover, a lack of cybersecurity awareness can lead to riskier behaviours (Torten et al., 2018; Li et al., 2019). Combined with inadequate awareness among the public (De Bruijn & Janssen, 2017), there are a number of challenges and concerns that need to be addressed.

Research also highlights a gap between individuals' perceptions of cybersecurity threats and their preparedness (Nam, 2019). Socio-demographic and contextual factors also affect individual preparedness (Lee & Kim, 2020; Blackwood-Brown et al., 2019). This underscores a need to improve user cybersecurity efficacy and awareness, while also considering the underlying complex and personal factors. More research is needed to explore the way these factors drive user behaviour in smart home environments.

This chapter examines how the human element in smart homes interacts with cybersecurity. It explores user cybersecurity efficacy in association with risks, vulnerabilities, and behaviour. It also highlights gaps in end-user awareness and the need to align cybersecurity requirements with awareness activities. Exploring this alignment serves the ultimate goal of building better cybersecurity hygiene in smart home users. A human-centric approach is crucial as the attack surface in smart homes expands in ways that are closely linked to user behaviour.

The rest of this chapter is organized as follows. Section 2.1 discusses the current state of smart home systems both generally and with respect to cybersecurity. Section 2.2 delves into the human element, exploring user capabilities, expectations, behaviour, and security requirements. Section 2.3 examines gaps between these requirements and the state-of-the-art. Section 2.4 offers recommendations for users, vendors, and policy-makers.

2.1. Today's Smart Home Systems

In the continuously evolving landscape of smart home systems, securing a home goes beyond simply installing the latest technologies. Like securing any other information system, it must be grounded in a broader approach that encompasses the principles of confidentiality, integrity, and availability. No one technology constitutes state-of-the-art smart home security. It is also important to remember that smart homes can differ greatly in design, technical components, and implementation, so those organizations developing the state-of-the-art can often only draw attention to a broader set of best practices. This section takes a similar approach and focuses on the overall strategies that inform commonly accepted security practices. The most secure approaches treat security as an ongoing process from purchase and configuration, to maintenance, and all the way to retirement and disposal. Defence in depth (DiD), secure defaults, and least privilege, which are described later in this section, form the backbone of any good security approach. Moving beyond a vendor-centric view, it would seem that the need to transition toward solutions focused on consumers' needs and behaviour is only partially realized. Best practices in smart homes should balance strong technical controls with user convenience and foster an ecosystem where security and user-friendliness are not in opposition.

2.1.1. Common Technical Components

Smart home systems refer to the integration of various interconnected devices and technologies within a domestic setting, enabling automation, control, and remote monitoring of household functions. Key components of a smart home system, as outlined by the Institute of Electrical and Electronics Engineers (IEEE, 2023), include a smart home gateway that acts as a central communication hub, a smart home control terminal for user interaction, smart home device terminals encompassing a range of IoT devices, and smart home service platforms that facilitate the deployment and management of services. The European Telecommunications Standards Institute (ETSI, 2020) envisions a similar architecture where standard and constrained devices are linked via a hub at the home's perimeter, connected to external services through the Internet.

Common elements within smart homes encompass networking components like routers and gateways, in-house appliances, audiovisual equipment, and security and monitoring systems, as highlighted by the International Standards Organization and International Electrotechnical Commission (ISO/IEC, 2017). These devices are integrated into a network, equipped with sensing and actuating capabilities and applications for generating, transmitting, and processing data (ISO/IEC, 2022). Smart home operations often involve companion application software, such as mobile apps, to provide users with intuitive control interfaces. Though many smart home devices can process data locally, cloud services are often employed to store and process device-generated data, forming the backend infrastructure (Fagan et al., 2022). This reliance on external service providers for applications and infrastructure creates an environment where responsibility for user data and device security is not primarily in the hands of end users.

Operational technologies (OT), which encompass hardware and software for monitoring and controlling physical devices, processes, and events, are becoming increasingly integrated into smart home environments. These technologies, once mainly used in industrial settings, are now applied in residential spaces for controlling home automation systems, managing energy usage, and maintaining security through surveillance systems. The convergence of OT and IT in smart homes is leading to increasing complexity that necessitates better security measures for both digital and physical vulnerabilities.

2.1.2. The State of Security in Smart Homes

Every smart home carries its distinct features, making it a challenge to pinpoint every security or privacy control that would suit a specific setting. Rather than delving into differing technical approaches, it is more beneficial to discuss overarching strategies that seek to uphold confidentiality, integrity, and availability. A widely acknowledged strategy in cybersecurity is DiD, which advocates for a multifaceted protection framework encompassing strategies such as robust password requirements or multifactor authentication (MFA) for smart home devices (ETSI, 2020). In a similar way, security maintenance is an important aspect of smart homes, and organizations emphasize secure, reliable, and verifiable updates to maintain the system's security over time (IEEE, 2023; ETSI, 2020; Fagan et al., 2022). Here, the notable point is that the state-of-the-art for smart home cybersecurity broadly mirrors the principles applied in organizational settings.

Important too is the degree of significance that can be assigned to best practices in organizational versus consumer settings. One very relevant example relates to secure defaults. Best practices for smart home security include secure defaults such as passwords, policies, and protocols (ETSI, 2020). And while secure defaults remain important in organizational settings, there is less of a focus because organizations are much more likely to have paid security experts aligning these settings with the needs of the organization. These settings are often not managed by experts in consumer settings, leading to an increased dependence on default settings for a secure smart home. Another example that seems to have unique implications in the consumer setting is managing guest users. Organizational infrastructure and protocol would be more complex and allow nuanced handling of network guests. A smart home requires its comparatively simple setup to balance appropriately limiting the privileges of guests without unnecessarily compromising privacy or functionality for that guest (Mare et al., 2019). This brings to the forefront the necessity to revisit and adapt the principles of organizational cybersecurity to cater to the distinct demands and realities of smart home contexts.

In some cases, approaches that are widespread in organizations are also recommended for consumer settings despite the fact that these approaches may cause completely different problems in a smart home. A critical part of an ongoing security process is being aware of the state of the system and the ability to flexibly respond to threats in a timely manner. A common recommendation for smart home security is that network and environmental data should be thoroughly examined to maintain general cybersecurity state awareness (ETSI, 2020; Fagan et al., 2022). This allows for timely threat detection and response and for the information to be used for continual improvement of security decision-making. The continuous authentication and evaluation of access requests is a best practice approach only possible if data are being managed effectively (Colombo et al., 2021). In an organizational setting, this is typically not problematic as traffic is mostly generated by employees performing their jobs. In a smart home, widespread data collection can pose serious problems to user privacy. In this case, there is potentially a direct conflict between perceived best practices and the legitimate needs and capabilities of smart home users.

State-of-the-art concepts such as adopting the principle of least privilege should be prominent in the security design, yet they face hurdles in real-world implementation because of their reliance on users' expertise and awareness. To implement a least privilege approach, granular access policies are recommended (Colombo et al., 2021), yet these environments usually lack users with the expertise to configure sufficiently granular policies. Even though the vendor may be capable of alleviating this pressure, the vendor may not have intimate knowledge of the needs and desires of a particular home's end users.

To address this, the "Secure by Design" principles, recently promoted by the Cybersecurity and Infrastructure Security Agency (CISA) in collaboration with international bodies, advocate for security to be integrated into products from the very beginning. This approach aims to minimize the security burden on consumers by ensuring that secure configurations are the default, and vulnerabilities are mitigated before products even reach the market (CISA, 2023, p. 8). This is a good place to start, but security-by-design must also include meaningful user engagement so that secure defaults can be readily adapted to unique and personal digital environments.

Reliance on vendors for state-of-the-art security has other barriers too. Though there is a degree of advocacy for increased user choice such as opt-in data collection (ETSI, 2020), there is also a reliance on the vendor to act in good faith. Users typically prioritize convenience and functionality, so vendors that are not required to implement user-centric security and privacy features by law will instead focus on bringing functionality and convenience that will increase sales.

Those familiar with organizational cybersecurity may not have found much that is new in this section, except for the misalignment between organizational cybersecurity best practices and what can be expected of a non-expert user. This is in large part because the state-of-the-art has largely been moulded from existing best practices for organizational cybersecurity. Yet, there is a significant disparity between state-of-the-art and the effectiveness of security practices for smart homes. Even though there are well-defined guidelines for smart homes and consumer IoT, they are often difficult to implement or ineffective for reasons such as the requirement of specific components or the assumption that the rest of the network can be trusted. Many of these solutions place the onus of security squarely on the vendors of individual devices and services. True state-of-the-art security is unlikely to be realized by many of the solutions offered by vendors because the security posture of vendors can vary greatly. It is likely the case that giants, like Google or Amazon, offer more secure products than relatively unknown vendors simply because they face more scrutiny than smaller vendors (Davis et al., 2020). Unfortunately, most people do not have the expertise to verify or even understand security claims and so many of these poorly secured products can end up in smart homes anyway. And even a competent vendor may achieve security without offering adequate privacy. Crucially, the organizational approach to cybersecurity that informs best practice has difficulty extending to those that are not members of the organization. This necessitates a radical rethinking that makes consumers the focus, moving beyond vendor-driven solutions to create a landscape where security and privacy are not just optional add-ons but fundamental constituents of smart home ecosystems. Smart home security must begin to consider the consumer-centric nature of the environment: the human element.

2.2. The Human Element in Smart Homes

As smart homes become an increasingly large part of daily life, the role of the human element comes sharply into focus. Homeowners transition from mere beneficiaries to pivotal decision-makers and must strike a balance between convenience and security. In this environment, standard security measures, which have largely been shaped by organizational security orthodoxy, may fall short. To facilitate a truly secure smart home environment, it is imperative to consider the diverse needs and capabilities of individual users to create a living space that is both secure and accommodates the intricacies of personal life. This demands a departure from rigid organizational security frameworks toward more flexible, user-centric paradigms that privilege user autonomy, embrace a nuanced understanding of privacy, and endorse collaboration between vendors and end users.

By understanding that homeowners are not just users, but stewards of their own security, the way can be paved for systems that meet the multidimensional needs of the individual. Users require security and privacy measures that encompass a broad spectrum of behaviours, expectations, and capabilities. By fostering a landscape where security is not just implemented but lived, choice, adaptability, and ease-of-use become cornerstones for the security of self.

Smart homes make homeowners both beneficiaries and chief decision-makers. Unlike organizations with dedicated security teams, homeowners must manage their own security, buying devices and using services based on personal needs and preferences. This requires a flexible security approach tailored to daily life, balancing convenience and safety for diverse users. State-of-the-art security often reflects an organizational perspective, but in smart homes, is security adequate if users have no control over their privacy? Or if tech-savvy users can misuse devices to spy on others in the home? Current approaches, borrowed from enterprise settings, lack the focus on consumer choice and make it hard for non-experts to manage their unique needs. Security solutions often assume smart homes can be managed like organizations. But smart homes are unique, with multiple users, each with different needs and preferences. This creates conflicts and complexities, as smart homes combine the challenges of diverse IoT devices and varied user behaviours.

2.2.1. Users' Capabilities, Expectations, and Behaviours

In an enterprise, a cybersecurity team configures, maintains, and troubleshoots a system's security. Not only are they employed full-time to perform these duties, but they also have both tools and expertise at their disposal. A smart home user might not have the time, knowledge, or necessary tools to properly use or secure a smart home. This creates vulnerabilities. Default settings might be left unchanged, or devices might be operating on outdated software, unknowingly leaving gaps in security. Additionally, homeowners might not always be aware of emerging threats or might not have the tools to monitor for breaches, reducing the possibility of taking a proactive stance.

For most end users, a smart home is more than just a collection of devices; it is a personal space. While enterprises might not need to trade some level of privacy for functionality or business insights, homeowners are left with a dilemma. Even though privacy means more to a homeowner than an employee, they must decide how to balance convenience and functionality with privacy and security, if they have the means to make that decision at all. Consumer expectations include the desire for increased control over the data generated by users (Mineraud et al., 2016; Worthy et al., 2016), along with the essential choice to participate in data collection processes (Jacobsson et al., 2016; Worthy et al., 2016). However, these choices are often hindered by user confusion surrounding the purpose and methods of data collection (Worthy et al., 2016). A smart device that captures more information than necessary or shares data without explicit consent can be seen as intrusive. Vendors, therefore, face the challenge of providing a better product without invading user privacy. Moreover, the boundaries of privacy in a home environment are fluid and can vary among different users, demanding adaptability and clear communication about data usage to and between users (Zeng et al., 2017).

The dynamics of user behaviour play a significant role in shaping the security profile of a smart home. While new features and increased convenience are appealing, they often come with compromises in security. A homeowner might opt for ease of use over MFA for a device, potentially leaving it vulnerable. The varying needs and perspectives of different household members further complicate the landscape. One member's preferences for security measures might clash with another's desire for simplicity. In other cases, users can even behave as adversaries, attempting to spy on one another. Furthermore, despite users often professing a high desire for privacy, their behaviour might sometimes be at odds with this stated priority. This inconsistency in behaviour, known as the privacy paradox (Kokolakis, 2017), underscores the importance of creating intuitive and user-friendly security measures. Users may not always be willing or capable of achieving the privacy they should have if they are not provided with the appropriate options.

2.2.2. User-Centric Security Requirements

Smart home users should be involved in key security and privacy decisions. These decisions, however, must be framed in an approachable and intuitive manner, given the varying capabilities of end users. Access control policies, network configurations, and security incident responses should be tailored for consumer understanding.

There is a need for vendors to provide secure default settings that require minimal adjustments alongside simple tools for customization if the users desire granularity. Moreover, balancing the tension between rigorous security measures, such as continuous authentication, and user convenience is paramount. Innovative solutions like biometrics can bridge this gap, providing both security and a frictionless user experience.

Data security and privacy are foundational in the realm of consumer IoT. Users often generate and interact with a vast array of data, from medical records to information surrounding daily routines. Protecting this data involves employing robust encryption methods and data management practices. Additionally, given the multi-user nature of most consumer networks, a nuanced approach is needed to respect privacy between users. Limited or incorrect threat models and varying levels of expertise can create power imbalances where some users are forced to rely on others for access (Zeng et al., 2017). Reliance on a single technically savvy user may sidestep expertise issues but centralized configuration can very easily lead to some users' concerns being dismissed and even facilitate abuse by the primary user (Leitão, 2019). To mitigate issues where other users can act as adversaries, informed consent mechanisms should be promoted for data use and sharing, making it clear who has access to what data, and for which specific purposes. While users should have visibility and control over their data, they may not have the expertise to manage complex configuration options. Providing too much granularity could paradoxically lead to weaker security. The degree of user involvement must be carefully considered, ensuring adequate choice without overwhelming the user.

The heterogeneous array of devices and services in smart homes also places an emphasis on network configuration and architecture. Network segmentation is a solution that ensures that devices and services interact in a way that minimizes the risk for other network segments. Segmentation is widely agreed to be good practice in IoT (Tanczer et al., 2018), but could result in networks that are difficult to manage for non-experts. To this end, users should be presented with effective device configurations and information regarding the segments in a way that resonates with non-experts. This ensures that the security infrastructure is both robust and user-friendly.

In this consumer IoT landscape, users bear the primary responsibility for security, irrespective of their level of expertise (Zheng et al.,

2018). The blurred lines between different categories of smart home devices further complicate matters, making it unclear which standards should be applied (Zheng et al., 2018). Addressing these challenges necessitates a comprehensive approach involving both users and vendors, emphasizing user education, transparent communication, and robust security measures to safeguard individuals' privacy and data in the ever-evolving realm of consumer IoT. Clear security and privacy labels could help users discern the security posture of a vendor and allow them to make more informed purchasing decisions (Emami-Naeini et al., 2020). Bringing education and empowerment past purchase and into configuration and maintenance ensures that secure consumers not only choose products with important features, but also use these features properly.

To improve security in smart homes, automated tools that are tailored for non-expert users could prove essential. Since individual consumer networks are unlikely to face highly specialized threats, a significant portion of automation can focus on education and empowerment. While routine security issues can be addressed automatically, these systems should engage users meaningfully for unique or important situations. This ensures that automation does not generalize a solution where human intervention is necessary. Robust data management policies informed by user choice can ensure that data collection for security improvements obeys the principles of least privilege. This balanced approach, combining automated measures with user empowerment, allows non-expert users to tailor security and privacy controls to their unique needs.

2.3. Gap Analysis Between the State-of-the-Art and User Expectations

Smart homes attempt to provide convenience and efficacy in our everyday lives. When examined from a user-centric perspective, however, the security and privacy of these systems appear to be inadequate while still remaining overly complex. While standards try to provide comprehensive technical guidelines, there remains an unresolved tension between state-of-the-art security and privacy practices and the application of these measures to smart home settings. This tension is especially palpable when considering the end-user experience and expectations. These tensions shed light on a number of gaps that exist for user-centric security in smart homes.

2.3.1. Gap Analysis

A major theme in the current security paradigm is reliance on vendor-specific solutions. While some products may be robust and secure, the landscape is muddled with offerings from a multitude of vendors with varying degrees of competency. This diversity means that even though standards organizations offer security guidance to vendors, consumers are still faced with an inconsistent security landscape. Even if some vendors offer better security and privacy, consumers require knowledge and motivation to choose them. In reality, users often face difficulties in verifying security and privacy claims made by IoT product vendors (Zheng et al., 2018). If vendors alone are trusted to provide security and privacy, then there is no DiD if that vendor is untrustworthy. Furthermore, relying solely on vendors for security without adequately defining and mandating privacy systems would be nominally secure in a way that may still compromise user privacy. Privacy may be important to users but not to vendors who seek to harvest data.

Another reason vendors alone cannot be relied upon is because the diversity of consumer IoT devices within a single environment amplifies security risks. These devices may interact complexly because they exist both physically and digitally (Bellman & Oorschot, 2019). Physical interconnectedness increases the risk of incorrect network state information, potentially leading to erroneous automations and program execution, even with individually secure devices. The number of non-standard interfaces creates additional vulnerabilities and further complicates device management (Mare et al., 2019).

Smart home systems should also accommodate a wide variety of people. Parents may struggle to grasp the privacy implications associated with their children's connected toys (McReynolds et al., 2017), while the elderly may grapple with a trade-off between privacy and autonomy within smart home environments (Townsend et al., 2011). Vulnerable individuals, such as those with cognitive impairments, stand to benefit from IoT technologies, but responsible data handling is crucial. Ensuring that the right individuals have access to sensitive information while preventing unauthorized access raises significant challenges (Poyner & Sherratt, 2018). Vulnerable individuals may also be more susceptible to security risks due to their limited ability to utilize security controls and their vulnerability to social engineering (Poyner & Sherratt, 2018). Current solutions are simply not flexible enough to support a wide range of demographics.

Modern security recommendations may be technically well defined but challenging to implement for the average user. In a similar vein, concepts like DiD, effective security maintenance, or least-privilege are paramount for security but can compromise user convenience. Recommendations are made for vendors but rely on individual users for some of the most important steps in securing their own unique environments. Moreover, state-of-the-art guidelines assume that consumers have the expertise to make informed decisions about their security. In reality, the complexity of the choices can be overwhelming, leading to potential misconfigurations and vulnerabilities. The tension between rigorous security measures and a seamless user experience remains unresolved.

Data play a key role in both the security and operation of smart homes. Given its importance, there is a prominent lack of user agency over these data. While best practices emphasize robust encryption and data management, the current landscape lacks clarity on who accesses these data and for what purpose. This is exacerbated by the multi-user nature of most consumer networks. Data are managed at the level of particular services or of the smart home as a whole, but rarely at an individual level. This is an important gap as there are security and privacy considerations at the level of the smart home as well as between users. One challenge lies in providing users with visibility and control over their data without overwhelming them with intricate configuration options. There is also a challenge balancing inter-user conflicts with privacy and efficacy goals. The data collected for improved security automation and decision-making must balance the benefit it provides to security at a potential cost to privacy. Data management must be approached with far greater nuance than comprehensive data collection and analysis.

2.4. Toward Shared Responsibility and a Proactive Smart Home Security Framework

While vendors should undoubtedly be held to rigorous standards in ensuring the security of their products, the reality is that they sometimes fall short in the context of smart home security. In line with the principles of DiD, one needs to consider what to do when vendors fail to meet our standards for security and privacy. There is an increasing need for technical, legal, and policy experts to come together and address these problems. The solution must be flexible and multifaceted. Regulatory bodies, in collaboration with legal experts, must work toward a framework that holds vendors accountable without deemphasizing the importance of redundant safety nets to protect people when our primary defences fail.

Serious commitment to secure-by-design represents another foundational approach that could alleviate many of the current challenges that smart home users face. Launched by CISA in 2023 in collaboration with a number of other major security agencies, the initiative outlines a set of guidelines and best practices to ensure that security is embedded into the lifecycle of any smart device. This approach focuses on reducing some of the burden on consumers by advocating for robust default security settings, secure update mechanisms, and a proactive stance on addressing vulnerabilities (Cybersecurity and Infrastructure Security Agency, 2023). By adhering to these principles, vendors can create products that are inherently more secure, thereby allowing consumers to benefit from smart home technologies without taking sole responsibility for safeguarding their own digital ecosystems.

While the secure-by-design approach should be a part of any robust smart home security strategy, it is also vital to create a paradigm where tech companies and end users operate as partners in cybersecurity. While companies should be mandated to deliver products with robust default security features and secure update mechanisms, there must also be mechanisms to empower and aid consumer involvement. Human-centric security measures should help individuals to take proactive actions to ensure strong cybersecurity. This will allow users to better secure unique environments without sacrificing ease of use or functionality. Users should be empowered, not just to secure individual networks, but to secure themselves as individuals. A shared responsibility model ensures that even if one line of defence encounters an issue, subsequent protective layers can thwart potential threats.

This shared responsibility model will only be helped with the aid of continuous cybersecurity education and awareness. The landscape of threats evolves constantly, and consumers need to be in a position to understand and demand protection from vendors and regulators. Education leads to empowerment and will only help consumers to participate in proactive measures to combat the latest threats. This education can be guided by policy-makers and vendors alike, bringing attention to issues in public places and through the various devices and services that need to be secured.

If the benefits of smart technologies are to be reaped, then one must remain vigilant. Even in people's most private moments, their devices are ceaselessly active, potentially vulnerable and relaying information. One must remember that while our physical walls might be sturdy, our digital ones require constant reinforcement.

Acknowledgements

The authors express their sincere gratitude to the Editors for their insightful and detailed feedback. This research was supported in part by the Natural Sciences and Engineering Research Council (NSERC RGPIN-2019-06150) of Canada and the Canada Research Chairs program (CRC-2021-09-01).

References

Abbass, W., Bakraouy, Z., Baina, A., & Bellafkih, M. (2019). Assessing the Internet of Things security risks. *Journal of Communications, 14*(10), 958–964. https://doi.org/10.12720/jcm.14.10.958-964

Abbass, W., Bakraouy, Z., Baina, A., & Bellafkih, M. (2018). Classifying IoT security risks using Deep Learning algorithms. In *2018 6th International Conference on Wireless Networks and Mobile Communications (WINCOM)* (pp. 1–6). IEEE. http://dx.doi.org/10.1109/WINCOM.2018.8629709

Bellman, C., & van Oorschot, P. C. (2019). Analysis, implications, and challenges of an evolving consumer IoT security landscape. In *2019 17th International Conference on Privacy, Security and Trust (PST)* (pp. 1–7). IEEE. http://dx.doi.org/10.1109/PST47121.2019.8949058

Blackwood-Brown, C., Levy, Y., & D'Arcy, J. (2019). Cybersecurity awareness and skills of senior citizens: A motivation perspective. *Journal of Computer Information Systems, 61*(3), 1–12. http://dx.doi.org/10.1080/08874417.2019.1579076

Blythe, J. M., & Johnson, S. D. (2021). A systematic review of crime facilitated by the consumer Internet of Things. *Security Journal, 34*(5), 97–125. https://link.springer.com/article/10.1057/s41284-019-00211-8

Choo, K. K. R., Gai, K., Chiaraviglio, L., & Yang, Q. (2021). A multidisciplinary approach to Internet of Things (IoT) cybersecurity and risk management. *Computers & Security, 102*, 102136. https://doi.org/10.1016/j.cose.2020.102136

Colombo, P., Ferrari, E., & Tümer, E. D. (2021). Access control enforcement in IoT: State of the art and open challenges in the Zero Trust era. *2021 Third IEEE International Conference on Trust, Privacy and Security in Intelligent*

Systems and Applications (TPS-ISA), 159–166. http://dx.doi.org/10.1109/TPSISA52974.2021.00018

Cybersecurity and Infrastructure Security Agency. (2023). *Secure by design: Principles and practices to enhance product security.* https://www.cisa.gov/sites/default/files/2023-10/SecureByDesign_1025_508c.pdf

Davis, B. D., Mason, J. C., & Anwar, M. (2020). Vulnerability studies and security postures of IoT devices: A smart home case study. *IEEE Internet of Things Journal, 7*(10), 10102–10110. https://doi.org/10.1109/JIOT.2020.2983983

De Bruijn, H., & Janssen, M. (2017). Building cybersecurity awareness: The need for evidence-based framing strategies. *Government Information Quarterly, 34*(1), 1–7. https://doi.org/10.1016/j.giq.2017.02.007

Emami-Naeini, P., Agarwal, Y., Cranor, L. F., & Hibshi, H. (2020). Ask the experts: What should be on an IoT privacy and security label? In *2020 IEEE Symposium on Security and Privacy* (SP) (pp. 447–469). http://dx.doi.org/10.1109/SP40000.2020.00043

European Telecommunications Standards Institute. (2020). *Cyber security for consumer Internet of Things: Baseline requirements.* https://www.etsi.org/deliver/etsi_en/303600_303699/303645/02.01.01_60/en_303645v020101p.pdf

Fagan, M., Megas, K. , Watrobski, P., Marron, J., & Cuthill, B. (2022). *Profile of the IoT core baseline for consumer IoT products.* National Institute of Standards and Technology. https://doi.org/10.6028/NIST.IR.8425

Grobelna, I., Grobelny, M., & Bazydło, G. (2018). User awareness in IoT security. A survey of Polish users. International Conference of Computational Methods in Sciences and Engineering 2018 (ICCMSE 2018), *2040*(1). Thessaloniki, Greece. http://dx.doi.org/10.1063/1.5079136

Human-Centric Cybersecurity Partnership. (2023). *Home.* https://www.hc2p.ca/

Hong, Y., & Furnell, S. (2021). Understanding cybersecurity behavioral habits: Insights from situational support. *Journal of Information Security and Applications, 57*(1), 102710. https://doi.org/10.1016/j.jisa.2020.102710

International Standards Organization/International Electrotechnical Commission. (2017). *Information technology—Internet of Things (IOT)—IOT use cases.* https://www.iso.org/standard/73148.html

International Standards Organization/International Electrotechnical Commission. (2022). *Cybersecurity—IoT security and privacy—Guidelines.* https://www.iso.org/standard/44373.html

Institute of Electrical and Electronics Engineers. (2023). *2785-2023: IEEE Standard for Architectural Framework and General Requirements for Smart Home Systems.* IEEE.

Jacobsson, A., Boldt, M., & Carlsson, B. (2016). A risk analysis of a smart home automation system. *Future Generation Computer Systems, 56*(1), 719–733. https://doi.org/10.1016/j.future.2015.09.003

Kim, J. H. (2017). A survey of IoT security: Risks, requirements, trends, and key technologies. *Journal of Industrial Integration and Management, 2*(02), 1750008. https://doi.org/10.1142/S2424862217500087

Kokolakis, S. (2017). Privacy attitudes and privacy behaviour: A review of current research on the privacy paradox phenomenon. *Computers & Security, 64*(1), 122–134. http://dx.doi.org/10.1016/j.cose.2015.07.002

Lee, C. S., & Kim, J. H. (2020). Latent groups of cybersecurity preparedness in Europe: Sociodemographic factors and country-level contexts. *Computers & Security, 97*, 101995. http://dx.doi.org/10.1016/j.cose.2020.101995

Leitão, R. (2019, June 18). Anticipating smart home security and privacy threats with survivors of intimate partner abuse. In S. Harrison & S. Bardzell (Eds.), *Proceedings of the 2019 on Designing Interactive Systems Conference* (pp. 527–539). Association of Computing Machinery. http://dx.doi.org/10.1145/3322276.3322366

Li, L., He, W., Xu, L., Ash, I., Anwar, M., & Yuan, X. (2019). Investigating the impact of cybersecurity policy awareness on employees' cybersecurity behavior. *International Journal of Information Management, 45*(1), 13–24. http://dx.doi.org/10.1016/j.ijinfomgt.2018.10.017

Lin, H., & Bergmann, N. W. (2016). IoT privacy and security challenges for smart home environments. *Information, 7*(3), 44–59. https://doi.org/10.3390/info7030044

Lu, Y., & Da Xu, L. (2018). Internet of Things (IoT) cybersecurity research: A review of current research topics. *IEEE Internet of Things Journal, 6*(2), 2103–2115. http://dx.doi.org/10.1109/JIOT.2018.2869847

Mare, S., Girvin, L., Roesner, F., & Kohno, T. (2019). Consumer smart homes: Where we are and where we need to go. In A. Wolman & L. Zhong (Eds.), *Proceedings of the 20th International Workshop on Mobile Computing Systems and Applications* (pp. 117–122). http://dx.doi.org/10.1145/3301293.3302371

Marikyan, D., Papagiannidis, S., & Alamanos, E. (2019). A systematic review of the smart home literature: A user perspective. *Technological Forecasting and Social Change, 138*(1), 139–154. http://dx.doi.org/10.1016/j.techfore.2018.08.015

McReynolds, E., Hubbard, S., Lau, T., Saraf, A., Cakmak, M., & Roesner, F. (2017). Toys that listen: A study of parents, children, and Internet-connected toys. In G. Mark & S. Fussell (Eds.), *Proceedings of the 2017 CHI Conference on Human Factors in Computing Systems* (pp. 5197–5207). Association for Computing Machinery. http://dx.doi.org/10.1145/3025453.3025735

Mineraud, J., Mazhelis, O., Su, X., & Tarkoma, S. (2016). A gap analysis of Internet-of-Things platforms. *Computer Communications, 89–90*, 5–16. http://dx.doi.org/10.1016/j.comcom.2016.03.015

Nam, T. (2019). Understanding the gap between perceived threats to and preparedness for cybersecurity. *Technology in Society, 58*(1), 101122. http://dx.doi.org/10.1016/j.techsoc.2019.03.005

National Institute of Standards and Technology. (2024). *DoD Rainbow Series.* https://csrc.nist.gov/pubs/other/1985/12/26/dod-rainbow-series/final

Poyner, I. K., & Sherratt, R. S. (2018). Privacy and security of consumer IoT devices for the pervasive monitoring of vulnerable people. In *Living in the Internet of Things: Cybersecurity of the IoT 2018* (pp. 1–5). IEEE. https://doi.org/10.1049/cp.2018.0043

Smith, K. J., Dhillon, G., & Carter, L. (2021). User values and the development of a cybersecurity public policy for the IoT. *International Journal of Information Management, 56*(1), 102123. http://dx.doi.org/10.1016/j.ijinfomgt.2020.102123

Tanczer, L. M., Blythe, J. M., Yahya, F., Brass, I., Elsden, M., Blackstock, J., & Carr, M. (2018). *Review of international developments on the security of the Internet of Things.* PETRAS National Centre of Excellence for IoT Systems Cybersecurity. https://discovery.ucl.ac.uk/id/eprint/10050104/

Torten, R., Reaiche, C., & Boyle, S. (2018). The impact of security awareness on information technology professionals' behavior. *Computers & Security, 79*(1), 68–79. http://dx.doi.org/10.1016/j.cose.2018.08.007

Townsend, D., Knoefel, F., & Goubran, R. (2011). Privacy versus autonomy: A tradeoff model for smart home monitoring technologies. In *2011 Annual International Conference of the IEEE Engineering in Medicine and Biology Society (EMBC 2011)* (pp. 4749–4752). IEEE. http://dx.doi.org/10.1109/IEMBS.2011.6091176

United Nations Development Programme. (1994). *Human development report 1994: New dimensions of human security.* https://hdr.undp.org/system/files/documents/hdr1994encompletenostats.pdf

Worthy, P., Matthews, B., & Viller, S. (2016, June 4). Trust me: Doubts and concerns living with the Internet of Things. In M. Foth, & W. Ju (Eds.), *Proceedings of the 2016 ACM Conference on Designing Interactive Systems* (pp. 427–434). Association for Computing Machinery. http://dx.doi.org/10.1145/2901790.2901890

Zeng, E., Mare, S., & Roesner, F. (2017). *End user security and privacy concerns with smart homes.* In M. E. Zurko, S. Chiasson & M. Smith (Eds.), *Thirteenth Symposium on Usable Privacy and Security (SOUPS 2017)* (pp. 65–80). USENIX Association. https://www.usenix.org/system/files/conference/soups2017/soups2017-zeng.pdf

Zheng, S., Apthorpe, N., Chetty, M., & Feamster, N. (2018). User perceptions of smart home IoT privacy. *Proceedings of the ACM on Human-Computer Interaction, 2*(CSCW), 1–20. https://doi.org/10.1145/3274469

The Vulnerability of Emerging Technologies of the Self: A Critical Analysis of Virtual Reality Through Psychedelic Self-Hacking

Jordan Loewen-Colón, Sharday Mosurinjohn,
and Amarnath Amarasingam

Abstract

This chapter investigates the dual-use potential of virtual reality (VR) and psychedelic self-hacking as Foucauldian "technologies of the self." While these technologies can foster personal empowerment and resilience, they also create opportunities for exploitation and manipulation. VR, like psychedelics, can disrupt selfhood and consciousness by altering memory, perception, and social pressures. Contexts that leave users unaware of these psychological effects erode their autonomy. The chapter highlights two axes of exploitation: "outside-in," where external entities manipulate users, and "inside-out," where individuals engage in self-hacking. Both axes involve ethical concerns about power, control, and the commodification of selfhood that require robust safeguards. Interdisciplinary collaboration is necessary between humanities, social sciences, and computer science to navigate the vulnerabilities introduced by these emerging technologies. Only the experiences of sentient beings and their nurturing good relationships to themselves, each other, and the world can be at the centre of this project.

While virtual reality (VR) technologies can be exploited to hack vulnerabilities in the "self" for monetary and anti-social ends, they also hold promise for individuals to fortify their own psychological and emotional defences. Foucault's concept of "technologies of the self" (Martin et al., 1988) offers insights into how individuals are often conditioned to harness technologies in ways that might increase their vulnerability, especially when observing the interplay of bodies, discourse, and institutions. Yet, diverging from the conventional self-help narrative that perpetuates governmentality through normalization, "self-hacking," especially its psychedelic variants, can serve as a tool for individuals to reclaim agency, bolster resilience, and redefine their relationship with digital technology, illuminating pathways to both understand and potentially safeguard the multifaceted aspects of their "self" in our interconnected digital age.

In this chapter, we delve into VR and psychedelic self-hacking, framing them as Foucauldian "technologies of the self" with a dual-edged potential. To support better governance, we identify four primary ways that VR might be used to hack the individual "self," and then structure this exploitation along two distinct axes: 1) from the outside in, driven by orchestrated endeavours of entities like megacorporations; and 2) from the inside out, navigated by individuals themselves through the avenue of "self-hacking"—with a particular emphasis on "consciousness hacking."

3.1. The Critical Vulnerabilities of the Self in Virtual Reality

Previous work highlights case studies demonstrating how popular VR experiences (VRX) can induce religious experience, trigger ecstatic states, and disrupt users' experience of selfhood through mechanisms like body possession and proprioceptive confusion (Glowacki et al., 2020; Loewen, 2022). VR can alter a user's consciousness and trigger boundary dissolving states, where they may report feeling—and even appear—quite lucid, however, it is unclear whether they are still able to evaluate any ideological material they might find themselves perceptually immersed in, or make sound decisions about what to do with it. It is already known from studies of social learning in the context of so-called "cults," military structures, advertising, and other contexts accused of "brainwashing" that there are entirely analogue means of manipulating people's sense of self. Moreover, now that we are well into the information age, we understand how data-processing algorithms are increasingly influential "instruments of perception" that can operate in both targeted ways (such as radicalization via YouTube rabbit holes) and passive ways (e.g., framing the social issues that are collectively attended to as well as those that are neglected) (Amoore & Piotukh, 2015; Brown et al., 2022; Govers et al., 2023; Ledwich et al., 2022). VR has the potential to go beyond even these manipulative and disinformational functions.

More than indoctrination and filter-bubbling, VR is most akin to the altered perceptual state of psychedelic experience, where it is well known that "an environment that lacks defined boundaries provides shelter for predatory behaviour as well as increased opportunity for [...] transgressions" both unintentional and intentional (Devenot et al., 2022). However, while "bad trips" may be feared in psychedelics, in VR they can be designed, and most users are oblivious to the fact that they can even occur (Loewen, 2019). Considering human-centred cybersecurity, it is imperative to acknowledge how emerging technologies like VR can be employed to initiate altered states of consciousness without users' consent. The vulnerable self in VR becomes a crucial point of attack that must be addressed in cybersecurity planning and governance, reflecting the complex dynamics of both social pressure and self-construction within contemporary technological landscapes.

3.2. Hacking from the Outside In

Despite the relatively long lineage of VR technology, the advent of economically accessible, high-performance headsets has ushered in a deeper and more comprehensive wave of research on its impact and capacities (Bown et al., 2017). To date, the VR industry has largely focused on spatial elements such as creating immersive and realistic simulated environments.[1] However, the more potent and less explored aspect of VR is its unparalleled ability to manipulate the mind, and with recent entries by Apple, Google, and others into the VR space, this manipulation becomes an even more significant concern. According to recent market research, as of 2023, there were over 171 million VR users worldwide, and the number is expected to grow. Unfortunately, the VR industry has taken a page from the psychedelic industry, where "the institutions and actors that require oversight and regulation are positioning themselves as regulators. This raises significant concern regarding regulatory capture and conflicts

---

1. This was the primary focus of Meta's (formerly Facebook) Metaverse, whose limited consumer reception was due, in part, to this narrow focus. See, for example: https://gamerant.com/meta-metaverse-losses-why-audience-reception/.

of interest, and may result in the type of 'ethics washing' that has been discussed in other industries" (Devenot et al., 2022). This lack of regulation is in spite of the fact that, in a relatively short timeframe, VR has been shown to improve mood (Chan et al., 2021), reduce loneliness (Antunes et al., 2017), induce and resolve body dysmorphia (Summers et al., 2021), induce and resolve vertigo (Mandour et al., 2022), treat obesity and eating disorders (Brown et al., 2020), and enhance learning (Lee et al., 2010).

This vast array of psychosocial manipulations that VR can administer, from mood alterations to learning enhancements, demonstrates its unrivalled potential. As compelling as these capabilities are for personal transformation, they also signal alarming opportunities for misuse, particularly in the realms of training simulations (e.g., recreating complex scenarios, recruitment processes, surveillance techniques, disinformation campaigns). For example, the US military has been using video games like *America's Army* to recruit young people since 2002 (Jacques, 2009). This possibility relates to the first axis we named above, the exploitation of individuals using VR by coordinated groups. While the misuse by certain groups is undeniably concerning, as the Cambridge Analytica scandal revealed (Chan, 2019), the potential manipulation by megacorporations represents a more pervasive and insidious threat to individual autonomy (Strycharz & Duivenvoorde, 2021).

In the case of exploitation of individuals by megacorporations, the possibilities are nearly endless, as they seek to "enhance" every aspect of our lives with digital-virtual replicas in the "metaverse," starting with advertising and consumerism (Takahashi, 2022). As Rigotti and Malgieri (2023, p. 10) write, "the ultimate goal of the metaverse will be to access goods and services in new and immersive ways." The digital economy that will characterize the metaverse "will eventually allow users to earn, pay, exchange, and invest," but the "framing power" will rest with Big Tech companies, who can "reconfigure choice architectures in line with whoever pays for them" (Hildebrandt, 2021, pp. 10, 56). That is, Big Tech companies can "nudge the user to accept unfair or undesirable terms and conditions in exchange for the satisfaction of their needs and the removal or mitigation of the human vulnerabilities they experience in the physical world" (Rigotti & Malgieri, 2023, p. 24). Additionally, the complexity of key technologies that underlie VR worlds like the "metaverse" will raise barriers for those without high digital and financial literacy to understand what they are really choosing. Difficulty understanding the complex functionality of these nested systems, when VR shopping experiences might require you to spend with bitcoin, for example, "will impair a user's autonomy and informational self-determination" (Rigotti & Malgieri, 2023, p. 11).

Most importantly, however, when theorizing about the critical vulnerabilities of VR, we need to account for how emerging technologies can be used to trigger altered states of consciousness that induce neural plasticity and allow new forms of self-concepts to be triggered without users' consent. This is why our study also accounts for insidious use cases that are harder to track, those associated with our axis number 2: individuals deliberately manipulating themselves via the project of "self-hacking," and especially "consciousness hacking."[2] While social media platforms have indeed sculpted the psyche through strategic ads and echo chambers, VR takes manipulation to a more intimate and somatic level. These complex somatic-subjectivity-altering elements include:

- Modifying the enduring memory of the body (Serino et al., 2016)
- Inducing "mystical"-type experiences (Glowacki et al., 2020)
- Inducing "out-of-body" experiences and affecting people's fear of death (Martial et al., 2023)
- Inducing symptoms of depersonalization and derealization (Barreda-Ángeles & Hartmann, 2023)
- Inducing proprioceptive confusion (confusing the sense of ownership over one's body) (Valori et al., 2020)

The development of regenerative virtual therapy (RVT), for example, will "offer an unprecedented experimental overview of the dynamics of our bodily representations, allowing the reverse-engineering of their functioning for hacking them using advanced technologies" (Riva et al., 2021, p. 1). These can potentially be healing, liberatory, and wonderful tools. But "if tech elites control the infrastructure for global access to these tools, the encoding of normative ideologies" in datasets and in use protocols "could have far-reaching implications by influencing beliefs and expectations in a manner that aligns with

---

2.   For more on this see: *Gaming and extremism: The radicalization of digital playgrounds* (2024).

elite interests. In both cases, echoes and reflections of the status quo of power relations can seem like evidence about the fundamental nature of reality, which undermines their utility as tools for healing and liberation" (Devenot, 2023, p. 14). Thus, through this list of VR's phenomenological and subjectivity altering use-cases, the vulnerable self becomes a point of attack.

Disturbingly, certain mass violence attacks witnessed in recent years, such as the Highland Park shooter and his engagement with "schizowave" content (Yousef, 2022), show that some violent actors are seeking out online content and community designed to bring about a kind of psychotic break in themselves in order to prime them to do violence. As Newhouse (2022) explains:

> People in these communities [schizowave, or schizoposting communities] create and post content that is purposefully designed to be incoherent, cobbled together from a mishmash of influences, and often with an overwhelming focus on graphic violence and aggressive visuals. This content is meant to be spread, and it is meant to transform a person's mind into a state where it is more amenable to actually carrying out real-world attacks. It is designed to make violence the only possible solution to a world without distinction between fiction and reality.

According to some monitors of violence in online culture, "'schizowave' [...] has broken into the mainstream. It's a large part of Zoomer online culture now" (Newhouse, 2022).[3] The case of the Highland Park shooter highlights that not only is there danger in the potential for external entities to "hack" another person's subjectivity without their knowledge or consent, but there is also danger in the individual's ability to shape their own reality by "self-hacking." Our emphasis in this report is that we need to consider this self-hacking in cybersecurity planning and governance.

In particular there are four key vulnerabilities of VR that can be used to hack the self:

---

3.   Schizowave's name references the disorders schizophrenia and schizoaffective disorder, both commonly characterized by paranoid delusions and hallucinations. Ideologically, it amalgamates various conspiracy ideas ranging from Nordic aliens to hollow earth civilizations, with a fascist interpretation related to the existence and ascendency of "higher races."

1) Induce dissociative states: VR is capable of using program-
   mable experiences and the body ownership illusion to significantly alter one's perception of reality, both spatially and
   temporally. As the VRX "Isness" demonstrates, these experiences can induce a state of dissociation, where the user feels
   detached from their own body and sense of self (Slater, 2018).
   The designers achieved this by programming experiences
   that consistently contradict the user's physical movements or
   actions, leading to a sense of disconnection from their body
   or identity. Mindset and setting of the VRX are determinants
   here: Isness produced a state of euphoria in users, while a
   maliciously designed VRX could produce a psychosis-like
   state (Loewen, 2019).

2) Manipulation of memory and perception: As shown by recent
   studies on forensic memory in VR, extremist actors could create VR experiences designed to manipulate the user's memory or perception of events (Casey et al., 2019). For example,
   they might subject the user to virtual experiences that repeatedly associate negative emotions or experiences with certain
   aspects of their identity, leading to a distorted self-perception
   over time, especially as they are forced to experience these
   memories visually from a "first-person" perspective that
   screen-based media cannot replicate.

3) Simulated peer pressure: In a virtual environment, users can
   interact with artificially created avatars, coupled with generative AI, that can exert social influence (Franceschi-Bicchierai,
   2019). Extremist actors could take advantage of the fabula-
   tive tendencies of our human bodies by creating humanlike
   crowds and individuals that produce a false sense of consensus, pressuring the user to conform to extremist ideologies
   (Loewen-Colon & Mosurinjohn, 2022).

4) Weaponize feedback and rewards: Utilizing addictive reward
   elements developed in video games and slot machines, VR can
   provide haptic, sound, and visual sensory feedback and emo-
   tional/psychological stimulation based on the user's actions
   (Bean et al., 2017). The risk of subtle belief change happens
   when the user's actions, which conform to certain extremist
   behaviours or beliefs, are consistently rewarded and intermit-
   tently reinforced (Lewandowsky, 2012). In other words, the
   VR user is rewarded when their actions and behaviours in

the virtual world align with the extremist ideological goals of the VR designer.

As noted above, by threatening a user's stability and security in their sense of self, VR may leave them to be extra vulnerable to exploitation by bad actors who seek to influence their identity and/or worldview. However, we must also consider how it can encourage individuals to alter themselves in such a manner that they feel they are in control of "hacking" themselves, but do not realize the unintended consequences of doing so. The phenomenon of "self-hacking" belongs to a larger umbrella that includes "life hacking," "personality hacking," and a host of other sub-communities already prevalent among popular, elite, and fringe groups seeking performance enhancement, and adds another layer to this discussion.[4] Historically, the discourse around self-hacking primarily focused on the automation of mundane tasks or the optimization of routines. However, as we ponder the expanding domains of "self-hacking" and its implications, it is essential to examine the philosophical underpinnings that shape our understanding of self and technology. It is within this framework that Foucault's perspective on technology, power, and subjectivity offers invaluable insights.

3.3. Hacking from the Inside Out: Foucault's "Technologies of the Self"

While Foucault considers there to be four major types of "technologies," the ones that capture his interest are these technologies of the self "which permit individuals to effect by their own means or with the help of others a certain number of operations on their own bodies

---

4.   Although we use the broad term "self-hacking," under its umbrella are various sub-genres of hacking techniques, including life, consciousness, spirit, personality, and a host of other hacking modalities. As legend has it, the movement began in 2004 when computer scientist Danny O'Brien gave a presentation on the topic of programming scripts and shortcuts into computer software in which he coined the phrase "life hack" (Tripani, 2005). O'Brien found himself frustrated with the relative sloppiness and inefficiency of his own work and realized that with a few simple tricks he could cut his programming time significantly. With more time came opportunities to do more things that he enjoyed so he solicited other "hackers" to share their scripts and methods, and a new discourse was born. Blending the language of computer science, biology, and capitalism, "lifehacking" was embraced by entrepreneurs, techgeeks, and computer nerds throughout the tech industry and broader Internet culture.

and souls, thoughts, conduct, and ways of being, so as to transform themselves in order to attain a certain state of happiness, purity, wisdom, perfection, or immortality" (Martin et al., 1988, p. 18). When thinking about technology as Foucault uses it, it can be understood as both "a form of power that 'produces' individuals in ways that integrate them into political and economic structures by supervising, subjecting, and normalizing them, and a term that dispels the illusion of the 'the individual as abstract subject, defined by individual rights'" (Behrent, 2013, p. 82). It also frees us from the machinic/digital focus of the term where technologies become abstract machines and tools that people use in the world and on their bodies in order to manage and govern. Technologies are dynamic and transversal in the sense that they can be turned inwards upon the individual, as well as outwards upon the world.

Technologies of the self, and self-hacks in particular, are methods, practices, and actions for "improving" productivity, or making life easier, and are a response to the cultural pressures of capitalism. Self-hacking is a prime example of a "technology of the self" and the influence of power formations of governmentality by which the individual applies themselves to new disciplinary methods for the sake of normalization (Foucault, 1982, p. 777).[5] The practices and discourse of self-hacking exhibits both constructive and destructive powers as it reinforces and undermines power. It participates in normalizing technologies of the self, associated with self-help discourse, while also exploiting and undermining these normalizing processes. Self-hacking can be used both to automatize habits and to break through automatizing processes or bad habits for different effects (Grenny, 2016). Communities engaged in self-hacking also utilize embodied rituals like meditation, technology, nootropics, and psychedelics (most of which remain illegal) to alter their mental states.

---

5.   Although Foucault uses the word "technology" he is not referring to any sense of electronic or digital machines and devices. He uses "technology" primarily in the Greek sense of *techne,* which he modifies as a way of exploring how power gets directed toward the individual as they take the form of a self. In elaborating this concept, Foucault charts out the development of this understanding of technology from the Greco-Roman *techne* pairing of "know thyself" and "care for oneself" as it transitions into the early Christian pastoral power focused on renhunciation and salvation through self-transformation and self-disclosure. Foucault declares that in doing so, his "objective [...] has been to create a history of the different modes by which, in our culture, human beings are made subjects" (p. 777).

Among the self-hacking community, there is an intersection of the language and hardware of computer technology and a prevalent view of the body as a machine whose parts can be upgraded, worn out, and optimized. The writings of these self-hackers do not seem to be about getting control of one's body but, rather, learning exploitative tricks in order to shortcut its processes. Institutions, however, like the megacorporations of Silicon Valley and the tech industry, are very interested in encouraging these techniques for what seems like the purposes of control and manipulation. Sherry Turkle argues that the modern state has made citizens who do not need to be monitored as their "always-on/always-on-you technology takes the job of self-monitoring to a new level" (2008, p. 130). Their lives are taken over by "a new disciplining technology" (Turkle, 2008, p. 130). Just as governments sought to "to punish less, perhaps; but certainly to punish better" (Foucault, 1975, p. 82), some self-hackers can be understood as having the mentality to work less, perhaps; but certainly to work better. However, a newer frontier is emerging: hacking consciousness itself.

Borrowing from the vernacular of psychedelic science, "consciousness hacking" is a form of self-hacking that aspires to transform or "reprogram" the mental and emotional states of individuals. Through the controlled use of substances like psilocybin and LSD, users claim to reach heightened states of awareness, unlock creative potential, and address psychological issues like depression or trauma that are holding them back from enacting their full capacity for production (Solon, 2016). However, much like other technologies of the self, the ethical dimensions of psychedelic use cannot be overlooked. Such endeavours raise ethical questions that echo Foucault's scrutiny of power relations. Who controls these tools for altering consciousness? Who determines the "right" way to use these substances? And how might they be abused, consciously or unconsciously, to exploit vulnerable populations or perpetuate power imbalances? This line of inquiry uncovers a critical need for ethical frameworks that govern the responsible use of self-hacking technologies as they become even more complex, as a growing body of research now positions VR as a powerful and legal alternative to psychedelics, allowing users to change their minds (Aday et al., 2020; Kaup et al., 2023).

Devenot has pointed out that some self-hackers who are part of elite transhumanism, like Christian Angermayer, want to use psychedelics "to medicate popular resistance to our impending, posthuman future. Angermayer's public statements regularly align with long-termism's belief that we should 'use advanced technologies to reen-gineer our bodies and brains to create a 'superior' race of radically enhanced posthumans' in order to realize humanity's ultimate—or 'longterm'—potential" (Devenot 2023, p. 30; quoting Torres 2021). Again, the megacorporations of this Silicon Valley transhumanism stand to benefit from the digital-pharmacological anaesthetizing of the exploitable gig work labour and consumer base for the increasingly encompassing market of the "metaverse" or other VR worlds like it.

If hacking consciousness raises ethical questions, then the realm and capacities of VR open an entirely new set of dilemmas related to power, control, and identity. The capability of VR to construct alter-nate realities offers not just escapism but also a modicum of power to individuals, who can create, modify, and interact with their digi-tal environments. Yet, this control is often illusory for most VRX par-ticipants. The true power resides with the architects of these digital landscapes and the corporations that commodify user data for tar-geted advertising or algorithmic sorting. In this sense, VR can be seen as a digital panopticon, wherein users may feel a sense of autonomy while being under subtle forms of surveillance and manipulation in the guises already mentioned above.

Speaking of the interrelated hype between emerging technolo-gies like AI, VR, and psychedelics, Devenot writes: "Utopian hype is desensitizing people from noticing how elite decisions are optimiz-ing both for profit [...] now is the time to name—and resist—the cor-porate takeover" (2023, p. 12). This call for sensitization and action should be echoed and amplified with respect to the VR element of these disciplining technologies, as well as the need to break out of disciplinary silos, and even our usual domains (i.e., across academic-business-government) in order to effectively do so. This collaborative work ought to include all "overhyped technologies that have been conscripted by 'the gospel of tech solutionism'" (2023, p. 13).

3.4. Securing Technologies of the Self

The emergence of self-hacking ideologies and self-directed techno-logies signifies more than a simple preoccupation with heightened efficiency or streamlined daily routines. They usher in a seismic shift in how we conceptualize the "self," transitioning us from a static, sin-gular identity to one of dynamic multiplicity. This transformation is both facilitated and regulated by digital technology. However, this liberation comes at a cost. Individuals are ensnared in intricate systems of corporate governance, societal expectations, and power structures inextricably linked to these very technologies.

In this context, the realms of VR and psychedelics stand out as striking examples that warrant our ethical scrutiny. Many in the psychedelic world suggest that these substances offer routes to self-transcendence, while VR promises alternative realities laden with both possibility and peril. In sum, the digital age has revolutionized not just the external world but also the internal multiplicities of the human "self." It offers a double-edged sword: tools for both emancipation and subjugation. When engaging in the ongoing project of hacking our various selves, it is key to remain vigilant of the ethical terrain being navigated. It is within this nuanced interplay of autonomy and control that the destiny of our multiple evolving selves will ultimately be crafted. As Robin Arnott, a leading VR designer has put it, "there's not a market understanding yet for the type of technology that can alter your state of consciousness" (Bye, 2020). While many of these scenarios are already possible, advances in VR technology will make them even more powerfully affective. It is a dangerous combination when the market lacks an understanding of how "the whole [VR] system is designed to numb out the narrative mind" by "overwhelm[ing] it and overload[ing] it," while extremists have a deep understanding of how to manipulate human psychology and cognition (Bye, 2020).

There may indeed be larger existential risks of VR technology, but as Devenot (2023) points out:

> [...] in the context of inflated hype, the mundane risks of capitalism and its ideological drivers are underemphasized topics [...] In parallel to these omissions, critical scholars and activists in both fields—often the very people who initiated public discussions of risk, at personal expense—have described continuing patterns of marginalization and exclusion for highlighting the real harms already caused by [advanced tech] industries. In identifying these patterns across apparently disparate fields, we can gain insight into the influence of Silicon Valley's power on the circulation of ideas and identify the real risks facing our planet. (p. 14)

In other words, and in conclusion, it is important to consider the two axes that were identified above in relation to two more named in this quotation: existential risks and mundane risks of our modern system of production and consumption. The latter is the ever-present and actively alienating apparatus in which coordinated groups of violent extremists and megacorporations can function, and which is the well-spring that supplies the pressures impelling individuals to self-hack.

Currently there are not enough safeguards and regulations to prevent VR misuse. The approaching horizon of VR demands a response from us that should include:

1) enhanced encryption methods informed by leading psycho-logical research on user effects of VR experiences;
2) built-in user safety protocols like warnings and options for content so that VRX users can be more informed about the types of affective encounters they might have;
3) leveraging community-based threat intelligence by actively scanning video game and VR review sites and communities for unexpected effects, and;
4) VR companies fostering collaborations with non-profit cyber-security organizations and law enforcement agencies to inform them about possible illicit and unintended uses of their products.

To establish such a robust response, it is crucial to unite VR developers, security experts, and scholars of technology and media who can model and analyze the phenomenology of this powerful medium. Using the results of this kind of convergence, tech companies can be better informed of the risks of VR as they enter the space. Ultimately, work such as what we are modelling here will allow tech companies to implement preventive measures, including better security protocols and user safeguards, and respond efficiently to the unique risks to self and society enabled by VR's evolution as a prime tool of self-hacking movements when they are turned toward malicious ends.

References

Aday, J. S., Davoli C.C., & Bloesch, E. K. (2020) Psychedelics and virtual reality: Parallels and applications. *Therapeutic Advances in Psychopharmacology*, 10, 1–9. https://doi-org.libezproxy2.syr.edu/10.1177/2045125320948356

Antunes, T. P. C., de Oliveria, A. S. B., Crocetta, T. B., de Lima Antao, J. Y. F., de Almeida Barbosa, R. T., Guarnieri, R., Massetti, T., de Mello

Monterio, C. B., & de Abreu, L. C. (2017). Computer classes and games in virtual reality environment to reduce loneliness among students of an elderly reference center: Study protocol for a randomised cross-over design. *Medicine (Baltimore)*, *96*(10), 1–7. https://doi.org/10.1097%2FMD.0000000000005954

Barreda-Ángeles, M., & Hartmann, T. (2023). Experiences of depersonalization/derealization among users of virtual reality applications: A cross-sectional survey. *Cyberpsychology, Behavior, and Social Networking*, *26*(1), 22–27. http://doi.org.libezproxy2.syr.edu/10.1089/cyber.2022.0152

Bean, A. M., Nielsen, R. K. L., van Rooij, A. J., & Ferguson, C. J. (2017). Video game addiction: The push to pathologize video games. *Professional Psychology, Research and Practice*, *48*(5), 378–389. https://doi.org/10.1037/pro0000150

Behrent, M. C. (2013). Foucault and technology. *History and Technology*, *29*(1), 54–104. doi:10.1080/07341512.2013.780351

Bown, J., White, E., & Boopalan, A. (2017). Looking for the ultimate display: A brief history of virtual reality. In J. Gackenbach & J. Bown (Eds.), *Boundaries of self and reality online* (pp. 239–259). Academic Press. https://doi.org/10.1016/B978-0-12-804157-4.00012-8

Brown, A., Bisbee, J., Lai, A., Bonneau, R., Nagler, J., & Tucker, J. A. (2022). Echo chambers, rabbit holes, and algorithmic bias: How YouTube recommends content to real users. SSRN. http://dx.doi.org/10.2139/ssrn.4114905

Brown, T., Nauman Vogel, E., Adler, S., Bohon, C., Bullock, K., Nameth, K., Riva, G., Safer, D. L., & Runfola, C. D. (2020). Bringing virtual reality from clinical trials to clinical practice for the treatment of eating disorders: An example using virtual reality cue exposure therapy. *Journal of Medical Internet Research*, *22*(4), 1–10. http://dx.doi.org/10.2196/16386

Bye, K. (2020). "SoundSelf" & the Technodelic Manifesto: Using VR to transform consciousness [Audio podcast episode]. Voices of VR Podcast. Retrieved April 29, 2020, from https://voicesofvr.com/906-sound-self-the-technodelic-manifesto-using-vr-to-transform-consciousness/

Casey P., Lindsay-Decusati, R., Baggili, I., & Breitinger, F. (2019). Inception: Virtual space in memory space in real space—Memory forensics of immersive virtual reality with the HTC Vive [Supplement material]. *Digital Investigation*, *29*, S13–S2. https://www-sciencedirect-com.libezproxy2.syr.edu/science/article/pii/S1742287619301562#:~:text=VR%20systems%20are%20no%20exception,forensics%20has%20become%20increasingly%20important

Chan, R. (2019). The Cambridge Analytica whistleblower explains how the firm used Facebook data to sway elections. *Business Insider*. https://www.businessinsider.com/cambridge-analytica-whistleblower-christopher-wylie-facebook-data-2019-10

Chan, S. H. M., Qiu, L., Esposito, G., Mai, K. P., Tam, K., Cui, J. (2021). Nature in virtual reality improves mood and reduces stress: Evidence from young adults and senior citizens. *Virtual Reality, 27*, 3285–3300. https://doi.org/10.1007/s10055-021-00604-4

Devenot, N., Tumilty, E., Buisson, M., McNamee, S., Nickles, D., & Ross, L. K. (2022, March 9). A precautionary approach to touch in psychedelic-assisted therapy." *Bill of Health.* https://blog.petrieflom.law.harvard.edu/2022/03/09/precautionary-approach-touch-in-psychedelic-assisted-therapy/

Devenot, N, (2023). TESCREAL hallucinations: Psychedelic and AI hype as inequality engines. *Journal of Psychedelic Studies, 7*(S1), 22–39. https://doi.org/10.1556/2054.2023.00292

Dziura, J. (2013, December 19). When "Life Hacking" is really white privilege. *Medium.* https://medium.com/get-bullish/when-life-hacking-is-really-white-privilege-a5e5f4e9132f.

Foucault, M. (1982). The Subject and power. *Critical Inquiry, 8*(4), 777–795.

Franceschi-Bicchierai, L. (2019, July 3). Hackers hijacked VR chatrooms to manipulate users' reality. *Vice.* https://www.vice.com/en/article/8xz33p/hackers-hijacked-vr-chatrooms-to-manipulate-users-reality

Glowacki, D. R., Wonnacott, M. D., Freire, R., Glowacki, B. R., Gale, E. M., Pike, J. E., de Haan, T., Chatziapostolou, M., & Metatla, O. (2020). Isness: Using multi-person VR to design peak mystical-type experiences comparable to psychedelics. In R. Bernhaupt, F. F. Mueller, D. Verweij, & J. Andres (Eds.), *Proceedings of the 2020 CHI Conference on Human Factors in Computing Systems,* (pp. 1–14). Association for Computing Machinery. https://doi.org/10.1145/3313831.3376649

Govers, J., Feldman, P., Dant, A., & Patros, P. (2023). Down the rabbit hole: Detecting online extremism, radicalisation, and politicised hate speech. *ACM Computing Surveys, 55*(14), 1–35. https://doi.org/10.1145/3583067

Grenny, J. (2016). Trick yourself into breaking a bad habit. *Harvard Business Review.* https://hbr.org/2016/01/trick-yourself-into-breaking-a-bad-habit

Hildebrandt, M. (2021). The issue of bias. The framing powers of machine learning. In M. Pelillo & T. Scantamburlo (Eds.), *Machines we trust: Perspectives on dependable AI* (pp. 43–60). The MIT Press.

Jacques, J. (2009). *US Army has spent $32.8M on America's army game.* Gamerant. https://gamerant.com/army-spent-328m-americas-army-game/

Kaup, K. K., Vasser, M., Tulver, K., Munk, M, & Pikamae, J. (2023). Psychedelic replications in virtual reality and their potential as a therapeutic instrument: An open-label feasibility study. *Frontiers in Psychiatry, 14*, 1–14. https://doi.org/10.3389/fpsyt.2023.1088896

Ledwich, M., Zaitsev, A., & Laukemper, A. (2022). Radical bubbles on YouTube? Revisiting algorithmic extremism with personalised recommendations. *First Monday, 27*(12). https://doi.org/10.5210/fm.v27i12.12552

Lee, E., Wong, K. W., & Fung, C. C. (2010). How does desktop virtual reality enhance learning outcomes? A structural equation modeling approach. *Computers & Education, 55*(4), 1424–1442. http://dx.doi.org/10.1016/j.compedu.2010.06.006

Lewandowsky, S., Ecker, U. K., Seifert, C. M., Schwarz, N., & Cook, J. (2012). Misinformation and its correction: Continued influence and successful debiasing. *Psychological Science in the Public Interest, 13*(3), 106–131.

Loewen, J. B. (2019). Death, fabulation, and virtual reality gaming, *Gamevironments, 9*, 202–221.

Loewen, J. B. (2022). The problem of the "virtual": Virtual reality, digital dualism, and religious experience [Dissertation]. Syracuse University.

Loewen-Colón, J., & Mosurinjohn, S. C. (2022). Fabulation, machine agents, and spiritually authorizing encounters. *Religions, 13(4),* 333–342. https://doi.org/10.3390/rel13040333

Mandour, A. E., El-Gharib, A. M., Emara, A. A., & Elmahallawy, T. H. (2022). Virtual reality versus optokinetic stimulation in visual vertigo rehabilitation. *European Archives of Oto-rhino-laryngology, 279*(3), 1609–1614. https://doi.org/10.1007/s00405-021-07091-y

Martial, C., Casol, H., Slater, M., Bourdin, P., Mensen, A., Oliva, R., Laureys, St., & Nunex, P. (2023). EEG signature of out-of-body experiences induced by virtual reality: A novel methodological approach. *Journal of Cognitive Neuroscience, 35*(9), 1410–1422. https://doi.org/10.1162/jocn_a_02011

Newhouse, F. B. (2022). *Note on the Highland Park shooting.* Dirty South Right Watch. https://dirtysouthrightwatch.org/2022/highland-park-shooter/

Rigotti C., & Malgieri, G. (2023). *Human vulnerability in the metaverse* [Working paper]. Alliance for Universal Digital Rights. https://audri.org/wp-content/uploads/2023/07/EN-AUDRi-Metaverse-Report-07-PDF.pdf

Riva, G., Serino, S., Di Lernia, D., & Pagnini, F. (2021). Regenerative virtual therapy: The use of multisensory technologies and mindful attention for updating the altered representations of the bodily self. *Frontiers in Systems Neuroscience, 15* (749268), 1–8. https://doi.org/10.3389/fnsys.2021.749268

Solon, O. (2016). Under pressure, Silicon Valley workers turn to LSD microdosing. *Wired.* https://www.wired.com/story/lsd-microdosing-drugs-silicon-valley/

Summers, B. J., Schwartzberg, A. C., & Wilhelm, S. (2021). A virtual reality study of cognitive biases in body dysmorphic disorder. *Journal of Abnormal Psychology, 130*(1), 26–33. https://doi.org/10.1037/abn0000563

Trapani, G. (2005). Interview: Father of "life hacks" Danny O'Brien. *Lifehacker.* http://lifehacker.com/036370/interview-father-of-life-hacks-danny-obrien

Serino, S., Pedroli, E., Keizer, A., Triberti, S., Dakanalis, A., Pallavicini, F.,

Chirico, A., & Riva, G. (2016). Virtual reality body swapping: A tool for modifying the allocentric memory of the body. *Cyberpsychology, Behavior, and Social Networking, 19*(2), 127–133. http://doi.org.libez-proxy2.syr.edu/10.1089/cyber.2015.0229

Slater, M. (2018). Immersion and the illusion of presence in virtual reality. *British Journal of Psychology, 109*(3), 431–433. https://doi.org/10.1111/bjop.12305

Statista. (2023). Number of virtual reality (VR) and augmented reality (AR) users in the United States from 2017 to 2023. https://www.statista.com/statistics/1017008/united-states-vr-ar-users/

Strycharz, J., & Duivenvoorde, B. (2021). The exploitation of vulnerability through personalised marketing communication: Are consumers protected? *Internet Policy Review, 10*(4). http://dx.doi.org/10.14763/2021.4.1585

Takahashi, D. (2022). *Mark Zuckerberg unveils ultra-realistic VR display prototypes.* GamesBeat. https://venturebeat.com/games/mark-zuckerberg-unveils-ultra-realistic-vr-display-prototypes/

Turkle, S. (1997) *Life on the screen: Identity in the age of the Internet.* Simon & Schuster.

Turkle, S. (2008). Always-on/always-on-you: The tethered self. In J. E. Katz (Ed.), *Handbook of mobile communication studies* (p. 130). The MIT Press.

Valori, I., McKenna-Plumley, P. E., Bayramova, R., Zandonella Callegher, C., Altoè, G., & Farroni, T. (2020). Proprioceptive accuracy in immersive virtual reality: A developmental perspective. *PLoS One, 15*(1), e0222253. https://doi.org/10.1371%2Fjournal.pone.0222253

Yousef, O. (2022, July 6). *Why the Highland Park suspect represents a different kind of violent extremism.* NPR. https://www.npr.org/2022/07/06/1110013040/the-highland-park-suspect-breaks-the-mold-on-violent-extremists

CHAPTER 4

Developing Human-Centric Informational Security

Jonathon W. Penney

Abstract

Disinformation and information manipulation are widely seen as an urgent threat to democracy, but less often as a cybersecurity threat. Historically, disinformation has rarely been included in lists of recognized threats in cybersecurity manuals and appendices of global standards organizations and only recently has disinformation been approached as a cybersecurity threat, with only a handful of works offering a more focused and systematic discussion on this point. This chapter aims to help fill this void by arguing not only that disinformation and information manipulation is a cybersecurity threat, but that the present predominant cybersecurity paradigm is largely inadequate to address it. Instead, a human-centric approach to cybersecurity, one that centres humans as the objects of security—"security of the self"—should be adopted to address disinformation and information manipulation. However, human-centric approaches are themselves relatively new and underdeveloped, and there is little consensus in the field about what is required. This chapter argues that human-centric cybersecurity need not be monolithic, and different conceptualizations can be employed for different threats and contexts. To that end, a framework for human-centric cybersecurity is set out that addresses disinformation threats centred on user protection and safety, integrates psychological and

behavioural factors—the human costs of information manipulation—and is broad enough to encompass robust structural law
and policy reforms. Lastly, this chapter offers recommendations for operationalizing human-centric informational security,
including that rights-based conceptualizations of human-centric
cybersecurity should be avoided when operationalizing as policy
to reduce gridlock and inaction due to competing rights claims.
Instead, a duty of care or consumer protection frameworks are
more likely to see success.

D isinformation—deliberately   false   news   and   information
    intended to mislead and manipulate—is now viewed as a sig-
nificant threat to democratic societies. In 2022, a survey of over
two thousand Canadians found 72 percent believed disinformation
or intentionally false news or information is a "threat to Canadian
democracy" (Higginbotham, 2022). An earlier survey in 2019 found
90 percent of Canadians had been misled or manipulated by false
and "fake" news (Thompson, 2019). Canadians are not alone—it is
a global challenge. Studies have found that 69 percent of Americans
view disinformation as a "major problem" in society (McCorkindale
& Henry, 2019, p. 2) and 83 percent of Europeans say it is a "threat
to democracy" (European Commission, 2018). In light of Russian
interference in the 2016 US presidential election involving a large-
scale operation involving disinformation and other forms of targeted
information manipulation, former Central Intelligence Agency acting
director Michael Morell stated that the operation was "an attack on
our very democracy. It's an attack on who we are as a people [...]
the political equivalent of 9/11" (Morell & Kelly, 2016). More recently,
the European Union, United Kingdom, Canada, and other countries
have undertaken efforts to battle disinformation online (see Casero-
Ripollés et al., 2023; Bontcheva et al., 2020) and the United Nations
Secretary General called for "global action" tackling disinformation
and hate (Lederer, 2023).

Overall, disinformation and information manipulation are
widely seen as urgent threats to democracy, but often are not viewed
as *cybersecurity* threats. Given how disinformation is generated,
spread, and amplified via vulnerable computer systems and networks
(Nagasako, 2020, pp. 125–127; McKay & Tenove, 2020, pp. 705–706), it
would seem to constitute a clear threat. Yet, disinformation is rarely

included in lists of recognized threats in cybersecurity manuals and appendices of global standardizing organizations (Caramancion, 2020, p. 440). Further, the case for approaching disinformation as a cybersecurity threat is largely "missing" from the literature (Caramancion et al., 2022). The few works that have made the case have been overly technical and largely focused on state-centred issues like cyberwar and information conflict (e.g., Caramancion, 2020; Caramancion et al., 2022; Mirza et al., 2023; Ignaczak et al., 2021; Hunt, 2021) with human-centric approaches largely neglected. This neglect compounds an existing gap in the literature on human-centric approaches to cybersecurity more generally (Penney, 2021a, pp. 417–418; Grobler et al., 2021; Kioskli, 2023, p. 8). This chapter aims to help fill this void by arguing not only that disinformation and information manipulation is a cybersecurity threat, but that the present predominant cybersecurity paradigm is largely inadequate to address it. Instead, a human-centric approach to cybersecurity, one that centres humans as the objects of security—"security of the self"—should be adopted to address disinformation and information manipulation.

However, human-centric approaches are themselves relatively new and underdeveloped, and there is little consensus in the field about what is required. I argue that human-centric cybersecurity need not be monolithic and different conceptualizations can be employed for different threats and contexts. To this end, I set out a framework for human-centric cybersecurity to address disinformation threats that is centred on user protection and safety and integrates psychological and behavioural factors, the human costs of information manipulation, and is broad enough to encompass robust structural law and policy reforms. Last, I argue that rights-based conceptualizations of human-centric cybersecurity should be avoided when operationalizing as policy to avoid gridlock and inaction due to competing rights claims. Instead, duty of care or consumer protection frameworks are more likely to see success.

4.1. Information Manipulation as a Cybersecurity Threat

Disinformation is typically defined as false information that is knowingly shared to mislead, manipulate, and otherwise cause harm (Wardle & Darakhshan, 2017, p. 5; Hameleers, 2023, p. 5). By contrast, misinformation refers mainly to false information shared with no intention to harm (Wardle & Darakhshan, 2017, p. 5; Hameleers, 2023,

p. 5; Nagasako, 2020, p. 133). Disinformation can have many aims and purposes, such as changing a person's thoughts and behaviours, or changing people's perceptions of reality, and thus aim to influence public opinion and behaviour at scale (Caramancion et al., 2022, p. 1). Disinformation is also often employed in "propaganda" campaigns and "influence" operations, which seek to influence people and their political views, often by presenting biased or misleading information (Bradshaw, 2020; Bradshaw et al., 2021). More recently, disinformation and misinformation have been labelled as "information disorders" (Wardle & Darakhshan, 2017, p. 10) or "information manipulation" (Laidlaw, 2022, p. 8). This chapter employs the latter term as encompassing all forms of information deception beyond disinformation alone, such as misinformation, propaganda, and influence operations.

Disinformation and information manipulation have not generally been approached as cybersecurity threats, either in industry practices and standards or in cybersecurity research and literature. But that is slowly changing, as it must. For instance, a recent industry survey found that 48 percent of cybersecurity professionals view disinformation as a threat, and among them, 49 percent say it is a very significant threat. The same study also found that 91 percent of cybersecurity professionals thought stricter online measures were necessary to address disinformation (Coble, 2020). This is not surprising. Indeed, public concern about the threat posed by disinformation did not occur in a vacuum. Following the widely covered Russian interference in the 2016 US election, there has been a cascade of similarly high-profile cases of disinformation and information manipulation operations around the world (Nagasako, 2020, pp. 130–131; Schia and Gjesvik, 2020). Most of those cases involve disinformation used in conjunction with targets, tools, and techniques that fall within the domain of cybersecurity such as hacking, leaking, information warfare, and cyber-attacks on critical infrastructure (Nagasako, 2020; Caramancion et al., 2022; Ramirez & Choucri, 2016, p. 2220). The COVID-19 pandemic has only magnified these challenges, creating an "infodemic" wherein widely available pandemic-related disinformation and misinformation has been exploited by malicious state and non-state actors to launch cyber-attacks on vulnerable systems and populations (Smith, 2021). More recently, Caramancion et al. (2022) made a compelling case that disinformation and information manipulation has all the required elements of even the most technical definitions of cybersecurity threats and is analogous to other common forms of cyber-attacks, like phishing, denial-of-service attacks, and malware.

Therefore, disinformation and information manipulation should be approached as a cybersecurity threat. However, the existing predominant cybersecurity paradigm is far too narrow and limited to effectively address this emerging cybersecurity challenge.

4.2. The Limits of the Existing Cybersecurity Paradigm

Disinformation and information manipulation are nothing new. They have been a feature of human communication since ancient times. Octavian, for instance, waged a propaganda campaign against Marc Antony to smear his reputation in his bid to become Roman emperor, and succeeded (Posetti & Matthews, 2018, p. 1). Yet, new technologies have significantly altered their impact and reach over time. The development of the printing press in the fifteenth century, which made mass communications possible, increased the dissemination of disinformation and misinformation (Posetti & Matthews, 2018). Radio technology, developed in the early twentieth century, was widely employed by states during the Second World War to increase the range and effectiveness of war propaganda. This was especially used by Nazi Germany, consisting of a substantial threat to peace that the international community sought to address in the post-war period (Penney, 2014).

Today, our digitally connected world has made disinformation and information manipulation "unparalleled in its reach" (Ecker et al., 2022, p. 13). Established technologies like the Internet, social media, ubiquitous computing, big data collection, retention, and analytics, combined with emerging ones, like artificial intelligence, machine learning, and automation, has significantly increased the scale, scope, and sophistication of information manipulation operations (Schia & Gjesvik, 2020, p. 413; Bradshaw et al., 2021; McKay & Tenove, 2021, pp. 705–706; Posetti & Matthews, 2018). Always-on Internet connectivity and popular social media platforms like Facebook, X (Twitter), Instagram, and YouTube have created the largest mass communication audience in history that is captive but also generative and distributive, with billions of users from around the world sharing news, information, images, videos, and memes—a target-rich environment for disinformation and information manipulation (Krafft & Donovan, 2020; Wardle & Darakhshan, 2017; Marwick & Lewis, 2017). Those same social media platforms employ monetization models, system designs, and content moderation strategies that encourage the spread of disinformation and misinformation (McKay & Tenove, 2020; Posetti, 2018). Automated technology and tools, including bots—an abbreviation for social robots—can be very effective at spreading false information at mass scale (Bontridder & Poullet, 2021, p. e32–5). Such "bots" are designed to communicate information and mimic human behaviour online; once credible and trusted within the online groups and communities they target, they can be used by malicious actors to amplify and spread disinformation at scale via botnets (networks of bots) or generate interest in misleading content by creating an impression of broader interest in false information or via artificial "viral" sharing campaigns (Bontridder & Poullet, 2021, p. e32–5). Generative artificial intelligence (AI) and deepfake technology can now fabricate fake and false content and media that is nearly impossible to detect (Dan et al., 2021; Bontridder & Poullet, 2021; Micallef et al., 2021). It is cheaper and easier than ever before to mislead and manipulate people.

All this is compounded by a deeply permissive regulatory environment. Most major social media platforms are US-based, wherein Section 230 of the US *Communications Decency Act* provides them with near-blanket legal immunity, shielding them from liability and legal accountability for user-generated content and from lawsuits relating to how they moderate content (Citron & Wittes, 2017; Laidlaw, 2019). Section 230's broad legal protections shelter these powerful platforms from legal accountability while providing little incentive to address online abuse and other harms (Citron & Wittes, 2017). Canada has few laws addressing disinformation and no general intermediary liability statute to police social media platforms (Laidlaw, 2022, p. 28), and until recently both federal and provincial governments have been very reluctant to change that (Elghawaby, 2018). Existing common law is often "unprincipled" and "ill-suited" to dealing with these issues (Laidlaw & Young, 2017), and like lawmakers, courts have also not been eager to change. Taken together, disinformation and information manipulation pose an "unprecedented" public policy challenge (Wardle & Darakhshan, 2017, p. 10).

Yet, the predominant cybersecurity paradigm, including research and practice, is wholly inadequate to meet this challenge. Cybersecurity remains a relatively young field, which largely began as a subfield of computer science but has since evolved and expanded (Rahman et al., 2021; Ramirez and Choucri, 2016). Yet, recent comprehensive literature reviews by Ramirez and Choucri (2016) and Suryotrisongko and Musashi (2019) demonstrate that the field remains highly technical, with cybersecurity researchers and practitioners focused primarily on encryption and other network security measures, while human factors are largely neglected (Rohan et al., 2021, p. 133; Rahman, et al., 2021, p. 1; Grobler et al., 2021; Jacob & Yang, 2020). Often, the only "human factor" in cybersecurity, if addressed at all, is that people are the weakest link (Rohan et al., 2021, p. 133; Rahman, et al., 2021, p. 1; Grobler et al., 2021). Moreover, the broader policy context of cybersecurity is also far too narrow, focused on state interests and national security. This is a product of a longer-term "securitization" and "militarization" of the field that began in the 2000s as states increased their interest in cyberwarfare capabilities for strategic advantage (Deibert, 2003, pp. 517–518; Deibert, 2012; Dunn Cavelty, 2012). Today, cybersecurity policy is predominantly framed as a matter of national security, focused mainly on the security of states, state infrastructure, and corporations, rather than citizens and civil society (Carr, 2016; Stevens, 2016; Penney, 2021a, p. 410).

This neglect of the human dimensions in cybersecurity is especially problematic when it comes to disinformation and information manipulation. Human psychology and behavioural science are critical to understanding the generation, distribution, and impact of disinformation and information manipulation. There are critical cognitive, social, and emotional factors that lead people to form, approve, and share false information, as well as to resist knowledge revision once false information has been corrected (Ecker et al., 2022, at p. 13; Pennycook & Rand, 2021). Those engaged in information manipulation operations actively exploit these behavioural and psychological tendencies in order to generate and spread disinformation. Caramancion et al. (2022) have argued disinformation and information manipulation are analogous to other common forms of cyber-attack. However, it is the individual's psychology and "cognitive" capacity that is exploited, referred to as cognitive hacking, and not some vulnerability in a computer system (p. 1).

Moreover, social media platforms that have played a central part in the spread of disinformation and misinformation similarly employ design features that exploit human psychological and behavioural tendencies for commercial advantage. For instance, content curation algorithms and platform dark patterns—user interfaces intentionally designed to confuse or manipulate users—exploit user behavioural tendencies, leading them to amplify and promote news, information, and media that are often false and misleading but sensational in order to drive engagement and profit (McKay & Tenove, 2020; Luguri & Strahilevitz, 2021; Sinders, 2021). For similar reasons, understanding and addressing the impact of established technologies like social media and emerging ones like generative AI and deepfake technology require an understanding of human–computer interaction, which itself is an extensive field of social and behavioural science (Dan et al., 2021; Bontridder & Poullet, 2021; Micallef et al., 2021). In other words, neglecting "human factors" will render cybersecurity not only unable to address or mitigate disinformation and information manipulation threats, but incapable of even understanding them.

Moreover, cybersecurity policy discourse is predominantly focused on the security of states and commercial organizations, especially geopolitical information conflict and cyberwarfare issues. As a result, cybersecurity will have little to offer on domestic generation, distribution, and consumption of disinformation and misinformation, and the permissive regulatory laws and policies that enable it. In many cases, it will advance cybersecurity policies that actively harm individuals and their interests as the interests of states and organizations are often incommensurable with those of individuals (Dunn Cavelty, 2012; Kumar, 2021). With digital media and networked technology, and now automation and machine-learning-powered content generation, it is cheaper and easier than ever before to manipulate people at a societal scale. Law and policy reform can help introduce new costs and accountability but neglecting individuals and how disinformation and information manipulation impact their rights and interests would undercut any effective response.

In short, the existing cybersecurity paradigm, which is highly technical with a national security focus, must be abandoned to deal with disinformation and information manipulation. Instead, a human-centric approach to cybersecurity focused on protection and duties of care should be adopted. But what might that look like? The next section offers some ideas and guidelines for future works on these points—how to frame human-centric cybersecurity for disinformation and information manipulation.

4.3. Framing Human-Centric Informational Security

Critics of the technical and heavily securitized focus of the existing cybersecurity field have increasingly argued for more human-centric approaches to cybersecurity (Grobler et al., 2021; Kioskli, 2023; Penney, 2021a, pp. 417–418;). However, human-centric cybersecurity is itself a new domain that is difficult to define and not well developed (Grobler et al., 2021, p. 2). The core element of a human-centric approach is that the human subject is the central object of security (Dunn Cavelty, 2014; Kumar, 2021, p. 376). Beyond that, there is little guidance. For instance, Dunn Cavelty (2014) and Klein and Hossain (2012) hold that human-centric cybersecurity requires that human interests take priority over state or economic interests. Deibert (2018) and Liaropoulos (2014), by contrast, advocate for a human-centric approach to cybersecurity that focuses predominantly on human rights. Boulanin (2016) argues that human-centric cybersecurity should ensure citizens can enjoy the benefits of information and communication technology safely, thus it should prioritize the well-being of human subjects. In other words, there is no clear consensus on what "human centric" requires and how it should be operationalized in practice. Nevertheless, what follows is an attempt to elaborate a useful framework and guidelines to build greater consensus and lay the foundation for the development of human-centric approaches to cybersecurity disinformation and information manipulation—what I will refer to, shorthand, as informational security.

An effective human-centric framework for informational security should be deeply interdisciplinary, balanced, comprehensive, and empirical. It should focus primarily on the protection and safety of the human subject while ensuring that safety and include protection are not just pursued in technical terms, like network security, but protection of other human interests and values as well, like privacy, equality, trust, and transparency. The framework should offer several critical features. First, it should centre on human behavioural factors and computer interactions in cybersecurity research and practice. A human-centric cybersecurity framework that centres on the human subject will still be inadequate if it remains overly technical and focused solely on human factors in system vulnerabilities. Instead, human psychological, cognitive, and behavioural factors in this approach must be central in addressing information manipulation. Of course, technical security vulnerabilities and protective measures will remain critical to human-centric cybersecurity, but the social context of these technical measures must also be considered and applied. That is, the measures should be understood in terms of both behavioural science and their social context, with insights from other fields like science and technology studies. One of the immense benefits of human-centric approaches in this context is that they can combine the technical dimensions of the existing cybersecurity paradigm with insights from social theory and behaviour science. This, in turn, should render security solutions and mitigation that much more effective in the long term.

Second, the framework should be comprehensive enough to elaborate the *human costs* of disinformation and information manipulation (Smith, 2021, pp. 186–187). No matter the aim or purpose of an information manipulation operation, be it financial cybercrime, cyberwarfare, political or otherwise, it is *people* that are chiefly exploited and impacted. It is their equality, autonomy, decision-making, and behaviour that is manipulated and influenced, often without their knowledge (Smith, 2023). It is also their human rights and interests that are violated and encroached upon. The Cambridge Analytica scandal is a high-profile example of this, involving a large-scale operation over several years that included massive data misappropriation, retention, and leaking, coupled with big data analytics, to create "psychographic profiles" to allow for targeted and highly personalized information manipulation on an ongoing basis to impact the US 2016 election (Susser et al., 2019, pp. 9–12). The scandal involved massive privacy violations as well as harms to the equality and autonomy of targeted users, who were often discriminated against and whose political decision-making was improperly influenced and undermined. Again, a clear benefit of human-centric approaches to informational security is that it will aim to foreground these human costs such that technical and technological cybersecurity knowledge and expertise will be leveraged in a way to reduce them. Moreover, it will ensure that human costs, in addition to technical effectiveness, will be a key factor in assessing the success of informational security measures.

Third, a proper human-centric framework should be broad enough to encompass not just the technical and functional components of cybersecurity and related legislative and regulatory measures, but also more comprehensive measures, such as those ensuring privacy protections, design standards, new legal or statutory rights, and international regulatory measures. While infrastructure has long been a key area of research in the cybersecurity field, it has largely been conceptualized in more narrow and technical ways. Infrastructure speaks to network infrastructure and their resiliency to attack and compromise by malicious actors and advanced persistent threats (Ramirez & Choucri, 2016). A human-centric informational security framework must also integrate design norms and standards centred not just on technical security objectives but other human values such as privacy, human rights, and deliberative democracy (Rubenstein & Good, 2013; Cavoukian, 2009; Penney et al., 2018). Naturally, a human-centric approach here will help ensure that cybersecurity solutions incorporate these other critical values in design. This will also help avoid design trade-offs, where technical solutions necessarily sacrifice other critical human interests. Where the trade-off is too great, the informational security "solution" may end up being just another problem. A human-centric approach to informational security design can help avoid these problems.

For example, one way to "inject" such human values into system and technology design is to slow them down, make them less efficient, less automated, and less seamless (Kim & Ohm, 2023). In other terms, introduce friction in the design of emerging technologies and related systems. There is now an emerging body of literature on friction-in-design, which explores different design features, values, and standards often mandated by law along those very lines (e.g., Kim & Ohm, 2023; Ohm & Frankle, 2018; McGeveran, 2013). Often, information and data misappropriated through hacks and leaks are used in conjunction with disinformation operations to generate media coverage and interest for greater impact. A design standard would prioritize security rather than interoperability. For example, a design rule to make it more difficult for data exfiltration within and between systems would assist human-centric cybersecurity to address information manipulation (Kim & Ohm, 2023, pp. 155–156). Meanwhile, at an international level, there is a need for greater transparency, accountability, and oversight in the trade and export of software vulnerabilities and other offensive tools and techniques that are used in conjunction with disinformation operations (Anstis et al., 2022). To address information manipulation, cybersecurity should move beyond technical measures and security-focused design.

The closest example of a human-centric cybersecurity framework with these features is found in Grobler et al. (2021), which seeks not to focus "purely" on the role that humans play in cyber security — as in, prioritize addressing the "weakest link" in security — but to develop "varied approaches that could ultimately lead to a balanced cyber security perspective" (p. 2). The authors set out a framework based on 3 U's — user, usage, and usability — with each encompassing different elements of cybersecurity (p. 3). The "user" components concern social, cultural, cognitive, and psychological factors in how users interact with systems. The "usage" components include technical, functional, and legislative/regulatory measures put in place to protect users. Lastly, "usability" components explore how well systems can be used by users and encompass experience and interaction factors (p. 3). This framework is comprehensive enough to cover off both the human behavioural factors and human costs of information manipulation, while also not neglecting the technical and functional elements of cybersecurity that remain critical to addressing disinformation and information manipulation. Recently, the framework has been applied to healthcare (Kioskli et al., 2023) and national digital identity system contexts (Hilowle et al., 2023).

Yet, this framework may also be too narrow in that it still focuses primarily on human involvement in systems and processes (Kioskli et al., 2023, p. 7), which may preclude broader structural reforms. This will come down to how "systems" are conceptualized. It must not be just technical systems like networks, but also cybersecurity within broader democratic systems as well. Disinformation and information manipulation have proven to be a serious threat to democracies and civil society, a threat that has been described as the "defining political communication topic of our time" (Freelon & Wells, 2020, p. 145; McKay & Tenove, 2020). Thus, a human-centric informational security framework must also account for the social, political, and economic context of disinformation and information manipulation, like surveillance capitalism, to address it effectively in the long term. For instance, one of the realities of surveillance capitalism is that users are consumers, but they are also the consumed. Information and data, predominantly about consumers themselves, are collected, analyzed, and monetized to drive the digital economy (Srnicek, 2017; Zuboff, 2014; Penney, 2019). Consumers have always been the targets of deception and manipulation, but a combination of big data, AI-driven analytics and targeting, and platforms with entrenched market monopolies seek to influence them, distort the information environment, and create profound new possibilities for digital manipulation and "systematic consumer vulnerability" (Calo, 2014; Zuboff, 2019). These broader market realities must be addressed through structural reforms to also mitigate, manage, and protect against information manipulation as both a cybersecurity threat and societal threat.

A final critical issue is how best to *operationalize* such a framework in cybersecurity policy and practice. This, to an extent, reintroduces some of the uncertainty around human-centric approaches to cyber-security, which, as noted earlier, are relatively new and undeveloped, especially when it comes to implementation in policy. One key challenge is that disinformation and information manipulation typically involve forms of speech and expression, so that laws and policies addressing them are criticized and opposed as likely to have a chilling effect on speech and expression (Cohen, 2019; Penney, 2021b) or as being selective based on the political preferences of the government. This is surely one reason why governments are so reluctant to enact reforms to address disinformation. For instance, one of the most common and forceful criticisms of the Government of Canada's proposed online harms legislation (now Bill C-63) is that it will have a large-scale chilling effect on social media platforms and the speech, sharing, and engagement of users (see e.g., Finckenstein & Menzies, 2022; Karadeglija, 2021a, 2021b).[1] On this count, one possible advantage of the framework set out here is that it offers a means to reduce reliance on rights-based conceptions of human-centric cybersecurity, which may assist operationalizing it in practice. Rights-based frameworks can lead to conflicting claims, where the rights of victims subjected to disinformation and misinformation conflict with those engaged in its generation and spread, leading to regulatory stalemates and inaction. Of course, freedom of expression will likely be implicated in any cybersecurity framework or policy operationalized to address disinformation and information manipulation. The point here is simply to mitigate those conflicting claims and discourses as much as possible.

Frameworks focused on the protection and well-being of users like Boulanin (2016) offer additional guidelines for informational security frameworks. For instance, duty of care frameworks, like the EU *Digital Services Act,* which impose broader duties and responsibilities on social media platforms and other private sector actors to ensure the protection and care of users would fit this model (Laidlaw, 2022). Instead of governments or state agencies taking action against disinformation or misinformation, under duty of care regulatory frameworks, social media platforms develop their own policies to

---

1.   Bill C-63, An Act to enact the Online Harms Act, to amend the Criminal Code, the Canadian Human Rights Act and An Act respecting the mandatory reporting of Internet child pornography by persons who provide an Internet service and to make consequential and related amendments to other Acts, 1st Sess., 44th Parl., 2021–2024 (first reading 26 February 2024).

operationalize and implement the mandated duty of care in practice. That leaves the balancing of rights and interests of creators, disseminators, and victims of information manipulation to the platforms and other private sector actors, avoiding government overreach. Similarly, there are advocates for "information consumer protection," a broader policy framework to address disinformation and information manipulation that builds on existing consumer protection laws, policies, and regulatory agencies (Penney, 2019). It emphasizes protection, harm reduction, and measures that foster trust based on consumer protection law and other precautionary regulatory frameworks that rarely raise issues for freedom of speech or expression. Of course, the recommendations set out here are not meant to be authoritative. Human-centric informational security need not be monolithic or a one-size-fits-all theory or provide a framework for every cybersecurity problem or threat—this is a misconception of the present cybersecurity paradigm that should be avoided. Different conceptualizations of human-centric approaches may be preferable to others, depending on the threat and context.

4.4. Recommendations for Policy and Research

This chapter has argued that the existing predominant cybersecurity paradigm is too technical and narrowly focused on state and national security issues to adequately address disinformation and information manipulation. A human-centric informational security paradigm would be more effective in both the near and long term. Such a framework should be interdisciplinary and centred on the human subject's protection and safety and integrate psychological and behavioural factors, the human costs of information manipulation, to allow for not just technical measures and related regulatory responses, but broader structural reforms as well. However, a truly human-centric approach should also be interdisciplinary and both evidence-based and empirical (Penney, 2021a, pp. 417–420). Any technical and regulatory measures taken to address information manipulation must be studied and their impact and efficacy explored. This is a critical requirement as human-centric cybersecurity develops and evolves.

In terms of policy recommendations, to avoid government and regulatory inaction due to conflicting and competing rights, rights-based conceptualizations of human-centric cybersecurity should be avoided when operationalizing these human-centred frameworks in law, policy, and practice. Instead, duty of care frameworks or those based on consumer protection, like information consumer protection, will likely face less opposition and prove more effective in addressing disinformation and information manipulation in the near and long term. Lastly, no informational security framework is authoritative and monolithic—informational security approaches and policies must be contextual and context-specific.

Acknowledgements

This chapter benefitted greatly from conversations with Ron Deibert, Siena Anstis, Chris Parsons, and other colleagues at the Citizen Lab, based at the University of Toronto's Munk Center for Global Affairs and Public Policy. It also benefitted greatly from conversations with Emily Laidlaw, Florian Martin-Bariteau, Joan Donovan, Gabby Lim, Taylor Owen, David O'Brien, Teresa Scassa, and Nathan Matias, as well as from panel discussions and conversations with participants at the CANIS 2023 International Conference on "Misinformation: Impact and Challenges in a Diverse Society" at the Banff Centre for Arts and Creativity, Banff, Alberta, March 22–24, 2023.

References

Anstis, S., Leonard, N., & Penney, J. W. (2023). Moving from secrecy to transparency in the offensive cyber capabilities sector: The case of dual-use technologies exports. *Computer Law & Security Review, 48,* 105787. https://doi.org/10.1016/j.clsr.2022.105787

Boulanin, V. (2016). Information and communication technology, cybersecurity and human development. In Stockholm International Peace Research Institute (Ed.), *SIPRI yearbook 2016: Armaments, disarmament and international security* (pp. 13–14). Oxford University Press. https://www.sipriyearbook.org/view/9780198787280/sipri-9780198787280-chapter-010.xml

Bontcheva, K., Posetti, J., Teyssou, D., Meyer, T., Gregory, S., Hanot, C., & Maynard, D. (2020). *Balancing act: Countering digital disinformation while respecting freedom of expression.* International Telecommunication Union (ITU) & United Nations Educational, Scientific and Cultural Organization (UNESCO).

Bontridder, N., & Poullet, Y. (2021). The role of artificial intelligence in disinformation. *Data & Policy, 3,* e32-1–e32-21. http://dx.doi.org/10.1017/dap.2021.20

Bradshaw, S. (2020). *Influence operations and disinformation on social media*. The Centre for International Governance Innovation. https://www.cigionline. org/articles/influence-operations-and-disinformation-social-media/

Bradshaw, S., Bailey, H., & Howard, P. N. (2021). *Industrialized disinformation: 2020 global inventory of organized social media manipulation*. Project on Computational Propaganda at the Oxford Internet Institute. https://demtech.oii.ox.ac.uk/wp-content/uploads/sites/12/2021/01/ CyberTroop-Report-2020-v.2.pdf

Calo, R. (2014). Digital market manipulation. *The George Washington Law Review, 82,* 995–1051. https://digitalcommons.law.uw.edu/faculty-articles/25/

Caramancion, K. M. (2020). An exploration of disinformation as a cyber-security threat. In *2020 3rd International Conference on Information and Computer Technologies (ICICT)* (pp. 440–444). IEEE. http://dx.doi. org/10.1109/ICICT50521.2020.00076

Caramancion, K. M., Li, Y., Dubois, E., & Jung, E. S. (2022). The missing case of disinformation from the cybersecurity risk continuum: A comparative assessment of disinformation with other cyber threats. *Data, 7*(4), 49. https://doi.org/10.3390/data7040049

Carr, M. (2016). Public—private partnerships in national cyber-security strategies. *International Affairs, 92*(1), 43–62. https://doi.org/10. 1111/1468-2346.12504

Casero-Ripollés, A., Tuñón, J., & Bouza-García, L. (2023). The European approach to online disinformation: Geopolitical and regulatory dissonance. *Humanities and Social Sciences Communications, 10*(1), 1–10. http:// dx.doi.org/10.1057/s41599-023-02179-8

Cavoukian, A. (2009). *Privacy by design: The 7 foundational principles*. Information and Privacy Commissioner of Ontario, Canada. https://privacy.ucsc. edu/resources/privacy-by-design-foundational-principles.pdf

Citron, D. K., & Wittes, B. (2017). The Internet will not break: Denying bad samaritans sect. 230 immunity. *Fordham Law Review, 86*(2), 401–423. https://ir.lawnet.fordham.edu/flr/vol86/iss2/3/

Coble, S. (2020). Cybersecurity community concerned about misinformation. *Infosecurity Magazine*. https://www.infosecurity-magazine.com/ news/us-concerned-about-misinformation/

Cohen, J. E. (2019). *Between truth and power*. Oxford University Press.

Dan, V., Paris, B., Donovan, J., Hameleers, M., Roozenbeek, J., van der Linden, S., & von Sikorski, C. (2021). Visual mis- and disinformation, social media, and democracy. *Journalism & Mass Communication Quarterly, 98*(3), 641–664. https://doi.org/10.1177/10776990211035395

Deibert, R. J. (2003). Black code: Censorship, surveillance, and the militarisation of cyberspace. *Millennium Journal of International Studies, 32*(3), 501–530. http://dx.doi.org/10.1177/03058298030320030801

Deibert, R. (2012). *Distributed security as cyber strategy: Outlining a comprehensive approach for Canada in cyberspace.* Canadian Defence and Foreign Affairs Institute. https://jmss.org/article/view/58030/43673

Deibert, R. J. (2018). Toward a human-centric approach to cybersecurity. *Ethics & International Affairs, 32*(4), 411–424. http://dx.doi.org/10.1017/S0892679418000618

Dunn Cavelty, M. (2012, June 5–8). *The militarisation of cyberspace: Why less may be better.* [Description of contribution—Research Paper]. 2012 4th International Conference on Cyber Conflict (CYCON 2012), Tallinn, Estonia. https://ccdcoe.org/uploads/2012/01/2_6_Dunn-Cavelty_TheMilitarisationOfCyberspace.pdf

Dunn Cavelty, M. (2014). Breaking the cyber-security dilemma: Aligning security needs and removing vulnerabilities. *Science and Engineering Ethics, 20*(3), 701–715. https://doi.org/10.1007/s11948-014-9551-y

Ecker, U. K., Lewandowsky, S., Cook, J., Schmid, P., Fazio, L. K., Brashier, N., Kendeou, P., Vraga E. K., & Amazeen, M. A. (2022). The psychological drivers of misinformation belief and its resistance to correction. *Nature Reviews Psychology, 1*(1), 13–29. http://dx.doi.org/10.1038/s44159-021-00006-y

Elghawaby, A. (2018, August 2). *Social media's self-regulation isn't enough.* Center for International Governance Innovation. https://www.cigionline.org/articles/social-medias-self-regulation-isnt-enough/

European Commission. (2018). *Fake news and disinformation online.* https://europa.eu/eurobarometer/surveys/detail/2183

Freelon, D., & Wells, C. (2020). Disinformation as political communication. *Political Communication, 37*(2), 145–156. http://dx.doi.org/10.1080/10584609.2020.1723755

Grobler, M., Gaire, R., & Nepal, S. (2021). User, usage and usability: Redefining human centric cyber security. *Frontiers in Big Data, 4*, 583723. http://dx.doi.org/10.3389/fdata.2021.583723

Hameleers, M. (2023). The (un)intended consequences of emphasizing the threats of mis- and disinformation. *Media and Communication, 11*(2), 5–14. http://dx.doi.org/10.17645/mac.v11i2.6301

Higginbotham, B. (2022, December 1). *New report finds Canadians believe disinformation is a major problem in society.* Institute for Public Relations. https://instituteforpr.org/new-report-finds-canadians-believe-disinformation-is-a-major-problem-in-society/

Hilowle, M., Yeoh, W., Grobler, M., Pye, G., & Jiang, F. (2023). Users' adoption of national digital identity systems: Human-centric cybersecurity review. *Journal of Computer Information Systems, 63*(5), 1264–1279. https://doi.org/10.1080/08874417.2022.2140089

Hunt, J. S. (2021). Countering cyber-enabled disinformation: Implications for national security. *Australian Journal of Defence and Strategic Studies, 3*(1), 83–88. https://doi.org/10.51174/AJDSS.0301

Ignaczak, L., Goldschmidt, G., Costa, C. A. D., & Righi, R. D. R. (2021). Text mining in cybersecurity: A systematic literature review. *ACM Computing Surveys, 54*(7), 1–36. http://dx.doi.org/10.1145/3462477

Jacob, J., Peters, M., & Yang, T. A. (2020). Interdisciplinary cybersecurity: Rethinking the approach and the process. In K. Kwang, R. Choo, T. H. Morris, & G. L. Peterson (Eds.), *National Cyber Summit (NCS) research track* (pp. 61–74). Springer International Publishing. http://dx.doi.org/10.1007/978-3-030-31239-8_6

Karadeglija, A. (2021a, October 1). Ditch "fundamentally flawed" online harms bill, experts say in submissions to Heritage Canada. *National Post.* https://nationalpost.com/news/politics/ditch-fundamentally-flawed-online-harms-bill-experts-say-in-submissions-to-heritage-canada

Karadeglija, K. (2021b, June 24). New hate law could have chilling effect, free speech advocates say. *National Post.* https://nationalpost.com/news/politics/new-hate-law-could-have-chilling-effect-free-speech-advocates-say

Kim, N., & Ohm, P. (2022). Legacy switches: A proposal to protect privacy, security, and the environment from the Internet of Things. *Ohio State Law Journal, 84*, 101. https://papers.ssrn.com/sol3/papers.cfm?abstract_id=4149789

Kioskli, K., Fotis, T., Nifakos, S., & Mouratidis, H. (2023). The importance of conceptualising the human-centric approach in maintaining and promoting cybersecurity-hygiene in healthcare 4.0. *Applied Sciences, 13*(6), 3410. http://dx.doi.org/10.3390/app13063410

Klein, J., & Hossain, K. (2020). Conceptualising human-centric cyber security in the arctic in light of digitalisation and climate change. *Arctic Review on Law and Politics, 11*, 1–18. https://doi.org/10.23865/arctic.v11.1936

Krafft, P. M., & Donovan, J. (2020). Disinformation by design: The use of evidence collages and platform filtering in a media manipulation campaign. *Political Communication, 37*(2), 194–214. https://doi.org/10.1080/10584609.2019.1686094

Kumar, S. (2021). The missing piece in human-centric approaches to cybernorms implementation: The role of civil society. *Journal of Cyber Policy, 6*(3), 375–393. http://dx.doi.org/10.1080/23738871.2021.1909090

Laidlaw, E. (2019). Notice-and-notice-plus: A Canadian perspective beyond the liability and immunity divide. In G. Frosio (Ed.), *The Oxford handbook of intermediary liability online.* Oxford University Press.

Laidlaw, E. (2022). *An examination of the role and responsibilities of social media.* Public Order Emergency Commission. https://publicorderemergencycommission.ca/files/documents/Policy-Papers/Mis-Dis-and-Mal-Information-and-the-Convoy-Laidlaw.pdf

Laidlaw, E., & Young, H. (2017). *Internet intermediary liability in defamation: Proposals for statutory reform.* Law Commission of Ontario. http://www.

lco-cdo.org/wp-content/uploads/2017/07/DIA-Commissioned-Paper-Laidlaw-and-Young.pdf

Lederer, E. M. (2023, June 12). *UN chief calls for coordinated global action on disinformation, hate and artificial intelligence.* AP News. https://apnews.com/article/disinformation-hate-artificial-intelligence-united-nations-6f3081ae39bfabc362588c5518df2793

Liaropoulos, A. (2015). A human-centric approach to cybersecurity: Securing the human in the era of cyberphobia. *Journal of Information Warfare, 14*(4), 15–24.

Luguri, J., & Strahilevitz, L. J. (2021). Shining a light on dark patterns. *Journal of Legal Analysis, 13*(1), 43–109. https://doi.org/10.1093/jla/laaa006

Marwick, A., & Lewis, R. (2017). *Media manipulation and disinformation online.* Data & Society Research Institute. https://datasociety.net/library/media-manipulation-and-disinfo-online/

McKay, S., & Tenove, C. (2021). Disinformation as a threat to deliberative democracy. *Political Research Quarterly, 74*(3), 703–717. http://dx.doi.org/10.1177/1065912920938143

McCorkindale, T., & Henry, A. (2021). *Third annual disinformation in society report: How Americans perceive intentionally misleading news or information.* Institute for Public Relations. https://instituteforpr.org/ipr-disinformation-study

McGeveran, W. (2013). The law of friction. *University of Chicago Legal Forum, 2013*(1), 15–68. https://chicagounbound.uchicago.edu/uclf/vol2013/iss1/3/

Micallef, N., Avram, M., Menczer, F., & Patil, S. (2021). Fakey: A game intervention to improve news literacy on social media. *Proceedings of the ACM on Human-Computer Interaction, 5*(CSCW1), 1–27. https://doi.org/10.1145/3449080

Mirza, S., Begum, L., Niu, L., Pardo, S., Abouzied, A., Papotti, P., & Pöpper, C. (2023, February 27–March 3). *Tactics, threats & targets: Modeling disinformation and its mitigation.* ISOC Network and Distributed Systems Security Symposium (NDSS), San Diego, CA, United States. https://www.ndss-symposium.org/ndss-paper/tactics-threats-targets-modeling-disinformation-and-its-mitigation/

Morell, M, & Kelly, S. (2016, December 11). *Fmr. CIA acting Dir. Michael Morell: "This is the political equivalent of 9/11."* The Cipher Brief. https://www.thecipherbrief.com/fmr-cia-acting-dir-michael-morell-political-equivalent-911-1091

Nagasako, T. (2020). Global disinformation campaigns and legal challenges. *International Cybersecurity Law Review, 1,* 125–136. https://link.springer.com/article/10.1365/s43439-020-00010-7

Ohm, P., & Frankle, J. (2018). Desirable inefficiency. *Florida Law Review, 70*(4), 777–838. https://scholarship.law.ufl.edu/flr/vol70/iss4/2/

Penney, J. W. (2015). The cycles of global telecommunication censorship and surveillance. *University of Pennsylvania Journal of International Law, 36,* 693–753.

Penney, J. W. (2019). Protecting information consumers. *Models for Platform Governance,* 69. https://www.jstor.org/stable/pdf/resrep26127.14.pdf

Penney, J. W. (2021a). Cybersecurity, human rights, and empiricism: The case of digital surveillance. In P. Cornish (Ed.), *The Oxford handbook of cyber security* (p. 409-426). Oxford University Press. https://doi-org.ezproxy. library.yorku.ca/10.1093/oxfordhb/9780198800682.013.56

Penney, J. W. (2021b). Understanding chilling effects. *Minnesota Law Review, 106,* 1451–1530.

Penney, J. W., McKune, S., Gill, L., & Deibert, R. J. (2018). Advancing human-rights-by-design in the dual-use technology industry. *Journal of International Affairs, 71*(2), 104–110. https://jia.sipa.columbia.edu/news/ advancing-human-rights-design-dual-use-technology-industry

Posetti, J. (2018). News industry transformation: digital technology, social platforms and the spread of misinformation and disinformation. In C. Ireton & J. Posetti (Eds.), *Journalism, "fake news" and disinformation: Handbook for journalism education and training* (pp. 57–73). United Nations Educational, Scientific, and Cultural Organisation (UNESCO). https://bit. ly/2XLRRlA

Posetti, J., & Matthews, A. (2018). A short guide to the history of "fake news" and disinformation. *International Center for Journalists, 7*(2018). https:// www.icfj.org/sites/default/files/2018-07/A%20Short%20Guide%20 to%20History%20of%20Fake%20News%20and%20Disinformation_ ICFJ%20Final.pdf

Rahman, T., Rohan, R., Pal, D., & Kanthamanon, P. (2021). *Human factors in cybersecurity: A scoping review.* In *Proceedings of the 12th International Conference on Advances in Information Technology* (pp. 1–11). Association for Computing Machinery. http://dx.doi.org/10.1145/3468784.3468789

Ramirez, R., & Choucri, N. (2016). Improving interdisciplinary communication with standardized cyber security terminology: A literature review. *IEEE Access, 4,* 2216–2243. http://dx.doi.org/10.1109/ACCESS.2016.2544381

Rohan, R., Funilkul, S., Pal, D., & Chutimaskul, W. (2021). Understanding of human factors in cybersecurity: A systematic literature review. In *2021 International Conference on Computational Performance Evaluation (ComPE)* (pp. 133–140). IEEE. http://dx.doi.org/10.1109/ComPE53109. 2021.9752358

Rubinstein, I. S., & Good, N. (2012). Privacy by design: A counterfactual analysis of Google and Facebook privacy incidents. *Berkeley Tech. Law Journal, 28,* 1333–1414. https://doi.org/10.15779/Z38G11N

Schia, N. N., & Gjesvik, L. (2020). Hacking democracy: Managing influence campaigns and disinformation in the digital age. *Journal of Cyber Policy, 5*(3), 413–428. 10.1080/23738871.2020.1820060

Sinders, C. (2021). *Designing against dark patterns.* The German Marshall Fund Policy Paper. https://www.gmfus.org/sites/default/files/Sinders%2520-%2520Design%2520and%2520Information%2520Policy%2520Goals.pdf

Smith, T. (2021). The infodemic as a threat to cybersecurity. *The International Journal of Intelligence, Security, and Public Affairs, 23*(3), 180–196. https://doi.org/10.1080/23800992.2021.1969140

Srnicek, N. (2017). *Platform capitalism.* Polity Press.

Stevens, T. (2016). *Cyber security and the politics of time.* Cambridge University Press.

Suryotrisongko, H., & Musashi, Y. (2019). Review of cybersecurity research topics, taxonomy and challenges: Interdisciplinary perspective. In 2019 IEEE 12th Conference on Service-Oriented Computing and Applications (SOCA) (pp. 162–167). IEEE. https://doi.org/10.1109/SOCA.2019.00031

Susser, D., Roessler, B., & Nissenbaum, H. (2020). Online manipulation: Hidden influences in digital world. *Georgetown Law Technology Review, 4*(1), 1–46. https://georgetownlawtechreview.org/online-manipulation-hidden-influences-in-a-digital-world/GLTR-01-2020/

Thompson, E. (2019, June 10). *Poll finds 90% of Canadians have fallen for fake news.* CBC News. https://www.cbc.ca/news/politics/fake-news-facebook-twitter-poll-1.5169916

Von Finckenstein, K., & Menzies, P. (2022, February 4). A lighter touch is needed for the government's online harms bill. *The Globe and Mail.* https://www.theglobeandmail.com/opinion/article-a-lighter-touch-is-needed-for-the-governments-online-harms-bill/

Wardle, C., & Derakhshan, H. (2017). *Information disorder: Toward an interdisciplinary framework for research and policymaking.* Council of Europe. https://edoc.coe.int/en/media/7495-information-disorder-toward-an-interdisciplinary-framework-for-research-and-policy-making.html

Zuboff, S. (2015). Big other: Surveillance capitalism and the prospects of an information civilization. *Journal of Information Technology, 30*(1), 75–89. https://doi.org/10.1057/jit.2015.5

Zuboff, S. (2019). *The age of surveillance capitalism: The fight for a human future at the new frontier of power.* Public Affairs. http://dx.doi.org/10.1007/s00146-020-01100-0

CHAPTER 5

The Technology-Facilitated Insecurity of Public and Private Selves

Chris Tenove and Heidi Tworek

Abstract

Conventionally, cybersecurity focuses on the confidentiality, integrity, and availability of data and data systems, rather than on how hostile or threatening communication affects human beings. This chapter expands that framing by showing how social media and messaging platforms can contribute to *technology-facilitated insecurity* by increasing their users' risks of experiencing diverse forms of harm. This insecurity results partly from how social media and messaging platforms blur the boundaries between individuals' "public" and "private" identities. That blurring can create intense security risks, which are compounded by intersectional identities. After reviewing existing literature on cybersecurity and online harassment, this chapter shows how social media and messaging platforms expose public figures to various harms, using in-depth interviews with thirty-five health communicators who engaged in public discussions of the COVID-19 pandemic. We explain why platforms exacerbate online and offline security risks, including through enhanced visibility, doxing, and the coordination of hostile networks. This chapter concludes by proposing that a human-centric cybersecurity approach should be used to address technology-facilitated insecurity as a systemic problem rather than an individual predicament. Two specific recommendations are made. First, institutions should adopt more proactive policies to support those targeted by online threats. Second, technologies and organizational policies should help individuals to maintain clearer and stronger separation between their public and private selves online. This chapter focuses on health communicators and other individuals in public communication roles because online harassment and technology-facilitated insecurity are particularly acute for them. However, these problems are a general feature of the contemporary digital media landscape. Any individual interacting online would benefit from greater security of the self.

During the COVID-19 pandemic, public health officials, medical practitioners, and journalists experienced intense levels of hostility and threats of violence online. Some, including British Columbia Provincial Health Officer Bonnie Henry, were even told they should face processes like the Nuremberg trials in 1945–1946, which sentenced many German war criminals to death by hanging (Gawley, 2021; Picard, 2021).

Threats and hostility did not remain online. Protestors marched on the private homes of public health officials in Ontario, Saskatchewan, and other provinces (Piller, 2021; Hodgins, 2022). Journalists reporting during the Freedom Convoy in January 2022 were threatened, and in several cases, physically assaulted (Lindgren et al., 2022). Members of marginalized groups, including racialized communities, felt doubly at risk given increases in hate incidents (Tenove & Tworek, 2022).

Individuals in public roles have always been exposed to additional risks of harm, while often also enjoying additional forms of power and support. However, these risks have taken on new dimensions and have increased in scope, scale, severity, frequency, and omnipresence with the rise of social media and messaging platforms. Critically, platforms have facilitated a dramatic increase in harassment targeting politicians (Tenove, Tworek, Lore, et al., 2023), journalists (IPSOS, 2021; Tenove, Al-Rawi, et al., 2023), and researchers (Gosse et al., 2021). Moreover, social media and messaging platforms enable the recruiting, radicalizing, and coordinating of individuals who may seek to harm public figures (Hart et al., 2021). Such dynamics magnify challenges faced by members of marginalized or underrepresented groups (Bardall & Tenove, 2024; Collignon & Rüdig, 2021; Posetti & Shabbir, 2022).

At the same time, public communicators cannot ignore online spaces for two reasons. First, many members of the public can best or only be reached via such platforms. Second, even those who do not have social media accounts, like Henry, can still be targeted by online harassment and by the online mobilization of offline threats.

Our chapter focuses on the potential harms that public communicators may experience as a result of online harassment and other platform-enabled activities, highlighting increased threats to physical, psychological, and professional security. We call this predicament *technology-facilitated insecurity* (TFI). This insecurity arises from the design and use of platforms by public communicators and other actors. One key element is how social media platforms blur the boundaries between individuals' "public" and "private" identities. That blurring also exacerbates risks faced by individuals because of their gender, race, disability, or other identity factors.

We suggest that adopting a *cybersecurity* lens can help to understand TFI and, more importantly, how to address it. Cybersecurity frameworks emphasize systemic issues including technology design and organizational policies, shifting the responsibility for security to organizations and away from targeted individuals. Conventionally, cybersecurity focuses on the confidentiality, integrity, and availability of data and data systems, rather than how communication on social media and messaging platforms affect human beings. However, more *human-centric* approaches to cybersecurity treat individuals as the object of security, and highlight the individual and societal factors that contribute to their insecurity.

This chapter first reviews existing literature on online harassment and cybersecurity. Second, we explore how online harassment and other forms of harmful communication affect public figures, drawing on in-depth interviews with thirty-five individuals who were health communicators during the COVID-19 pandemic. We explain how social media and messaging platforms expose individuals to diverse security risks, including through doxing, protest organization, and threats to employment.

This chapter concludes with recommendations to address technology-facilitated insecurity by adopting insights from human-centric cybersecurity. That means focusing on systemic sources of insecurity and shifting responsibility for security away from individuals, just as we emphasize the role of institutions in cybersecurity rather than leaving people to shore up their cyber defences on their own. Both social media companies and employers of public communicators benefit from the blurring of private and public selves; therefore, they have a responsibility to address the ensuing vulnerabilities and harms. Two directions of improvement are proposed: first, more extensive institutional policies to protect and support those targeted by online harassment; and second, the establishment of policies to enable individuals to maintain clearer and stronger separation between their public and private selves online.

This chapter focuses on health communicators and other individuals in public communication roles because technology-facilitated insecurity is particularly acute for them. However, these problems are a general feature of the contemporary landscape. Any individual interacting online would benefit from greater security of the self.

5.1. Harassment, Technology-Facilitated Violence, and Cybersecurity

During the COVID-19 pandemic, many public health officials, medical practitioners, and other health experts dramatically increased their use of social media to inform the public and counteract widespread misinformation (Mello et al., 2023; Royan et al., 2022). Forms of online communication could range from promoting official health messages to health workers' personal advocacy for public action and descriptions of the pandemic's toll (Al-Rawi & Zemenchik, 2023; Pangborn et al., 2021).

While social media and messaging platforms provided greater opportunities for public communicators to productively engage with citizens and stakeholders, they also exposed communicators to new forms of violence and anti-social behaviour. Different terms to define problematic communication include harassment (Basky, 2021; Chen et al., 2020; Holton et al., 2021; Royan et al., 2023), hate speech (Cinelli et al., 2021; Obermaier et al., 2018), incivility (Rossini, 2022; Tenove, Tworek, Lore, et al., 2023), and dark participation (Wintterlin et al., 2021).

While there are important reasons to align terms for this phenomenon across the literature, this chapter focuses on how our interviewees experienced this issue rather than terminological distinctions. They most often used the terms harassment and abuse. Their usage of these terms aligns with Miller (2021, p. 4), who defines harassment as "unwanted abusive behavior." The focus on unwanted activities empowers "the target of the abusive behavior to deem it as unwanted" (Miller, 2021, p. 4).

Online harassment is often intertwined with offline activities (Posetti & Shabbir, 2022; Tenove, Tworek, Lore, et al., 2023). For instance, individuals may face threats from the same person online and offline, and online networking may be used to mobilize offline attacks. Scholars have shown how it is simply untrue that "people are somehow less vulnerable as humans in online spaces and can thus easily protect themselves from harm and abuse" (Gosse et al., 2021, pp. 57–58).

To conceptualize the various ways that digital technology may be used to perpetrate harm, including their potential linkage to offline activities, scholars have coined the term *technology-facilitated violence* (TFV). Researchers taking feminist and critical race theory approaches have highlighted how this violence builds on systemic factors. Thus, Dunn (2021, p. 40) notes that in addition to the role of technology, "TFV can be recognized by looking for behaviors that control, dominate, and instill fear in the person targeted, particularly those behaviors that rely on existing systemic power structures to further dehumanize and limit the autonomy of a particular person or group."

We build on this concept of technology-facilitated violence and propose the term *technology-facilitated insecurity* (TFI), which refers to the predicament in which communicators' use of social media and messaging platforms increases their risks of experiencing a range of harms. These risks are not entirely the result of online activities, but may also include associated offline activities and broader structures of violence and oppression.

The term TFI helps to straddle the online/offline and public/private divides that may obscure the challenges that individuals face. Furthermore, a focus on insecurity takes the diagnosis and potential solutions to these problems in a new direction by incorporating the literature on cybersecurity. A cybersecurity analysis addresses insecurity as a problem to be addressed at organizational and systemic levels, and not left to individuals to manage. Cybersecurity emphasizes technological and infrastructure design, national laws and regulations, organizational policies and resources, and diverse behaviours by hostile actors as well as those who may be targeted. Similarly, we argue, these and other dimensions should be the focus of efforts to address TFI.

Many activities contributing to TFI fall outside the usual focus of cybersecurity laws and policies. Conventional cybersecurity approaches focus on a computer system, including its confidentiality, integrity, and availability, and emphasize threats to organizations, particularly government agencies and businesses (Grobler et al., 2021). This "'national security first' approach to cybersecurity" often dominates the field (Deibert, 2018, p. 411). Even when individual harms are contemplated, cybersecurity laws and policies often focus on economic harms. Some see the largely male leadership of cybersecurity as one reason for the narrow focus on economic harms "at the exclusion of other harms that often are disproportionately suffered by women and minority groups" (Kosseff, 2018, pp. 244–245).

However, more human-centric approaches to cybersecurity have gained prominence, which "champion the human in cybersecurity" (NIST, 2024). These focus on securing human beings and human rights (not just data and technical systems), highlight factors that exacerbate individual risk (including technical literacy as well as societal and identity-related factors), and attend to the real-world challenges that individuals face when trying to implement security practices (Hofstetter & Pourmalek, 2023; Grobler et al, 2021). We suggest that a shift to a human-centric cybersecurity framework for solutions may address the types of insecurities explored in this chapter, including the intersectional nature of technology-facilitated insecurity, and highlights the importance of institutional solutions that move beyond individual responsibility.

5.2. How Platforms Facilitate Insecurity and Harm

To understand online harassment and broader issues of security, thirty-five health communicators were interviewed, including public health officials or their communication staff (8), medical professionals (10), health journalists (9), and university-based or civil society health experts (8). Sixteen identified as racialized and twenty as women. They worked in Alberta, British Columbia, Ontario, Quebec, and the Yukon.

The semi-structured interviews were conducted using Zoom between December 2021 and June 2023 and lasted forty to ninety minutes. Interviews were transcribed. Three team members used a combination of deductive and inductive coding on Atlas.ti to organize and analyze interviews (for similar methodology see Tenove, Tworek, Lore, et al., 2023).

5.2.1. Negative Impacts on Safety, Health, and Professional Security

All thirty-five health communicators identified that harassment and other potentially harmful forms of communication on social media and messaging platforms had negative consequences for their physical safety, mental health, and/or professional credibility and employability. These impacts are often interlocking by nature. For example, harassment targeting professional credibility could exacerbate harms to mental health.

5.2.1.1. Safety

Close to half of interviewees (15 of 35) described receiving threats of violence or physical harm. Several other interviewees described receiving comments about being watched or monitored, suggesting future violence. A prominent medical practitioner, and head of a civil society organization, noted that the most threatening communications came as "direct messages, both on Instagram and Twitter."

The four most senior health officials in our study all received explicit threats of violence, some of which referred to submitting them to trials like those held for Nazi officials in Nuremberg. One official gave the example of a social media post "calling for my live execution on video feed." Another official described receiving an email "that basically said, our entire church group is praying that you and your family all get some sort of incurable, horrific cancer."

Many interviewees suggested that while they may not have faced explicit threats of violence, they felt that hostility directed at them directly or circulating on social media and messaging platforms had increased the likelihood of violent encounters in their workplace. This is a classic example of technology-facilitated insecurity, as interviewees felt unsafe as employees because platforms increased risks of experiencing a range of potential harms.

Health journalists noted that during the pandemic, newsroom and journalist safety became an increasing concern, though most threats of violence were veiled. Some newsrooms even took their decals off company vehicles to avoid attracting attention from hostile individuals. One interviewee conducted a safety audit of her apartment, which included taking her name off the building's buzzer list and being careful to not post anything online to indicate her address. A 2021 survey of Canadian journalists regarding online harassment found that 20 percent reported feeling scared for physical safety (IPSOS, 2021, p. 25). In a convenience sample of scientists surveyed by *Nature*, 22 percent had received threats of physical or sexual violence after their media interviews or social media commenting regarding COVID-19 (Nogrady, 2021).

5.2.1.2. Mental Health

Harm to mental health was the most commonly mentioned impact of online harassment. Twenty-eight out of thirty-five interviewees described feelings of despair, fear, emotional exhaustion, and sadness (for more, see Wight et al., 2025). Sometimes harms to mental health were intertwined with interviewees' concerns about the relationship between online harassment and their safety, professional reputation, and their broader relationship with patients or members of the public.

A racialized health communicator explained that getting hateful or violent messages "instills fear in me, and I get the sensations and the triggers that usually comes from somebody who has PTSD." A physician said, "I've had nightmares about people like coming to my clinic and shooting me." Other health communicators explained that engaging hostile comments on Twitter (now X) as "really not good for your well-being and then your physical functioning."

Finally, several interviewees described negative mental health impact on family members, who see or know of the online harassment faced by the health communicator.

These comments resonate with surveys on mental health impacts of online harassment. For instance, a survey found that 42 percent of Canadian journalists who faced more frequent harassment (on a weekly basis or more frequently) said it left them struggling with their mental health (IPSOS, p. 6). In the survey of scientists by *Nature* survey, more than 40 percent of scientists reported experiencing emotional or psychological distress due to the responses they received to their comments on COVID-19 on social media or in journalism interviews (Nogrady, 2021).

5.2.1.3. Ability to Communicate

Twenty out of thirty-five respondents said that the harassment had affected their ability to engage in professional communication with the general public, and, for some, with patients or colleagues.

The mental health burden of online harassment caused many participants to scale back their online communication (on this and other coping measures, see Wight et al., 2025). In addition to the abuse they received, participants also noted the burden of communicating in a climate of potential harassment. Multiple participants left social media platforms completely because of harassment. One communicator said that by "speaking out, we are targets." Several senior health officials decided not to use social media personally. As one described: "I'm not on Twitter, for my mental health. The only time I know that something happened on Twitter is I get random, supportive emails from colleagues and family members."

An interviewee who leads a national advocacy body for health practitioners said that among its members, "You may have excellent health communicators who are just like, 'I can't live my life with this level of abuse.' And that's obviously the goal of the people doing the abusing, right, to silence you."

Three journalists said that online harassment prompted them to cut back on their Twitter use, one wondering: "Why would I just put something out, get attacked again and again for a couple of likes and retweets?" Another commented that, because of their decision to stop using a platform where they faced harassment "I feel like the trolls have kind of won."

Some respondents thought that communicators are scared to handle certain topics because of potential harassment. For example, one person said they asked interviewers on mainstream media to avoid bringing up the small but potential risks of COVID-19 vaccination for adolescents, since it could provoke harassment online and being "cancelled" by colleagues. Another said they avoid controversial topics since it could attract physical threats. Technology thus facilitated a range of new insecurities, both online and offline, mental and physical.

5.2.1.4. Exacerbating Factors

Many interviewees noted that health communicators' gender affected the kinds of online harassment they faced, as did their race, ethnicity, or religion.

Several racialized health communicators described receiving hate speech and explicit death threats. A racialized female health communicator described some extreme messages from "people who would literally write an entire email outlining the different ways they want to kill you." Another noted that, "before 2020, the type of hate and harassment that I would get exposed to did not have this flavor of misogyny and xenophobia."

A racialized female journalist, who reports on far-right communities as well as the COVID-19 pandemic, noted that violence by individuals with far-right ideologies targets certain groups: "It's people that walk into a mosque and shoot people in prayer. It's people walking to a classroom and in separating the men from women and shooting as many women as they can... it's like they are engaged in random stochastic violence."

Several female university-based experts and journalists stated that they received harassment that their male colleagues do not, such as body-shaming comments or being called a bad mother. Similarly, four male health communicators stated that they received less harassment compared to female peers. Two interviewees received transphobic comments, although they do not identify as being transgender.

These interview findings reflect recent research. A 2021 survey of Canadian journalists found that respondents identifying as women or BIPOC reported higher incidents of online harassment (IPSOS, 2021, p. 5), and a 2022 survey found that Canadian women journalists reported higher levels of their mental health being harmed than men (74 percent vs. 51 percent) and having seriously considered quitting journalism (56 percent vs. 32 percent) due to harassment and attacks on their reputations (Tenove, Al-Rawi, et al., 2023, p. 82).

5.2.2. Socio-Technical Factors Contributing to Insecurity

Socio-technical factors exacerbate risks from online harassment, creating broader offline and online insecurity. Experiences of technology-facilitated insecurity puncture the oft-assumed separation between online communication and offline security.

5.2.2.1. Platform-Enhanced Visibility

To reach the public with health information, health communicators must often increase their own "visibility," meaning accessibility of information about them. Visibility can be understood both in terms of breadth, or the number of people who access information about an individual, and depth, or how much information is accessed. Digital platforms have greatly increased the breadth, depth, and pervasiveness of visibility for many people, including journalists, influencers, publicly engaged academics, and artistic content creators (Duffy & Hund, 2019; Miller & Lewis, 2022). However, the structure or terms of service of social media platforms often make it challenging to separate one's professional and personal social media accounts. Moreover, individuals frequently receive more visibility by projecting greater authenticity, which often comes through sharing personal details, which, in turn, can enhance their vulnerability (Duffy & Hund, 2019) and "further erodes the supposed line between one's personal and professional self" (Miller & Lewis, 2022, p. 2).

Multiple interviewees described a sharp increase in their online visibility during the pandemic to address intense demand for health information. "The public turned to us in a way we'd never seen before, and we had massive increases in followers," said the social media manager for a public health agency. While the increased reach was viewed positively, over time, "people definitely started getting more abusive as they grew frustrated with the situation, and the changing health messages as the pandemic itself changed."

Another health communicator explained that she had long engaged on issues of pediatric health and vaccinations by including her own experiences as a mother, but that these personal revelations made her feel more vulnerable when she attracted large numbers of online followers during the pandemic. "I wanted to keep a bit of a safer space, [but] when you have 18,000 followers, it's not exactly easy," she said.

While communicators' efforts to reach broader audiences partly drove their increased visibility, many interviewees experienced sudden increases in visibility when identified or "tagged" by other individuals with much larger followings. One physician noted that whenever prominent pro-vaccine or anti-vaccine accounts retweeted her, "the bots showed up," as well as accounts accusing her of committing crimes against humanity and deserving Nuremberg-style trials. A public health official described having a prominent American academic with "half a million followers who tweeted out that I should be fired."

Visibility was particularly challenging when attention was drawn to people's appearance or physical location. For instance, one health journalist said that because she is prominent online and featured in TV broadcasts, she is regularly recognized in public spaces when she is not working. "Is an anti-masker going to come spit in my face because they didn't like that I suggested that the mask mandate should come back? [...] You start thinking about how vulnerable you really are at the grocery store in those sorts of situations, and how things can go sideways really quickly."

5.2.2.2. Doxing and Online Release of Personal Details

Ten of thirty-five interviewees described having personal details revealed, such as their home address, their private social media or email accounts, or details about family members. The connections to their private life caused significant concerns for their safety and were linked to more mental health harms.

There were many different versions of doxing. Protestors targeted the private residences of four interviewees, all prominent health officials. They had reason to believe that their addresses were shared via online platforms and messaging accounts. For instance, we interviewed a health official's security officer who had tracked the online spread of the official's address, and used this information to help develop a security plan for the official's residence. In other cases, interviewees described activities that suggested their private address was being shared widely. One interviewee noted, "The police had to come to my house as people were trying to break in, but there was nothing [they] could do [to keep it from happening again]. The police just moved them along. This has happened week after week after week... it was terrifying." Another public health official also had people protest at their house, prompting them to temporarily move to avoid threats.

Communication staff at another health agency received media attention for their high-profile social media campaigns. Critics tracked down the private social media accounts of the individuals who normally contributed to the institutional social media accounts. The intense concentration on individuals' personal details prompted police to encourage one staff member to move their family away from their home residence to avoid potential violent threats.

A racialized health communicator said that among the death threats she has received, "I had somebody post a picture of my intersection, telling me that they know where I live. I had to go sleep at my boss's house for a few nights, I was so scared."

In a high-profile case of doxing, a prominent alternative media commentator announced he would pay $5,000 to anyone who recorded a video of certain doctors meeting with family or friends during the holidays in December 2021, effectively creating a bounty to violate their privacy (Tworek, 2022).

The knowledge that personal details could be found online caused severe distress to several interviewees. A family doctor said, "As a physician, my work address is easily searchable. Anyone can look it up and anyone can show up. And I'm not in a hospital. There's no security."

5.2.2.3. Facilitating Hostile Networks

Social media platforms can also facilitate the networking of individuals engaging in harassment. Social media algorithms can promote clusters of people based on in-group similarity and outgroup hostility, forming "agitated clusters of comforting rage" (Chun, 2021). Social media platforms play a role in promoting networks or clusters of individuals who may be hostile to health communicators. For instance, individuals who watch anti-vaccine videos on YouTube are more likely to be recommended anti-vaccine videos than those who watch pro-vaccine videos. Similarly, "morally motivated harassment" can occur when "a member of a social network accuses a target of violating the network's norms, triggering moral outrage. Network members send harassing messages to the target, reinforcing their adherence to the norm and signalling network membership" (Marwick, 2021, p. 4).

Quite a few health communicators described facing what they perceived to be networks of hostile or harassing communication. A public health official who runs his own prominent Twitter (now X) account said that in response to some posts around public health measures, he would get hundreds of negative comments, ranging from criticism to "hate speech, intimidation, harassment," often from "troll-like accounts" with few followers and generic pictures. "It felt like [my posts] had been shared or highlighted somewhere," he said, prompting these sudden coordinated spikes in negative messaging.

A Canadian journalist described her experience like this: "all throughout the night, my phone notifications kept going off. It was almost like my story had been posted on a group chat somewhere and everybody was like, 'You've got to go write to this chick and take her down a notch.' […] I've had that kind of experience before, and I found out then that my articles were posted in an anti-vaccine Facebook group."

Multiple interviewees credited the "anti-vaccine movement" and "organized anti-vaccine groups" for much of the hostility they face. But some also faced hostile or even threatening messages from accounts accusing health communicators of insufficiently strict policies, or for failing to pursue "COVID Zero," meaning the full-scale elimination of COVID-19. While hostile accounts calling for tougher public health measures appeared to come from individuals in the same community or in Canada, those who experienced the highest volumes of anti-vaccine or anti-mask messages observed that many accounts appeared to be from outside Canada, primarily in the United States.

The communication manager for a regional health authority described the networked international hostility when their work became prominent online or in news accounts: "Even though we're at the local level, we do have a large voice, our followers do span across Canada, and we get trolls from across Canada, across North America."

Several racialized health communicators noted that some accounts that harassed them engaged in what appeared to be part of networks promoting xenophobic or racist discourse more broadly. Platforms facilitated the mobilization or redirection of these networks when health policy became politicized during the pandemic.

5.3. Systemic Suggestions to Address Technology-Facilitated Insecurity

Hostile, harassing, and threatening online messaging have negative consequences for Canadian health communicators. We suggest that the term TFI is a useful concept to understand how social media and messaging platforms contribute to increased risks of harm to physical safety, mental health, and professional efficacy and employability. There are three linkages to highlight between online communication and offline threats:

- Explicit or ambiguous threats of violence posted online;
- The vilification of individual health communicators, which may not explicitly call for violence, but which might help justify it or motivate people to take violent action, a mechanism sometimes called "stochastic terrorism" (Kolentsis & MacDonald, 2023);

- Intentional sharing of private information, in particular home addresses, which leads individuals to feel insecure, and which in some cases facilitated threatening protests at individuals' homes.

These and other mechanisms contribute to TFI: when individuals' security and feelings of security offline are threatened by how they and other actors make use of social media and messaging platforms. This situation can and should be addressed, and we propose that a framework of cybersecurity—and especially of *human-centric* cybersecurity—may help do so. This framework highlights how sociotechnical factors contribute to insecurity. For instance, platform design exposes individuals with greater visibility to face increased exposure to harassment, and enables individuals to find and maintain networks that promote hostility toward individuals and that may coordinate activities posing offline threats to targeted individuals' safety.

Additionally, a human-centric cybersecurity frame highlights how individuals' intersectional identities, including their gender or racialization as well as their health communication roles, can put them at greater risk. Not only did some health communicators face racialized and/or gendered harassment online, platforms also promoted visibility, exposure of private information, and networked action in ways that targeted their identities and undermined their offline security.

Our recommendations seek to move beyond placing the burden on individuals to protect themselves. We thus suggest more institutional approaches at workplaces and more effective responses from platforms and police. The term *cybersecurity* helps to make this point. While individuals may be required to download anti-virus software, that software is provided by their employer and most of the patching or other upgrades occur without employees having to do anything. Much of the labour of addressing TFI should fall to institutions, not individuals.

Two directions of improvement are proposed, which align with human-centric cybersecurity frameworks. First, there should be more extensive support for those targeted by online harassment, to help address harms to public and private identities. These recommendations are somewhat more advanced for journalists (PEN America, 2021; Storm, 2022), than for university-based experts or health experts (though see Researcher Support Consortium, 2024). Employer support mechanisms should not treat online harassment as a problem for individuals to address, but rather as a collective and organizational problem, requiring multidimensional responses including cybersecurity and physical security assistance, mental health and human resources support, and—in some circumstances—counter-messaging. Support policies should be designed to address the factors that exacerbate risks for some individuals and groups, such as practices to address the gendered or racialized nature of some harassment (Holton et al., 2021; Tenove, Al-Rawi et al., 2023). Employers cannot address online harassment on their own, and more effective policies are also needed from additional organizations, including police and social media companies.

Second, we encourage technological design and institutional policies that help individuals to maintain clearer and stronger separation between their public and private selves online. Employers often explicitly or implicitly encourage individuals to use their private identities for public roles; instead, they should clearly articulate the risks of this communication strategy and offer alternatives. Social media platforms should make it easier for individuals to control their personal and professional communication, including features that enable easier toggling between personal and professional accounts, more granular user control over how they engage and with whom, and pre-designed, opt-in "safety modes" (PEN America, 2021). Moreover, platforms should reduce their extraction of people's data, including inferred or social data, that unduly impinges on their privacy and puts them at risk (Chun & Sylvester, 2023). Further policies could include quicker and more accessible legal action to address online defamation (Law Commission of Ontario, 2020), or to de-index or remove information that violates a "right to reputation" (Therrien, 2021).

Insecurity arising from the use of social media and messaging platforms, and the need for more effective security responses, are particularly acute for health communicators and other individuals in public communication roles. Such dangers are a general feature of the security of the self in the contemporary digital media landscape. Any individual could be thrust into the spotlight or experience these issues. Therefore, policies should aim to protect all individuals online whether their following is large or small.

Acknowledgements

We gratefully acknowledge the time and insights of colleagues who worked on the broader research project, including Dr. Elizabeth Dubois, Dr. Saima Hirani, Dr. Jaigris Hodson, Dr. George Veletsianos,

Sabah Haque, Hanna Hett, and Oliver Zhang. Research for this project was supported by funding from the Government of Canada's New Frontiers in Research Fund (NFRFR-2021-00289) and the Canada Research Chair programme (CRC-2020-00132).

References

Al-Rawi, A., & Zemenchik, K. (2023). Tiktoking COVID-19 with frontline workers. *Digital Health, 9*, 1–8. https://doi.org/10.1177/20552076231152766

Bardall, G., & Tenove, C. (2024). Online violence against women in politics: Global trends and the Canadian experience. In T. Raney & C. N. Collier (Eds.), *Gender-based violence in Canadian politics in the #MeToo era* (pp. 22–44). University of Toronto Press.

Basky, G. (2021). Health advocates want help handling online harassment. *Canadian Medical Association Journal (CMAJ), 193*(8), E292–E293. https://doi.org/10.1503/cmaj.1095921

Carpiano, R. M., Callaghan, T., DiResta, R., Brewer, N. T., Clinton, C., Galvani, A. P., Lakshmanan, R., Parmet, W. E., Omer, S. B., Buttenheim, A. M., Benjamin, R. M., Caplan, A., Elharake, J. A., Flowers, L. C., Maldonado, Y. A., Mello, M. M., Opel, D. J., Salmon, D. A., Schwartz, J. L., & Hotez, P. J. (2023). Confronting the evolution and expansion of anti-vaccine activism in the USA in the COVID-19 era. *The Lancet, 401*(10380), 967–970. https://doi.org/10.1016/S0140-6736(23)00136-8

Chen, G. M., Pain, P., Chen, V. Y., Mekelburg, M., Springer, N., & Troger, F. (2020). "You really have to have a thick skin": A cross-cultural perspective on how online harassment influences female journalists. *Journalism, 21*(7), 877–895. https://doi.org/10.1177/1464884918768500

Chun, W. H. K., & Sylvester, P. (2023). *Platform data is social: How publicity and privacy are vital to data governance.* Centre for the Study of Democratic Institutions. https://democracy.ubc.ca/platforms/platform-governance-in-canada/platform-governance-essay-series/data/platform-data-is-social-how-publicity-and-privacy-are-vital-to-data-governance/

Chun, W. H. K. (2021). *Discriminating data: Correlation, neighborhoods, and the new politics of recognition.* The MIT Press.

Cinelli, M., Pelicon, A., Mozetič, I., Quattrociocchi, W., Novak, P. K., & Fabiana Z. (2021). Dynamics of online hate and misinformation. *Scientific Reports, 11*, 22083. https://www.nature.com/articles/s41598-021-01487-w

Collignon, S., & Rüdig, W. (2021). Increasing the cost of female representation? The gendered effects of harassment, abuse and intimidation towards Parliamentary candidates in the UK. *Journal of Elections, Public Opinion and Parties, 31*(4), 429–449. https://doi.org/10.1080/17457289.2021.1968413

Deibert, R. J. (2018). Toward a human-centric approach to cybersecurity. *Ethics & International Affairs, 32*(4), 411–424. https://doi.org/10.1017/S0892679418000618

Duffy, B. E., & Hund, E. (2019). Gendered visibility on social media: Navigating Instagram's authenticity bind. *International Journal of Communication, 13,* 4983–5002. https://ijoc.org/index.php/ijoc/article/view/11729

Dunn, S. (2021). Is it actually violence? Framing technology-facilitated abuse as violence. In J. Bailey, A. Flynn, & N. Henry (Eds.), *The Emerald international handbook of technology-facilitated violence and abuse* (pp. 25–45). Emerald Publishing Limited.

Gawley, K. (2021, February 24). *Conspiracists fantasizing Dr. Henry's execution part of troubling trend, experts say.* CityNews Vancouver. https://vancouver.citynews.ca/2021/02/24/conspiracists-fantasizing-henry-execution/

Gosse, C., Veletsianos, G., Hodson, J., Houlden, S., Dousay, T. A., Lowenthal, P. R., & Hall, N. (2021). The hidden costs of connectivity: Nature and effects of scholars' online harassment. *Learning, Media and Technology, 46*(3), 264–280. https://doi.org/10.1080/17439884.2021.1878218

Grobler, M., Gaire, R., & Nepal, S. (2021). User, usage and usability: Redefining human centric cyber security. *Frontiers in Big Data, 4,* 583723, 1–18. https://doi.org/10.3389/fdata.2021.583723

Hart, M., Davey, J., Maharasingam-Shah, E., Gallagher, A., & O'Connor, C. (2021). *An online environmental scan of right-wing extremism in Canada.* Institute for Strategic Dialogue. https://www.isdglobal.org/isd-publications/an-online-environmental-scan-of-right-wing-extremism-in-canada/

Hodgins, B. (2022, January 17). Police investigating protest held near home of Peterborough Medical Officer of Health Dr. Thomas Piggott. *The Peterborough Examiner.* https://www.thepeterboroughexaminer.com/news/police-investigating-protest-held-near-home-of-peterborough-medical-officer-of-health-dr-thomas-piggott/article_f4dc465e-7394-5498-9d43-63546bfcb66a.html

Hofstetter, J. S., & Pourmalek, P. (2023). *Gendering cybersecurity through women, peace and security: Designing conflict-sensitive strategy documents at the national level.* Global Network of Women Peacebuilders & ICT4Peace Foundation. http://gnwp.org/gender-cybersecurity-through-women-peace-security

Holton, A. E., Bélair-Gagnon, V., Bossio, D., & Molyneux, L. (2021). "Not their fault, but their problem": Organizational responses to the online harassment of journalists. *Journalism Practice, 17*(4), 859–874. https://doi.org/10.1080/17512786.2021.1946417

IPSOS. (2021). *Online harm in journalism: Research report.* https://site-cbc.radio-canada.ca/documents/media-centre/Ipsos-Online-Harm-in-Journalism-Report.pdf

Kolentsis, A., & MacDonald, S. (2023, June 30). *The stabbing attack at the University of Waterloo underscores the dangers of polarizing rhetoric about gender.* The Conversation. http://theconversation.com/the-stabbing-attack-at-the-university-of-waterloo-underscores-the-dangers-of-polarizing-rhetoric-about-gender-208904

Kosseff, J. (2018). Cybersecurity of the person. *First Amendment Law Review,* 17, 343–366. https://heinonline.org/HOL/Page?handle=hein.journals/falr17&id=358&div=&collection=

Law Commission of Ontario. (2020). *Defamation law in the Internet age: Final report.* https://www.lco-cdo.org/wp-content/uploads/2020/03/Defamation-Final-Report-Eng-FINAL.pdf

Levy, K., & Schneier, B. (2020). Privacy threats in intimate relationships. *Journal of Cybersecurity,* 6(1), 1–13. https://doi.org/10.1093/cybsec/tyaa006

Lindgren, A., Wechsler, S., & Wong, C. (2022, August 26). *The COVID years: Risk, reward and rethinking priorities.* J-Source. https://j-source.ca/the-covid-years-risk-reward-and-rethinking-priorities/

Marwick, A. E. (2021). Morally motivated networked harassment as normative reinforcement. *Social Media + Society,* 7(2), 1–12 20563051211021378. https://doi.org/10.1177/20563051211021378

Mello, S., Glowacki, E., Fuentes, I., & Seabolt, J. (2023). Communicating COVID-19 risk on Instagram: A content analysis of official public health messaging during the first year of the pandemic. *Journal of Health Communication,* 28(1), 38–52. https://doi.org/10.1080/10810730.2023.2175278

Miller, K. C. (2021). Hostility toward the press: A synthesis of terms, research, and future directions in examining harassment of journalists. *Digital Journalism,* 11(7), 1230–1249. https://doi.org/10.1080/21670811.2021.1991824

Miller, K. C., & Lewis, S. C. (2022). Journalistic visibility as celebrity and its consequences for harassment. *Digital Journalism,* 11(10), 1886–1905. https://doi.org/10.1080/21670811.2022.2136729

National Institute of Standards and Technology. (2024, October 4). *Human-centered cybersecurity.* Computer Security Resource Center, National Institute of Standards and Technology. https://csrc.nist.gov/projects/human-centered-cybersecurity

Nogrady B. (2021). "I hope you die": how the COVID pandemic unleashed attacks on scientists. *Nature,* 598(7880), 250–253. https://www.nature.com/articles/d41586-021-02741-x

Obermaier, M., Hofbauer, M., & Reinemann, C. (2018). Journalists as targets of hate speech. How German journalists perceive the consequences for themselves and how they cope with it. *Studies in Communication, Media,* 7(4), 499–524. https://doi.org/10.5771/2192-4007-2018-4-499

Pangborn, S. M., Boatwright, B. C., Miller, C. L., & Velting, M. N. (2021). "I don't feel like a hero": Frontline healthcare providers' social media storytelling during COVID-19. *Health Communication, 38*(8), 1508–1518. https://doi.org/10.1080/10410236.2021.2017108

Pascual-Ferrá, P., Alperstein, N., Barnett, D. J., & Rimal, R. N. (2021). Toxicity and verbal aggression on social media: Polarized discourse on wearing face masks during the COVID-19 pandemic. *Big Data & Society, 8*(1), 20539517211023533, 1–17. https://doi.org/10.1177/20539517211023533

PEN America. (2021). *No excuse for abuse. What social media companies can do now to combat online harassment and empower users.* https://pen.org/report/no-excuse-for-abuse/

Picard, A. (2021, August 16). Opinion: The troubling Nazi-fication of COVID-19 discourse. *The Globe and Mail.* https://www.theglobeandmail.com/opinion/article-the-troubling-nazi-fication-of-covid-19-discourse/

Piller, T. (2021, January 24). *"Idiots" protest at Saskatchewan chief medical health officer's home: Moe.* Global News. https://globalnews.ca/news/7596300/protest-saskatchewan-chief-medical-health-officers-home-moe-shahab/

Posetti, J., & Shabbir, N. (2022). *The chilling: A global study of online violence against women journalists.* International Center for Journalists. https://www.icfj.org/our-work/chilling-global-study-online-violence-against-women-journalists

Researcher Support Consortium. (2024). *Researchers increasingly face campaigns of intimidation and harassment. They need your support.* Researcher Support Consortium. https://researchersupport.org/

Rossini, P. (2022). Beyond incivility: Understanding patterns of uncivil and intolerant discourse in online political talk. *Communication Research, 49*(3), 399–425. https://doi.org/10.1177/0093650220921314

Royan, R., Pendergrast, T. R., Del Rios, M., Rotolo, S. M., Trueger, N. S., Bloomgarden, E., Behrens, D., Jain, S., & Arora, V. M. (2022). Use of Twitter amplifiers by medical professionals to combat misinformation during the COVID-19 pandemic. *Journal of Medical Internet Research, 24*(7), Article e38324, 1–6. https://doi.org/10.2196/38324

Royan, R., Pendergrast, T. R., Woitowich, N. C., Trueger, N. S., Wooten, L., Jain, S., & Arora, V. M. (2023). Physician and biomedical scientist harassment on social media during the COVID-19 pandemic. *JAMA Network Open, 6*(6), Article e2318315, 1–5. https://doi.org/10.1001/jamanetworkopen.2023.18315

Storm, H. (2022, May 26). *Newsroom guide for managing online harm.* #NotOK Stand Up for Journalism and Democracy. https://notok.cestassez.ca/media/ct1jz3oo/newsroom-guide-for-managing-online-harm.pdf

Tenove, C., Al-Rawi, A., Merchan, J., Sharma, M., & Villela, G. (2023). *Not just words: How reputational attacks harm journalists and undermine press freedom.* Global Reporting Centre. https://globalreportingcentre.org/reputational-attacks/

Tenove, C., & Tworek, H. (2022). *Online hate in the pandemic*. British Columbia's Office of the Human Rights Commissioner (BCOHRC). https://hateinquiry.bchumanrights.ca/wp-content/uploads/Online-hate-in-the-pandemic-by-Dr.-Tenove-Dr.-Tworek_BCOHRCs-Inquiry-into-hate-in-the-pandemic.pdf

Tenove, C., Tworek, H., Lore, G., Buffie, J., & Deley, T. (2023). Damage control: How campaign teams interpret and respond to online incivility. *Political Communication, 40*(3), 283–303. https://doi.org/10.1080/1058460 9.2022.2137743

Therrien, D. (2021, May 11). *Submission of the Office of the Privacy Commissioner of Canada on Bill C-11, the Digital Charter Implementation Act, 2020*. Office of the Privacy Commissioner of Canada. https://www.priv.gc.ca/en/opc-actions-and-decisions/submissions-to-consultations/sub_ethi_c11_2105/

Tworek, H. (2022, January 12). *As Omicron surged, so did abuse of health communicators online*. Centre for International Governance Innovation. https://www.cigionline.org/articles/as-omicron-surged-so-did-abuse-of-health-communicators-online/

Wight, L., Tenove, C., Hirani, S., & Tworek, H. (2025). Mental health and coping strategies of health communicators who faced online abuse during the COVID-19 pandemic: Mixed Methods Study. *JMIR Infodemiology, 5*(1), e68483. https://doi.org/10.2196/68483

Wintterlin, F., Langmann, K., Boberg, S., Frischlich, L., Schatto-Eckrodt, T., & Quandt, T. (2021). Lost in the stream? Professional efficacy perceptions of journalists in the context of dark participation. *Journalism, 23*(9), 1846–1863. https://doi.org/10.1177/14648849211016984

PART II

TOWARD THE SECURITY OF SELF

Achieving the Security of Self in Machine Learning: Empowering Individuals Through Self-Security Enhancing Technologies

Sébastien Gambs

Abstract

Broadly, the security of self relates to the capacity of an individual to protect their personal information through direct actions and initiatives under their control, and thus their privacy. In this chapter, I investigate how this notion could be achieved within the context of machine learning in which one of the challenges is to protect personal profiles that have been aggregated and assimilated within a machine learning model. More precisely, the objective is to discuss in a prospective manner how recent advances in the field of security and privacy of machine learning could be leveraged to empower users. For instance, recent techniques such as membership inference attacks and dataset watermarking can be used as tools for auditing machine learning models, thus increasing the transparency, in particular in situations in which an individual's data have been incorporated in the model without their consent. Furthermore, "data poisoning" could be used as a preventive strategy against unauthorized data usage while machine unlearning, by enabling the removal of one's data from the model, can mitigate long-term privacy risks. Nonetheless, the security of self in machine learning is still in its infancy and many open issues remain to be solved such as the legal robustness of auditing techniques as evidence in court, the integration of these rights into artificial intelligence (AI) regulations, and the necessity of significant development efforts to move from proof-of-concepts to technologies that are mature and accessible to the general public.

In our current information society, there is a strong asymmetry in terms of power between the entities that gather and process personal data—major Internet companies, telecom operators, cloud providers—and the individuals who own these data (Bashir et al., 2015). As a consequence, users of information technologies have no choice but to blindly believe that the entities to which they have entrusted their data will use them in a manner that is respectful of their privacy. Yet, once personal data has been released, the user has lost an important part of their *sovereignty* over how their data are used, processed, and disseminated.

At the macro-level, data sovereignty is often associated with the capacity of countries to ensure that the personal data of their citizens remain within their sphere of influence using, for instance, on-premises equipment (Bellanger, 2014), instead of these data being located in remote servers through cloud computer infrastructure (Peterson et al., 2011). In contrast, at the individual level, data sovereignty can be defined as the control that individuals have over their personal data. More precisely, the data sovereignty principle is one of the fundamental principles to embed into technology when following the "privacy-by-design" approach, which integrates the privacy issues starting from the conception phase of a service up to its full lifecycle (Schaar, 2010). The data sovereignty principle states that the data related to an individual belong to them and that they should stay in control of how these data are used and for which purpose. As such, sovereignty can be seen as a necessary ingredient to achieve privacy, along with other fundamental privacy principles such as *data minimization*—the practice of only disclosing the minimal amount of information necessary for realizing a particular task (Anciaux et al., 2024)—and *transparency*—the practice of explaining to the user how data are collected and processed (Janic et al., 2013).

A fundamental hindrance to the achievement of sovereignty is that the trust assumptions given to external entities are often too optimistic, and that there are many realistic situations in which they might be betrayed. This implicit high level of trust that users give to service providers in charge of their personal data has been identified as one of the main issues to solve to close the gap between information privacy laws and technologies (Diaz et al., 2013). In addition, the centralization and concentration of a huge amount of personal data in large databases are a target of choice for hackers and malicious insiders, raising the risk of privacy breaches. As such, the current architecture of trust surrounding personal data includes many breaking points endangering sovereignty. A paradigm shift is needed to address this and support users in asserting sovereignty over their personal data and redress the balance between individuals and major online actors. However, moving sovereignty from an abstract principle to a practical reality requires the appropriate technological means, and the "security of self" is a relevant approach to achieve this objective.

Although the notion is not yet well-established and defined, the security of self, as used in this chapter, refers to the capacity of an individual to protect their personal information through direct actions under their control, and thus their privacy. For instance, this includes the ability of individuals to control their personal data as well as the traces left by their actions in both the physical and digital worlds, either through the use of privacy-enhancing technologies that can be used by users to defend themselves (e.g., an anonymous communication network) or that can be put in place by a service provider (e.g., transparency mechanisms or fine-grained privacy settings).

In cybersecurity, the concept of a *self-sovereign identity* (SSI) in which individuals have control over their own digital identities without relying on external authorities also aligns well with the notion of security of self. This is also directly linked to information security, in the sense that security risks such as identity theft, profiling, or manipulation are directly associated with the exposure surface of their digital identity. Thus, the practical enforcement of the notion of the security of self calls for the conception of new primitives, which we coin as *self-security enhancing technologies* (SSETs), in the same spirit as the well-established concept of *privacy-enhancing technologies* (PETs) (Goldberg, 2017) and the more recent concept of *transparency-enhancing technologies* (TETs) (Janic et al., 2013).

This chapter looks at how the security of self could be instantiated within the context of machine learning (ML) in which the data of an individual are integrated into a model outputted by a learning algorithm.[1] It is particularly challenging as, once the data of a user are

---

1.   For the sake of simplicity, this chapter uses the term "model" to refer to any model learned by a machine learning algorithm, agnostic to its internal structure. For instance, it can refer to a deep neural network or a random forest.

part of a model, they are then diluted and mixed with the data of others that were also part of the training set of the model. In Section 6.1, recent works on privacy and security attacks against ML models will be reviewed. Section 6.2 will present a first approach by which users can assess whether their data have been integrated in a ML model either by adopting an auditing approach based on privacy attacks or by watermarking their own data. This can be considered as a first implementation of a "right of transparency by default" from the platform on whether the data of the user have been used or not to generate the model. Section 6.3 will discuss the more aggressive stance in which a user would like to deter a company from including their data in a model without their consent by poisoning it. It means that the inclusion of these "poisoned" data in the training has a negative effect on the performance of the model, leading it to make erroneous predictions. This can be considered as a form of PET in which a user *a priori* modifies their data to prevent unwanted uses. In contrast, Section 6.4 presents an approach based on machine unlearning, which can be considered as a form of "right to be forgotten" in the ML context. Finally, Section 6.5 highlights fundamental open questions that need to be solved for the security of self in ML to be accessible to the general public.

6.1. Machine Learning Privacy and Security

In ML, the access to "big data" has enabled a "quantum leap" in the prediction accuracy in many domains. However, the collection and analysis of large-scale datasets as well as the ubiquity of ML models in our society due to their success raises serious ethical issues. Privacy is only one side of the coin as other ethical issues associated with "big data" analysis should be addressed, such as the *fairness* (Barocas et al., 2023) and *explainability* (Molnar, 2023) of the models that are learned from these data. Indeed, ML now has a central role in high-stakes decision systems, such as college admissions or loan attribution, as most of these systems are based on models learned from data rather than written by programmers. However, often their complex design makes it difficult to understand and explain their decision, which leads to a lack of transparency as well as a lack of trust (Pasquale, 2015).

With respect to privacy, in addition to the inferences that can be made from the data itself, it is important to understand how much the output of the learning algorithm itself—the model—leaks information about the input data it was trained on. For example, privacy attacks, also called *inference attacks*, have been developed against ML models to reconstruct the training data from the model (Fredrikson et al., 2015) or to predict whether the profile of a particular individual known to the adversary was in the training dataset (Shokri et al., 2017). Generally, this membership inference is deemed problematic if revealing that a profile belongs to this database enables the adversary to uncover sensitive information about this individual (e.g., being part of a cohort of patients for a disease). The security of ML is also a very active research topic as ML models are also vulnerable to attacks targeting confidentiality, integrity, or availability (Goldblum et al., 2022). For instance, *adversarial examples* (Biggio et al., 2013) can be used to alter a model behaviour at inference time, a classical example of adversarial examples being the addition of noise to a picture in such a way that the model will completely mislabel the content of the picture while a human would see no difference. In contrast, *poisoning attacks* (Jagielski et al., 2018) have an objective to manipulate the training dataset before the learning to cause an unexpected behaviour in the context of the model learned (e.g., predicting the wrong class). Overall, these two techniques have the same objectives of causing the misbehaviour of the model in terms of prediction, but one targets the inference time while the other impacts the training phase. More recently, the concept of *sponge examples* (Shumailov et al., 2021) has also targeted the availability of the ML model by crafting inputs to increase the model's inference time as well as its energy consumption. This is especially problematic in a scenario such as machine learning as a service (MLaaS), in which the model provider is making a client pay for each query done to the model rather than directly selling it. Indeed, by sending a high number of sponge examples to the MLaaS, it would become possible to cause a huge increase of the resources needed to answer them, thus possibly causing a crash of the service.

6.2. Auditing and Watermarking Data

The membership inference attack mentioned previously could possibly be used to detect that data was included in the training set of a ML model without the consent of the data subject. Indeed, the objective of the membership inference attack is to decide whether or not a specific profile was part of the training set of a model by observing its predictions or by analyzing its structure. If it is possible to build such an attack with high accuracy, it is also possible to transform it into an auditing approach. By conducting the attack on a particular dataset, such as the proprietary dataset of a company, it is possible to have a reliable estimate of whether or not this dataset was part of the training set of the model.

This proposed usage of membership inference attack is quite different from their common use, which is to assess the privacy protection provided by a model before it is released. Another limitation of the proposed approach is recent work on proof-of-repudiation (Kong et al., 2023), a form of *a posteriori* privacy-washing approach in which, upon a particular audit query, the model owner forges a proof that the model currently being audited could have been generated without the profile associated with the membership inference. Such proof-of-repudation for some profiles makes it difficult to envision that the outputs of successful membership inference attacks could be used as evidence in front of a judge due to the plausible deniability that they offer to the model owner.

One way to avoid the collection and use of data to train a ML model without the consent of the legitimate owner of the data is to *watermark* it. More precisely, a digital watermark corresponds to the introduction of a specific mark in a medium (e.g., picture, video, or sound) that can be used to provide ownership identification but also deter the unwanted dissemination of copyright information (Cox et al., 2007). Any watermarking scheme is composed of two phases: 1) the embedding phase in which the watermark is integrated in the medium, and 2) the verification phase during which the watermark can be retrieved. To be secure, both the embedding and verification also involve the use of a secret key necessary to be able to perform these two operations—that is, without the use of a secret key, anyone knowing the specification of the watermaking algorithm could extract it. In the case, for example, of a picture, the watermark can be visible or invisible. Usually, to be considered secure, the watermark has to be robust against perturbations and transformations of the medium such as, in the case of a picture, cropping, resizing, or rotations. Usually, a watermark can contain more complex information than simply the name of the creator, such as metadata on the time and location of creation of the medium, or other provenance information. The presence of a watermark can deter unauthorized entities from using the watermarked content without permission as it makes it possible to trace the source of the content or its creator. In particular, watermarking is one of the fundamental building blocks behind digital rights management techniques (Subramanya & Yi, 2006) used by online platforms to copyright distributed content, such as video-on-demand, or used by artists to brand their creations so they can be recognized easily.

One of the limits of classical watermarking techniques is that they normally do not survive their integration in a ML model. For instance, even if a large fraction of an image database is watermarked, it would be very difficult to test it once it is represented in a black-box model such as a neural network. More recently, the concept of dataset watermarking has been proposed as an approach for verifying whether a ML model has been trained with a particular watermarked dataset. To be efficient, such techniques need to work independently of the type of model, to be robust against image alterations, and to be visually imperceptible—otherwise the watermarked images could be detected by a human and discarded. An example of such an approach is the concept of *radioactive data* (Sablayrolles et al., 2020). The idea behind this approach is that a subset of the images of the training dataset is modified imperceptibly during the embedding phase in such a way that, if a ML model is trained on these data, it will be possible to recognize this by performing statistical assessments on the prediction behaviour of the model during the verification phase. This approach is promising and has been shown to be resistant to transformations applied to the training dataset of more sophisticated approaches, such as model extraction attacks (Atli et al., 2020).

One of the shortcomings of dataset watermarking approaches is the requirement to have access to a complete dataset, and not simply an individual profile. This is possible only if a user provides a dataset of their images or if a community of users coordinates to implement this approach. In contrast, the approach described in the next section can be performed directly by a single user on their own piece of content.

6.3. Poisoning Data

Recently, new approaches have been proposed to rely on the use of adversarial examples mentioned in Section 6.1. More precisely, the objective there is to modify a picture in such a way that the computer would wrongly classify the picture—for example, labelling a dog as a cat, or a car as a cow—while these modifications remain imperceptible to a human. Afterwards, if such adversarial pictures are integrated as part of the training set of generative text-to-image methods, such as Dall-E or Stable Diffusion, they will "poison" the outputs produced by these methods to render them meaningless.

A tool called Glaze (Shan et al., 2023) has been designed for artists to modify their work before uploading it online so that the computers will interpret it as a different artistic style than that of the original artist. Once the poisoned images are integrated into the generative model, they will basically perturb the concepts implicitly learned by the model itself. For instance, the concept of "fantasy art" could be shifted to "impressionism" in such a way that when the generative model is asked to generate a fantasy art picture, it will instead create one in an impressionist style.

More recently, another tool called Nightshade (Sand Lab, n.d.) designed by the same team that created Glaze was precisely developed to create adversarial inputs with the objective of helping artists to proactively defend themselves against unwanted uses of their work. Indeed, one of the issues of generative AI methods is that they are often trained with creative content publicly available on the Internet but collected as part of the training set without the consent of the associated artist. Techniques such as copyright form, opt-out lists, or robots.txt offer limited protection as their efficiency depends on the good will of the entity scraping this content. The objective of Nightshade is to introduce a perturbation in the poisoned images, which will lead the model to associate a wrong concept with the image. The magnitude of the change of the concept depends on the number of poisoned examples learned from, but researchers have demonstrated that a few hundred poisoned images are enough to completely perturb images generated by the models with respect to a particular concept—rendering them meaningless (Shan et al., 2024). In addition, the researchers have shown that Nightshade can also corrupt neighbour concepts. For example, if the model considers the concept of "dragon" to be related to "fantasy art," producing poisoned images of one of these concepts is also likely to perturb the performance on the model of the other concepts.

It is also possible to envision the use of such techniques for individuals to protect their own data before it is uploaded online. For example, it could be used to protect images containing the face of a user against facial recognition software. A similar approach has been proposed in the audio domain to avoid voice cloning by adding adversarial noise to an uploaded voice recording to ensure that it will be wrongly classified, in terms of the identity of the person, by a speech recognition system.

All these techniques could be considered as SSETs deployed by a user to proactively protect their privacy. Another way to increase the control of a user over their data involves a model provider implementing mechanisms that can be activated on demand by a user.

6.4. Unlearning Data

Under data protection legislation such as the *General Data Protection Regulation* (GDPR) in Europe, new rights have emerged such as the right to portability, requiring a service provider to give to a user a copy of their own data in a standardized format, and the right to erasure, also called the *right to be forgotten*.

Machine unlearning refers to the process in which the contribution of the data of a single user is removed from a trained ML model (Fosch-Villaronga et al., 2018). As such, it can be considered an implementation of the right to be forgotten in the ML context where an individual could request that their data be removed from a model. In practice, this could occur when a user withdraws consent to the use of their data with respect to a particular model, or following an audit (see Section 6.2) showing their data has been used without consent. Contrary to the watermarking, auditing, and poisoning approaches described in previous sections that can be performed directly by the user, machine unlearning requires the active collaboration of the model provider as the model is already trained and deployed and proactive approaches are no longer possible.

The most direct way to implement the right to be forgotten would involve deleting the targeted profile from the training dataset and then retraining the model completely. However, this is very inefficient in terms of both computational resources and associated energy costs. In addition, in distributed settings such as federated learning, the training dataset is actually split across several entities, making retraining the model more complex, if not impossible, if some of the original entities are no longer available. Consequently, the research on machine unlearning has mainly focused on efficiency in terms of the computational cost.

One possible architecture to realize machine unlearning consists of partitioning the training dataset into several subsets, learning a model for each subset, and, finally, aggregating the predictions similarly to ensemble methods approaches such as random forests. This is the approach taken by the Shared, Isolated, Sliced and Aggregated (SISA) framework where datasets are randomly split into k shards (Bourtoule et al., 2021) and a specific submodel is trained for each shard. When a particular profile needs to be unlearned, only the model corresponding to the shard in which the considered data point belongs needs to be retrained.

A completely different approach could be to directly try to surgically modify the structure of the trained model to remove the influence of the data point that we aim to unlearn. For example, in a neural network, the weights of the different links heavily influenced by the targeted profile could be updated to erase its contribution on the model (Wang et al., 2022).

One of the challenges of machine unlearning is for a user to be able to verify that their data has indeed been erased from the model. It is a difficult task for a model provider to prove the machine unlearning of a profile after a data deletion request. Such proof could be produced through a membership inference attack (see Section 6.2). If, after deletion, the output of a membership inference attack returns with a high confidence that the particular profile considered is a non-member (i.e., it was not part of the training set), while it was before, the user can be convinced with high probability that their particular profile has been removed from the model (Chen et al., 2021). In this approach, the user is directly acting as the auditor. Another possibility is to use a machine unlearning approach that provides a certificate after deletion confirming the unlearning (Guo et al., 2020), which provides a more systematic way to prove to a user that their deletion request has been diligently processed.

6.5. Toward a New Machine Learning Security of Self Paradigm

As argued in this chapter, implementing security of self in the ML context is much more difficult than protecting oneself against profiling when surfing the web—for example, through the use of an anonymous communication network such as Tor—because the model is in essence inferred from the collection of aggregated profiles through the learning process. Nonetheless, recent advances made by the research community on privacy and security of ML could be leveraged to empower users. For instance, membership inference attacks and dataset watermarking techniques can be used to audit a model to detect whether the data of an individual has been integrated in a ML model without their consent. Even more, the possibility of poisoning data could act as a deterrent to avoid the integration of content into a model without the owner's consent. Finally, new paradigms such as machine unlearning could be used in collaboration with a model provider to adapt new rights such as the right to be forgotten in the ML context.

Overall, the concept of security of self in ML is still a nascent idea and there remain significant open questions to address for the future. First, it is not clear if auditing approaches based on membership inference attacks or watermarking techniques could be considered robust enough to be used as legal evidence in front of a judge. Nonetheless, it is likely that such approaches will be tested legally in the future, in particular by artists or copyright owners whose content has been integrated in a generative model without their consent. Second, upcoming AI regulations will have to have explicit provisions for such a right to be recognized and enforced. For instance, machine unlearning should appear explicitly as a form of right to be forgotten for high-stakes decision systems or there will be little incentive for companies to offer it. Finally, there is a huge development effort needed to democratize the use of SSETs for the public and support individuals, authors, and artists to leverage these promising techniques.

Acknowledgements

This research is supported by the Canada Research Chair program as well as a Discovery Grant from NSERC.

References

Anciaux, N., Frittella, S., Joffroy, B., Nguyen, B., & Scerri, G. (2024). *A new PET for data collection via forms with data minimization, full accuracy and informed consent.* 27th International Conference on Extending Database Technology (EDBT), Paestum, Italy. https://inria.hal.science/hal-04149000/document

Atli, B. G., Szyller, S., Juuti, M., Marchal, S., & Asokan, N. (2020). Extraction of complex DNN models: Real threat or boogeyman? In O. Shehory, G. Barash, & E. Farchi (Eds.), *Engineering dependable and secure machine learning systems* (pp. 42–57). Springer Nature Switzerland AG. https://doi.org/10.48550/arXiv.1910.05429

Barocas, S., Hardt, M., & Narayanan A. (2023). *Fairness and machine learning: Limitations and opportunities*. The MIT Press.

Bashir, M., Hayes, C., Lambert, A. D., & Kesan, J. P. (2016). Online privacy and informed consent: The dilemma of information asymmetry. *Proceedings of the Association for Information Science and Technology, 52*(1), 1–10. https://doi.org/10.1002/pra2.2015.145052010043

Bellanger, P. (2014). *La souveraineté numérique*. Éditions Stock.

Biggio, B., Corona, I., Maiorca, D., Nelson, B., Šrndic, N., Laskov, P., Giacinto, G., & Roli, F. (2013). Evasion attacks against machine learning at test time. In H. Blockeel, K. Kersting, S. Nijssen, & F. Železný (Eds.), *Machine learning and knowledge discovery in databases: European conferder, ECML-PKDD, Proceedings, Part III, vol. LNAI 8190*, (pp. 387–402). Springer Berlin Heidelberg.

Bourtoule, L., Chandrasekaran, V., Choquette-Choo, C. A., Jia, H., Travers, A., Zhang, B., Lie, D., & Papernot, N. (2021, May 24–27). *Machine unlearning*. 42nd IEEE Symposium on Security and Privacy, SP 2021, San Francisco, CA, United States. https://doi.org/10.48550/arXiv.1912.03817

Chen, M., Zhang, Z., Wang, T., Backes, M., Humbert, M., & Zhang, Y. (2021). When machine unlearning jeopardizes privacy. In Y. Kim & J. Kim (Eds.), *CCS '21: Proceedings of the 2021 ACM SIGSAC Conference on Computer and Communications Security* (pp. 896–911). Association for Computing Machinery. https://doi.org/10.1145/3460120.3484756

Cox, I., Miller, M., Bloom, J., Fridrich, J., & Kalker, T. (2007). *Digital watermarking and steganography*. Morgan Kaufmann. https://doi.org/10.1016/B978-0-12-372585-1.X5001-3

Diaz, C., Tene, O., & Gürses, S. (2013). Hero or villain: The data controller in privacy law and technologies. *Ohio State Law Journal, 74*(6), 923–964. https://papers.ssrn.com/sol3/papers.cfm?abstract_id=2321480

Fosch-Villaronga, E., Kieseberg, E., & Li, T. (2018). Humans forget, machines remember: Artificial intelligence and the right to be forgotten. *Computer Law & Security Review, 34*(2), 304–313. https://doi.org/10.1016/j.clsr.2017.08.007

Fredrikson, M., Jha., S., & Ristenpart, T. (2015, October 12–16). Model inversion attacks that exploit confidence information and basic countermeasures. In I. Ray (Ed.), *Proceedings of the 22nd ACM SIGSAC Conference on Computer and Communications Security* (pp. 1322–1333). Assocation for Computing Machinery. https://doi.org/10.1145/2810103.2813677

Goldberg, I. (2007). Privacy-enhancing technologies for the Internet III: Ten years later. In A. Acquisti, S. Gritzalis, C. L. Ambrinoudakis, & S. di Vimercati (Eds.), *Digital privacy: Theory, technologies, and practices* (pp. 3–19). Auerberg Publications. https://doi.org/10.1201/9781420052183

Goldblum, M., Tsipras. D., Xie, C., Chen, X., Schwarzchild, A., Song, D., Madry, A., Li, B., & Goldstein, T. (2023). Dataset security for machine learning:

Data poisoning, backdoor attacks, and defenses. *IEEE Transactions on Pattern Analysis and Machine Intelligence*, 45(2), 1563–1580. https://doi.org/10.1109/tpami.2022.3162397

Guo, C., Goldstein, T., Hannun, A. Y., & van der Maaten, L. (2020). Certified data removal from machine learning models. *Proceedings of the 37th International Conference on Machine Learning*, 119, 3832–3842. https://proceedings.mlr.press/v119/guo20c.html

Jagielski, M., Oprea, A., Biggio, B., Liu, C., Nita-Rotaru, C., & Li, B. (2018). Manipulating machine learning: Poisoning attacks and countermeasures for regression learning. In *2018 IEEE Symposium on Security and Privacy (SP)* (pp. 19–35). IEEE. https://doi.org/10.1109/SP.2018.00057

Janic, M., Wijbenga, J. P., & Veugen, T. (2013). Transparency enhancing tools (TETs): An overview. In *2013 Third Workshop on Socio-Technical Aspects in Security and Trust* (pp. 18–25). IEEE. https://doi.org/10.1109/STAST.2013.11

Kong, Z., Chowdhury, A., & R., Chaudhuri, K. (2023). *Can membership inferencing be refuted?* arXiv. https://doi.org/10.48550/arXiv.2303.03648

Molnar, C. (2023). *Interpretable machine learning* (second edition). Leanpub.

Pasquale, F. (2015). *The black box society: The secret algorithms that control money and information*. Harvard University Press.

Peterson, N. J. Z., Gondree, M., & Beverly, R. (2011). *A position paper on data sovereignty: The importance of geolocating data in the cloud*. In I. Stoica & J. Wilkes (Eds.), *HotCloud' 11: Proceedings of the 3rd USENIX Workshop on Hot Topics in Cloud Computing* (p. 9). USENIX Association. https://www.usenix.org/legacy/event/hotcloud11/tech/final_files/Peterson.pdf

Regulation 2016/679. *Regulation (EU) 2016/679 of the European Parliament and of the Council of 27 April 2016 on the protection of natural persons with regard to the processing of personal data and on the free movement of such data, and repealing Directive 95/46/EC (General Data Protection Regulation)*. https://eur-lex.europa.eu/eli/reg/2016/679/oj/eng

Sand Lab (n.d.). *Nightshade*. University of Chicago. https://nightshade.cs.uchicago.edu

Sablayrolles, A., Douze, M., Schmid, C., & Jégou, H. (2020). *Radioactive data: tracing through training. Proceedings of the 37th International Conference on Machine Learning*, 119, 8326–8335. https://proceedings.mlr.press/v119/sablayrolles20a.html

Schaar, P. (2010). Privacy by design. *Identity in the Information Society*, 3(2), 267–274. http://dx.doi.org/10.1007/s12394-010-0055-x

Shan, S., Cryan, J., Wenger, E., Zheng, H., Hanocka, R., & Zhao, B. Y. (2023). Glaze: Protecting artists from style mimicry by {Text-to-Image} models. In J. Calandrino & C. Troncoso (Eds.), *Proceedings of the 32nd USENIX Conference on Security Symposium* (pp. 2187–2204). USENIX Association.

Shan, S., Ding, W., Passananti, J., Wu, S., Zheng, H., Zhao, B. Y. (2024). Nightshade: Prompt-specific poisoning attacks on text-to-image generative models. In *Proceedings of the 2024 IEEE Symposium on Security and Privacy* (SP) (pp. 807–825). IEEE.

Shokri, R., Stronati, M., Song C., & Shmatikov, V. (2017). Membership inference attacks against machine learning models. In *2017 IEEE Symposium on Security and Privacy (SP)* (pp. 3–18). IEEE. https://doi.org/10.1109/SP.2017.41

Shumailov, I., Zhao, Y., Bates, D., Papernot, N., Mullins, R.D., & Anderson, R. (2021). Sponge examples: Energy-latency attacks on neural networks. In *2021 IEEE European Symposium on Security and Privacy (EuroS&P)* (pp. 212–231). IEEE. https://doi.org/10.1109/EuroSP51992.2021.00024

Subramanya, S. R., & Yi, B. K. (2006). Digital rights management. *IEEE potentials*, 25(2), 31–34. https://doi.org/10.1109/MP.2006.1649008

Wang, J., Guo, S., Xie, X., & Qi, H. (2022). Federated unlearning via class-discriminative pruning. In F. Laforest, R. Troncy, E. Simperl, D. Agawarl, A. Gionis, I. Herman, & L. Médini (Eds.), *Proceedings of the ACM Web Conference 2022* (pp. 622–632). Association for Computing Machinery. https://doi.org/10.1145/3485447.3512222

CHAPTER 7

Addressing the Harms
of Data Security Breaches

Teresa Scassa

Abstract

Data security breaches are rapidly increasing in number and impact. For individuals whose personal information is collected and retained across a vast number of companies and service providers, data breaches have become a source of anxiety and frustration. For the most part, data protection laws in Canada are relatively toothless, focusing on a soft touch ombuds approach to resolving complaints. In recent years, individuals have increasingly turned to class action lawsuits to seek redress and behaviour modification in cases of data breaches. Nevertheless, privacy torts and other existing causes of action are often a poor fit with data breach cases, and courts are increasingly unwilling to stretch these causes of action to fit the data protection context. Bill C-27, currently before Parliament, proposes to reform Canada's data protection law. In doing so, it will create a new private right of action and put in place an administrative monetary penalty regime to impose sanctions on companies that disregard their obligations. This chapter considers how these reforms mesh with evolving class action jurisprudence, and whether they will, in combination, satisfy the goals of compensation and behaviour modification to better safeguard the security of the self.

When Canada's *Personal Information Protection and Electronic Documents Act* (PIPEDA) was enacted in 2000, the overriding public policy preoccupation was to increase trust in e-commerce by providing a measure of data protection (Deturbide & Scassa, 2021). The data protection context has changed dramatically since that time. Today, organizations collect vast quantities of data from users of the Internet, mobile services, and Internet-of-Things connected devices. Such data are valuable for more than just providing client services; personal data are used to profile individuals and groups, to develop new products and services, and in analytics and artificial intelligence. Personal data are used internally, shared, and sold by organizations. In such an environment, there are incentives for businesses to collect as much data as possible, to retain them for as long as is feasible, and to seek to use them for new purposes. The large volume of personal data collected by organizations in turn become a tempting target for malicious actors. Data security breaches have increased significantly in recent years and across all sectors (Bush, 2024; Statistics Canada, 2022; Office of the Privacy Commissioner, 2019; Boutilier, 2021). And, though the data context has changed dramatically, data protection laws in Canada have not, for the most part, kept up.

Class action lawsuits have emerged as a way to hold companies to account for privacy breaches in this context where weak recourse under existing data protection laws provide no real incentive for organizations to strengthen lax privacy practices and offer little satisfaction for frustrated individuals. Privacy class actions, however, are a blunt tool, and existing legal recourse is not particularly well adapted to the data economy context. Emerging jurisprudence makes it clear that courts are attempting to curb the circumstances in which privacy class action lawsuits can advance. Proposed reforms to PIPEDA will also impact class action recourse.

Data privacy breaches impact millions of Canadians, although individual harms are difficult to quantify. Nevertheless, in circumstances in which individuals must inevitably share large volumes of personal data with an increasingly broad range of organizations, data breaches pose a risk to the security of the self. This chapter looks at the role that class-action lawsuits have played in providing a means to hold companies to account for data security breaches. They have filled a gap left by soft touch, ombuds-style data protection laws, and private law remedies poorly calibrated to the data protection context. I then consider proposed amendments in Bill C-27 that would introduce a new private right of action along with stiff administrative monetary penalties for certain breaches of the law. I assess how these measures will impact the class action landscape, and whether they fill the gap effectively in terms of providing both remedies for those impacted by breaches and incentives for organizations to improve data security.

7.1. Legislative Context

Canada's first private sector data protection law, the *Personal Information Protection and Electronic Documents Act* (PIPEDA), took effect in 2001 and reflected a soft-touch approach to data protection that was principally designed to build trust in the emerging e-commerce environment (Deturbide & Scassa, 2021). The law set out a series of obligations shaped around the Canadian Standards Association *Model Code for the Protection of Personal Information*, a code of practice developed and adopted as a national standard and subsequently incorporated as Schedule I to PIPEDA. PIPEDA contains several obligations designed to limit security breaches or their impact. These include requirements for organizations to minimize the collection of personal data, to set data retention limits, and to securely dispose of data at the end of these limits. PIPEDA also requires organizations to maintain appropriate security measures (PIPEDA, Schedule I). The law adopts an ombuds approach to enforcement of obligations (Stoddart, 2005). Yet, incentives to over-collect and over-retain personal data have increased over time with the growth in value of personal data within the burgeoning data economy. These incentives have not been countered by stronger enforcement measures.

PIPEDA was amended in 2015 to include a data breach notification requirement in new sections 10.1 to 10.3. These provisions, which took effect in November of 2018, required organizations to inform both the Commissioner and affected individuals where a breach created "a real risk of significant harm to an individual." This notification requirement undoubtedly increased individuals' awareness of data breaches that might otherwise have gone unnoticed and may have contributed to the rise in class action litigation (Cofone, 2021).

Under PIPEDA, those affected by data breaches can file complaints with the Office of the Privacy Commissioner of Canada. The complaints can lead to an investigation culminating in a report of findings and non-binding recommendations. After receiving a report, a complainant can choose to apply to the Federal Court for an order, which can include an award of damages (PIPEDA, s. 14, s. 16). Although the Federal Court has awarded moral damages for privacy breaches without proof of actual harm, it will only do so in the "most egregious situations" (*Randall v. Nubodys Fitness Centres,* para. 55). In addition, the amounts awarded are small enough to deter litigation by all but the most stubbornly aggrieved (*Nammo,* 2010). It is also unlikely that s. 14 can provide the foundation for class proceedings. In a 2023 decision, the Federal Court ruled that s. 14 of PIPEDA did not support a class action lawsuit in the case before it, and that it was unlikely to do so in other cases (*Doan,* 2023). The court's reasoning turned in part on the fact that standing to bring an application under s. 14 required the applicant to have been a complainant under PIPEDA. Even if a representative class plaintiff might be a former complainant, it is unlikely that this would be the case for the entire class.

Three provinces have private sector data protection laws that have been considered substantially similar to PIPEDA (von Tigerstrom, 2020; Deturbide & Scassa, 2021). The first, Alberta, added data breach notification requirements to its *Personal Information Protection Act* in 2009. Meanwhile, the second, British Columbia (BC), has no data breach notification requirements in its own *Personal Information Protection Act.* Regardless, both Alberta and BC have a complaint mechanism, and their respective commissioners can make binding orders to require organizations to change practices. Neither statute provides for damages for harms resulting from data breaches, but both allow individuals to sue for damages arising from breaches of the law. However, under both BC and Alberta legislation, the right of action is only for an individual "affected by the order" (PIPA [Alberta], s. 60; PIPA [BC], s. 57.) issued by the Commissioner following a complaint. The third province, Quebec, has recently reformed its *Act respecting the protection of personal information in the private sector,* and its revised legislation goes significantly beyond PIPEDA in several respects. Along with data breach notification requirements, it has incorporated provisions allowing for the imposition of substantial administrative monetary penalties.

7.2. Class Action Lawsuits

Class action lawsuits for privacy breaches have been on the rise in Canada (Cofone, 2021). Gratton & Phizicky (2021) indicate that the majority of such lawsuits relate to failures by organizations to properly protect personal data. A class action lawsuit does not preclude a complaint being filed with a privacy commissioner, but there is no requirement to pursue a complaint prior to filing a suit. Although individual class members have received relatively little in compensation in those lawsuits that have reached the settlement stage (*Karasik*, 2021), the overall compensation envelope combined with legal costs and reputational harm to the defendant at least send a message to organizations that there are real consequences for poor data management practices (Lenz, 2021). The Supreme Court of Canada has noted that:

> Without class actions, those who cause widespread but individually minimal harm might not take into account the full costs of their conduct, because for any plaintiff the expense of bringing suit would far exceed the likely recovery. Cost-sharing decreases the expense of pursuing legal recourse and accordingly deters potential defendants who might otherwise assume that minor wrongs would not result in litigation. (*Western Canadian Shopping Centres Inc. v. Dutton*, para. 29)

Most privacy class action lawsuits that have been certified in Canada have settled before the final determination on the merits. Class action lawsuits that proceed to settlements are not necessarily meritorious; defendants may choose to settle even if they might ultimately be successful because of the cost and reputational harm of pursuing this expensive and time-consuming form of litigation (Gratton & Phizicky, 2021). A recent assessment of settlement amounts in privacy class action cases makes it clear that individual class members receive relatively little in the form of compensation, although the collective compensation combined with the expense of litigation may amount to a significant cost to the defendant. As a result, class action lawsuits do provide a means of recourse where individual claims would be too small to make litigation worthwhile and where there is a perceived need for access to justice (Lenz, 2021).

7.3. Privacy Law and Class Actions

Class action lawsuits relating to privacy breaches have had to rely on multiple causes of action. This approach reflects the fact that existing causes of action are often poorly suited to the data breach context. As a result, pleadings will try to identify as many causes of action as possible in the hope that one or more will succeed. This approach has received judicial criticism (*Del Guidice*, 2021). Possible causes of action have most notably included statutory privacy torts in those jurisdictions that have enacted them, common law privacy torts, recourse under Quebec's Civil Code for plaintiffs resident in Quebec, breach of confidence, negligence, breach of statutory obligations, and breach of contract. Statutory and common law privacy torts have been heavily relied upon because they do not require proof of actual damage to succeed (Gratton & Phizicky, 2021). Plaintiffs in privacy tort cases can receive nominal damages on the basis that the intrusion into a person's privacy is a harm in its own right. Many of the other causes of action, including negligence, require proof of actual damage. This can be very challenging in data breach cases since it may be difficult for plaintiffs to show that they have yet been victims of identity theft, or, if they have suffered identity theft or other related harms, it may be difficult for them to establish a causal link between the defendant's breach and the harm they experienced (*Karasik*, 2021; *Sofio*, 2015; *Lamoureux*, 2021). Courts in Quebec, where the law also allows for damages without proof of harm, have attempted to stem the spate of privacy class actions in that jurisdiction by requiring that allegations of moral harm go beyond the ordinary stresses and anxieties of daily life in contemporary society (*Sofio*, 2015; *Lamoureux*, 2021). Thus, in Quebec, the normal frustrations and inconveniences associated with receiving and reacting to a data breach notification are insufficient to support an award of damages without proof of something more (*Sofio*, 2015; *Lamoureux*, 2021).

If the proliferation of class action lawsuits for large-scale privacy breaches suggests an unmet need for effective recourse, the case law reveals the underdeveloped state of Canadian privacy law when it comes to providing adequate resources and remedies. The underdevelopment lies in part in the impoverished concept of privacy harms (Lenz, 2021) and in part in the poor fit of privacy torts with the contemporary context of business practices governed by data protection laws (Gratton & Phizicky, 2021). Essentially, the law does not effectively recognize the particular vulnerability of individuals who have little choice in most cases regarding providing personal data, and little or no say in how that data will be governed. Data protection laws have been focused on changing corporate practices rather than compensating victims. Privacy torts, first recognized in common law Canada by the Ontario Court of Appeal in 2012 (*Jones*, 2012) are clumsy and better calibrated to addressing more individualized and deliberate intrusions. The tort of intrusion upon seclusion has been limited to only those intrusions characterized as "significant invasions" (*Jones*, 2012, para. 72) and those that are "highly offensive" (*Broutzas*, 2023, para. 39).

Although privacy class-action lawsuits have proliferated, with many passing the low threshold for certification, there are now clear signs that courts are attempting to limit the availability of class action recourse for privacy breaches. A major way to do this has been by constraining the tort law cause of action, highlighting the poor fit of these torts with the commercial data protection context. For example, a recent trilogy of cases decided by the Ontario Court of Appeal—with leave to appeal to the Supreme Court of Canada denied—has largely closed the door on arguing the tort of intrusion upon seclusion against "database defendants" (*Owsianik v Equifax Canada Co.*, 2022, para. 1; *Obodo*, 2022; *Winder*, 2022), which are companies whose databases have been hacked. The tort of intrusion upon seclusion requires a defendant to have intentionally intruded upon an individual's privacy. The Ontario Court of Appeal has confirmed lower court rulings that found that defendants hacked by third parties have not intentionally invaded the privacy of the plaintiffs; rather, it is the hackers who have done this (*Owsianik*, 2022). This has important implications for privacy class action lawsuits. Hackers are seldom caught, and if they are, they may not be solvent enough to be worth pursuing in court. Although class plaintiffs may still have other possible recourse against the hacked company (such as arguments that the company was negligent in the handling of personal data or breached contractual undertakings to safeguard personal data according to industry standards), as noted above, suits for negligence require proof of compensable harm. Where the data of hundreds of thousands of people has been accessed by hackers, it may be difficult to show that it has been used by the hackers to defraud those individuals. Even if individuals within the class have experienced identity theft or other harms, they may have difficulty proving that it was this specific data breach that resulted in those harms.

7.4. Private Right of Action

The *Digital Charter Implementation Act* (Bill C-27) is before Parliament at the time of writing.[1] If passed, this Bill will replace PIPEDA with

---

1.   Bill C-27 died on the Order Paper when Parliament was prorogued in January 2025. This chapter is up-to-date as of the state of the Bill in December 2024.

a new *Consumer Privacy Protection Act* (CPPA). One element of the reform will be the introduction of a new private right of action. As it currently stands in Bill C-27, this right of action provides:

> 107(1) An individual who is affected by an act or omission by an organization that constitutes a contravention of this Act has a cause of action against the organization for damages for loss or injury that the individual has suffered as a result of the contravention if
>> (a) the Commissioner has made a finding under paragraph 93(1)(a) that the organization has contravened this Act and
>>> (i) the finding is not appealed and the time limit for making an appeal under subsection 101(2) has expired, or
>>> (ii) the Tribunal has dismissed an appeal of the finding under subsection 103(1); or
>> (b) the Tribunal has made a finding under subsection 103(1) that the organization has contravened this Act.
>
> A cause of action will also exist where an organization has been convicted of an offence under the new legislation, and the plaintiff has suffered damages as a result of the commission of the offence (s. 107[2]).

Unlike s. 14 of PIPEDA, the private right of action may be exercised in Federal Court or in a provincial superior court (Bill C-27, s. 107[4]). This is advantageous to plaintiffs who wish to assert multiple causes of action, since a s. 14 proceeding before the Federal Court is not well suited to advancing claims that are not grounded in breaches of PIPEDA. It would also allow plaintiffs to assert a breach of an obligation under the CPPA. These obligations are the ones most directly tied to the activities of organizations that collect and process personal data in a commercial context. Unlike s. 14 of PIPEDA, s. 107 of the CPPA does not seem to require that the plaintiff or plaintiffs are actual complainants to the Privacy Commissioner. Those who may bring an action need only be "affected by an act or omission that constitutes a contravention of this Act," and there must also be a finding by the Commissioner (that is not overturned by the Tribunal) that such a contravention has occurred. Thus, although the complaints process is a prerequisite for the private right of action, it does not appear to be necessary for the plaintiffs in a suit to have been complainants themselves.

Nevertheless, s. 107 is not likely to improve plaintiffs' odds of success in class action litigation, nor is it likely to reduce attempts to plead multiple causes of action, including the ill-fitting privacy torts. This is because Bill C-27's private right of action is framed as a recourse for "damages for loss or injury that an individual has suffered as a result of the contravention" (s. 107). Under s. 14 of PIPEDA, the Federal Court has had a more general power to "award damages to the complainant, including damages for any humiliation that the complainant has suffered." The wording of the new private right of action suggests that it will require proof of quantifiable harm. This will present the same difficulties already seen in the case law, where data may have been handled in breach of the law, but where harm remains an as-yet unrealized risk or cannot be causally linked to this specific data breach. Section 107 is likely to expand recourse and remedies only for those who can prove compensable harm; it will, at the same time, remove the s. 14 (PIPEDA) recourse to Federal Court, which, however problematic it may have been, at least sometimes led to awards of moral damages.

Interestingly, in addition to the private right of action, Bill C-27 also creates the possibility for the imposition of substantial administrative monetary penalties (AMPs) in cases of serious breaches of certain provisions of the law. Under proposed section 94(1), the Privacy Commissioner is empowered to recommend the imposition of such a penalty when specific provisions of the Act have been contravened. Among others, these include the failure to put in place appropriate security safeguards, as required by s. 57(1), and failure to provide appropriate data breach notification. Section 94 of the CPPA, combined with the rather limited private right of action, might be seen as a deliberate public policy choice to reserve recourse in the courts to cases that have caused compensable harm while using AMPs to punish and deter conduct that leads to breaches. However, there are indications in Bill C-27 that AMPs will be used very sparingly. For example, before recommending AMPs, the Commissioner must take into account a variety of factors, including the due diligence of the organization in attempting to avoid a breach of the law, whether it made reasonable efforts to "mitigate or reverse" the effects of its contravention (s. 94[2][c]), the organization's history, and any other factors that may be set out in regulations. Any recommendation for the imposition of an AMP will be reviewed by a newly created Personal Information and Data Protection Tribunal, which is empowered to make a final decision regarding the imposition of any penalty. Penalties can range from 3 percent of an organization's gross global revenue in the preceding financial year or $10,000, whichever is higher (s. 95[4]).

It is likely that only time will tell whether this new scheme will prove satisfactory in meeting public policy goals of punishing and deterring improper corporate behaviour with respect to personal data on the one hand, and compensating individuals for actual harm suffered because of breaches on the other. There seems to be little doubt that the new private right of action will not be of much use to class action plaintiffs who cannot establish either causation or compensable harm flowing from the data breach. They will continue to face similar challenges with the privacy torts, and courts may be even less inclined to expand or at least flexibly interpret the torts if there is a data protection-specific recourse for which they do not qualify. Whether the statutory amendments strike the right balance will turn, therefore, on whether penalties are seen to be meted out appropriately—both in terms of circumstances and quantum.

7.5. An Uncertain Future

The landscape this chapter describes reveals what is currently a significant gap between a desire on the part of the public for meaningful consequences in the case of data breaches and what legislators and courts have provided. Class action lawsuits may not be a well-calibrated tool to address harms to the security of the self in all cases. For example, such lawsuits are hugely costly to defend, even where organizations may not be at fault, or where the costs are significantly disproportionate to any fault. Concerns over the appropriateness of privacy class-action lawsuits have even led courts in Ontario to take a narrower approach to the interpretation of privacy torts. In Bill C-27, the federal government has proposed a scheme that combines a private right of action where individuals have suffered compensable harm as a result of a data breach, with AMPs to punish and deter organizations who have facilitated breaches through poor data protection practices.

The scheme in Bill C-27 seems to address the concerns of organizations that they not be inundated with class-action lawsuits for breaches of data protection laws. Individuals who experience compensable loss following a data breach will have recourse via the private right of action, and where there are many such individuals, a class action lawsuit might be possible. For those whose injuries amount to frustration and anxiety over yet another data breach with uncertain personal consequences, there will be no improvement—except the possibility of seeing AMPs imposed on companies that have acted in flagrant disregard of their obligations. Where breaches are considered serious enough to merit the imposition of an AMP, the nature of the contravention may also support a finding of breach of contract or negligence in any associated class action lawsuit. Much may therefore turn on how the awarding of AMPs is approached, and this is something that should be carefully monitored and assessed. Attention will need to be paid to those mitigation practices that emerge as the norm in data breaches, and that may be a factor in decisions about whether an AMP should be imposed. For example, some period of credit protection is increasingly provided by organizations to individuals whose data has been improperly accessed—either as part of settlements or in mitigation of potential harm. It may be that credit protection will emerge as a default mitigation strategy for avoiding AMPs.

A question that deserves further study is whether the risks for individuals that are created by organizations that amass personal data as part of increasingly complex data-driven business models require new approaches to compensation and redress for data breaches. The due diligence question raised with respect to compliance with accepted cybersecurity norms is an interesting one, as it may need to be assessed in light not just of the measures put in place to protect personal data, but also the risks of exposure imposed on individuals by decisions to collect and retain large volumes of personal data— particularly where the added benefits to individuals of such collection and retention are remote or non-existent. This approach, which takes into account the risk to *security of self* posed by commercial business choices may help address some of the frustration with current data breach outcomes. Possibilities for other approaches to redress could range from a no-fault compensation scheme for those affected by data breaches, to statutory damages for breaches for which non-compliance with data protection laws is a factor.

Acknowledgements

The author gratefully acknowledges the support of the Social Sciences and Humanities Research Council of Canada for the Human-Centric Cybersecurity Partnership, of which she is a part. Many thanks to the contributors of this volume for their feedback on the concept for this chapter at an earlier workshop and to the editors for their comments and feedback and for bringing this project together.

References

Act respecting the protection of personal information in the private sector, RSQ P. 39.1.

Bill C-27, *An Act to enact the Consumer Privacy Protection Act, the Personal Information and Data Protection Tribunal Act and the Artificial Intelligence and Data Act and to make consequential and related amendments to other Acts*, 44th Parliament, 1st Session, 2022 (first reading 16 June 2022), online: www.parl.ca/DocumentViewer/en/44-1/bill/C-27/first-reading

Boutilier, A. (2021, December 6). *Canadian health, energy sectors increasingly targeted by ransomware attacks*. Global News. https://globalnews.ca/news/8427930/canadian-health-energy-sectors-increasingly-targeted-by-ransomware-attacks/

Broutzas v Rouge Valley Health System, 2023 ONSC 540.

Bush, O. (2024, June 11). Cyber crime statistics in Canada. *Made in CA*. https://madeinca.ca/cyber-crime-canada-statistics/

Cofone, I. N. (2021). Introduction to privacy class actions. In I. N. Cofone (Ed.), *Class actions in privacy law* (pp. 1–12). Routledge Focus.

Del Guidice v Thompson, 2021 ONSC 5379 [*Del Guidice*].

Deturbide, M., & Scassa, T. (2021). *Digital commerce in Canada*. LexisNexis Canada.

Doan v Canada (Attorney-General), 2023 FC 236 [*Doan*].

Gratton, E., & Phisicky, L. (2021). Uncertainties and lessons learned from data protection laws. In I. N. Cofone (Ed.), *Class actions in privacy law* (pp. 30–55). Routledge Focus.

Jones v Tsige, 2012 ONCA 32 [*Jones*].

Karasik v Yahoo! Inc., 2021 ONSC 1063 [*Karasik*].

Lamoureux c Organisme canadien de réglementation du commerce des valeurs mobilières (OCRCVM), 2021 QCCS 1093 [*Lamoureux*].

Lenz, J. J. A. (2021). Privacy class actions' unfulfilled promise. In I. N. Cofone (Ed.), *Class actions in privacy law* (pp. 13–29). Routledge Focus.

Model Code for the Protection of Personal Information, CAN/CSA-Q830-96.

Nammo v TransUnion of Canada Inc., 2010 FC 1284 [*Nammo*].

Obodo v TransUnion of Canada Inc., 2022 ONCA 814, leave to appeal to the Supreme Court of Canada denied, 2023 CanLII 62026 (SCC) [*Obodo*].

Office of the Privacy Commissioner of Canada. (2019, October 31). *A full year of mandatory data breach reporting: What we've learned and what businesses need to know*. https://www.priv.gc.ca/en/blog/20191031/

Owsianik v Equifax Canada Co., 2021 ONSC 4112.

Owsianik v Equifax Canada Co., 2022 ONCA 813, leave to appeal to the Supreme Court of Canada denied, 2023 CanLII 62019 (SCC) [*Owsianik*].

Personal Information Protection and Electronic Documents Act [PIPEDA] (2000), SC 2000, c. 5.

Personal Information Protection Act (2003), SA 2003, c. P-6.5.

Personal Information Protection Act (2003), SBC 2003, c. 63.

Randall v Nubodys Fitness Centres (2010), 2010 FC 681 [*Randall*].

Sofio c Organisme canadien de réglementation du commerce des valeurs mobilières (OCRCVM), 2015 QCCA 1820 [*Sofio*].

Statistics Canada. (2022, October 18). *Impact of cybercrime on Canadian businesses, 2021.* https://www150.statcan.gc.ca/n1/daily-quotidien/221018/dq221018b-eng.htm

Stoddart, J. (2005). *Cherry picking among apples and oranges: Refocusing current debate about the merits of the ombuds-model under PIPEDA.* Office of the Privacy Commissioner of Canada. https://www.priv.gc.ca/en/opc-actions-and-decisions/research/explore-privacy-research/2005/omb_051021/

von Tigerstrom, B. (2020). *Information & privacy law in Canada.* Irwin Law.

Western Canadian Shopping Centres Inc. v Dutton (2001), 2001 SCC 46 (CanLII), [2001] 2 SCR 534.

Winder v Marriott International Inc. (2022), 2022 ONSC 390, leave to appeal to the Supreme Court of Canada denied, 2023 CanLII 62025 (SCC) [*Winder*].

CHAPTER 8

Algorithmic Impact Assessment: From Risk Assessments to Community Research

Fenwick McKelvey, Nick Gertler, and Alex Megelas

Abstract

Security of self has to be exercised, not just considered. This chapter considers ways to create opportunities for people to exercise their human rights in technological development. Human-centric cybersecurity should improve capacity to exercise human rights. Drawing on debates about the social impact of artificial intelligence (AI), we consider innovations in public participation in AI design as a lesson for greater participation in human-centric cybersecurity. AI's social impact has prompted calls for new measures and assessment tools. The Government of Canada has promoted the Algorithmic Impact Assessment as a key tool to assess the risk of its AI deployments. Unconventional in procurement, the tool focuses on potential social impacts beyond the traditional security and privacy assessment used. The chapter introduces Canada's efforts, then discusses its limitations and next steps, as a way toward better assessment tools capable of understanding how to enhance and innovate in public participation in human-centric cybersecurity.

How might a human-centric approach to cybersecurity inform the integration and adoption of AI? What are the new techniques and methods to integrate human rights and digital rights evaluations in the development of new technologies? Algorithmic impact assessments (AIAs) or AI impact assessments are a critical nexus between AI and a human-centric approach to cybersecurity. These assessments draw on human rights, privacy, and environmental assessment traditions as a process to expose the situations and context of a proposed AI development.

Algorithmic impact assessments have attracted attention as a policy innovation for better development and deployment practices. A major review of AIAs found that the concept has gained credibility "as a potential process for addressing algorithmic harms that moves beyond narrowly constructed metrics towards real justice" (Reisman et al., 2018, p. 4). Within this moment of heightened scrutiny, this chapter considers AIAs as a possible albeit limited means to give people an opportunity to exercise their human rights.

Assessments are integral to key pieces of national technology policy. Canada has been an early adopter of AIAs, and future AI regulation might further embed AIAs as a key regulatory tool with likely implications for cybersecurity. The previously proposed *Artificial Intelligence and Data Act* (AIDA) in Bill C-27 created the conditions for "the development of an independent sector of licensed private regulators" (Hadfield & Clark, 2023, p. 2) by sanctioning a new industry of firms in lieu of government institutions to assess AI risks and harms. Arguably, the new class of private regulators would have ensured AI's trustworthiness and minimize risks through a market of assessment techniques compliant with AIDA's harm framework. Canada's experimental approach to AI legislation, tied to its early advocacy of impact assessments, offers a novel case to consider how and whether the approach does create opportunities to exercise human rights.

This chapter begins by exploring the development of the concept, focusing principally on the Treasury Board of Canada Secretariat's own AIA. Promising as these developments may be, matters of national security creep back in with Canada's tool, less as a focus on threats than largely by reducing its considerations of risks to the state. The concluding discussion posits that while AIAs are a first step, more innovation is required to develop more local expertise and capacity for participating in cybersecurity and adjacent issues, described as an AI community-based action research network.

8.1. Algorithmic Impact Assessments

Broadly speaking, AIAs are processes for defining, evaluating, and mitigating risks or harms and/or protecting rights posed by algorithmic systems—including AI systems. AIAs were initially developed as a means of evaluating public sector automated decision-making systems. Concern over unaccountable "black box" algorithms grew as AI and algorithmic systems were poised to automate administrative processes in governments and companies. As the AI Now Institute argued in a 2018 report, opaque algorithmic systems precluded public scrutiny; AIAs are meant to provide information about how a system works, how it is being used, and what the consequences of its use are. In this way, AIAs could support stakeholders and affected communities in scrutinizing and challenging the use of algorithmic systems (Reisman et al., 2018).

There is no consensus about what an algorithmic impact assessment should be. The AI Now Institute's proposal, for example, is a model of self-assessment followed by external review and public consultation (Reisman et al., 2018). A broad-scale review of AIAs by Data & Society described the term more as a boundary object, where actual applications differ according to ten criteria: "1) Sources of Legitimacy, 2) Actors and Forum, 3) Catalyzing Event, 4) Time Frame, 5) Public Access, 6) Public Consultation, 7) Method, 8) Assessors, 9) Impact, and 10) Harms and Redress" (Moss et al., 2021). The broad criteria offer both hope and reality for AIA as a human-centric approach, at one point grounding consultations and redress. However, a major limitation is that these aspirations do not match its applications.

The Canadian government promoted itself as offering the first public sector implementation of an AIA (McKelvey & Macdonald, 2019; Gertler, 2023). Along with responsible procurement, the AIA was part of a Treasury Board of Canada Secretariat (TBS) program for responsible AI. The TBS AIA, which was released in 2019 and came into force in 2020, takes the form of a self-administered online questionnaire which Canadian government agencies developing automated decision-making systems are expected to complete. Respondents answer questions about the system they are developing, such as, "Are clients in this line of business particularly vulnerable?" or "Will the system be making decisions or assessments that require judgment or discretion?"

In the TBS system, the AIA outputs a score that determines the system's "impact level." This impact level corresponds to different sets of requirements in the TBS's *Directive on Automated Decision-Making*, such as whether the system can render decisions without a human-in-the-loop and whether (or to what extent) users of an automated decision making (ADM) system must be informed of that fact. In addition to these specific requirements, the directive requires that all completed AIAs be made public on Canada's open government database. The TBS AIA therefore serves a dual purpose: it attempts to create public accountability for the system, but it also attempts to enforce a set of predefined standards and impact-mitigation measures. Despite the completed AIA questionnaires being published, the TBS model does not officially provide for any public consultation or feedback.

8.2. Lessons Learned from the Limits of Canada's AIA

Regrettably, and despite the government's efforts to the contrary, Canada's Algorithmic Impact Assessment has suffered several setbacks notable for considering how this approach might inform human-centric cybersecurity. The tool had a mixed record of adoption, failed to function as a consultation tool, and its design lacks critical elements needed for due process. Rather than list these concerns alone, the next section briefly summarizes these concerns but also draws out key lessons for the future of AI assessment and consultation. We find that future consultations need to have greater enforcement powers, a focus on consultation, and new methods of research and engagement—factors that have led to the consideration of community-based assessment methods.

The first issue is that submitting an AIA is unevenly enforced and even considered by some departments as optional. The enforcement gap came into effect as a result of reporting by *The Globe and Mail*'s Tom Cardoso, on the case of the Department of National Defence, which turned to AI solutions to help improve diversity in its hiring processes (Cardoso & Curry, 2021). Next came disclosure that the Canadian Border Services Agency had piloted an AI-based system for travellers' risk assessment without carrying out a review (Keung, 2023). The limited scope of the directive raises the first concern with AIAs: they are disconnected from the development process, optional, and largely a symbolic good. Much of the debate in Canada had hinged on the TBS Directive interpretation with frequent and largely inaccurate claims of exception (Karanicolas, 2019). The first takeaway is that AIAs have become positioned as optional, rather than best practice, and as a parallel process to deployment and development. The lesson for human-centric cybersecurity is that any consultation mechanism must have obligations to the people directly affected.

Canada's AIA is a risk assessment tool, not a consultation tool. The criteria for who should fill it out are vague, and there are no criteria for what research is required while filling it out. At least twelve AIAs have been produced with highly different degrees of disclosure and internal consultation. At best, certain high-risk systems require external peer review before they can be put into production. In most cases, the risk assessment is completed internally with no consultation, and only numerical questions contribute to the designation of risk. Lacking sufficient oversight, the effectiveness of the tool largely depends on the honesty of a few internal stakeholders to reflect human-centric concerns translated into risk assessment (Gertler, 2023). Even with good faith actors, these assessment methods require some omnipotence to be able to anticipate all problems and know a black-boxes system in depth. These concerns are even more pronounced in the Toronto Police Services procurement mechanism that set similar unrealistic capacity on the internal ability to provide technological evaluation (Brandusescu et al., 2022; McKelvey et al., 2023). These concerns lead to a second question: How does an AIA constitute a public or audience capable of offering a fair assessment of the technology in question?

The third concern follows closely, but the AIA's function fits within a long history of consultation theatre in Canada and the use of the public as something of an on-demand resource. These issues of fair and effective public consultation are nothing new, but the AIA, even if effectively enforced, raises concerns about the burden to participate, particularly on equity-seeking groups who face a constant pressure to participate. Facial recognition is a good example, as these technologies have clear bias issues with racialized bodies, and yet with the way an AIA would function, these same groups would face increased demands to participate (without compensation) per application of the technology (Scassa, 2020). How can AIAs be shifted from being an on-demand, ad hoc approach to human-centric technology issues to an enduring one that builds capacity and treats participants with respect?

Enforcement, assessment, and consultation are all major barriers to effective AIAs as a means to create opportunities to exercise human rights. In the following section, an alternative approach to human-centric cybersecurity drawing on community research methods is discussed.

8.3. Toward a Community-Based Approach

Our critiques of AIAs point toward a need to flip the process and think of assessment as an enduring institution focused on the participants and their capability to meaningfully steer technology development. There is interest in a growing turn toward community-based methods for algorithmic assessment (Reilly & Morales, 2023). Here, we turn to community-based action research (CBAR) as a collaborative and relational approach to research that seeks to frame it in relation to local concerns and commitments to reciprocity and social justice, often through methods that see practitioners grounding their work as concrete offshoots of local community activism. As part of this, research often draws on local desires and agency, as expressed by residents and organizers, whose perspectives are integrated across all aspects of a research project, including in identifying underlying issues and determining appropriate methods (Coghlan & Brydo-Miller, 2014).

CBAR typically adheres to a range of principles, including: committing to close collaboration with community; fostering research that contributes to subsequent action in redressing local inequalities; ensuring that local perspectives are central to the research process; committing to acknowledging power differentials as they relate to the local context housing the research; and allowing the research to commit to a reflective and ongoing practice, so that research can lead to results that are meaningful to the host community (Troppe, 1994).

Since 2017, there has been a CBAR network dedicated to supporting critical engagement on the part of researchers and students in the Montreal neighbourhood of Parc-Extension, one of the poorest neighbourhoods in Canada, with 79 percent of its approximately thirty-three thousand residents living in rental housing, of whom 39.7 percent spend more than a third of their income on rent each month (CBAR Network in Parc-Extension, 2022). The Parc-Extension CBAR network, co-created by researchers and community organizers, operates independently of any specific university institution and, over the course of its history, has: informed the research practices of multiple scholars through exposure to participatory and CBAR; supported the emergence of educational collaborations with local community groups; brokered relationships between students, professors, and neighbourhood stakeholders; and engaged in a number of advocacy campaigns such as open letters, demonstrations, and action research projects that have led to the creation of advocacy tools (Jolivet et al., 2020).

Community-based research has already influenced some AI policy in Canada. In 2019, in response to community requests, the Parc-Extension CBAR Network undertook the Digital Divides research project, which proposed solutions for addressing the unequal distribution of economic benefits stemming from Montreal's AI sector and the evident disparity between Montreal's AI technology hub and adjacent neighbourhoods. The recommendations within the report encompassed alternative housing models, collective benefit agreements (CBAs), as well as smaller-scale grassroots efforts. The Digital Divides' researchers concluded their report by advocating for several reforms in AI and housing policies, emphasizing justice-oriented objectives over profit-driven motives, and emphasizing the significance of meaningful community engagement. The report underscored the importance of grassroots social movements as influential drivers in pursuing these objectives, alongside academic and governmental interventions (CBAR Network in Parc-Extension, 2022).

Efforts are underway to develop an AI CBAR in Montreal.[1] In 2023, some of the contributors to Digital Divides involved with the Applied AI Institute at Concordia University formalized the creation of another CBAR network, this time dedicated to engaging with the sphere of Montreal AI, and the extensive ecosystem which supports it. Initial meetings were held among Montreal researchers and organizers who had previously contributed to the Parc-Extension CBAR network or the Digital Divides project, had led research projects with a critical perspective on AI, or worked for a community group or non-profit organization involved in digital rights or advocacy.

These meetings led to the formulation of a mandate and terms of engagement with a strong slant away from entrepreneurial enthusiasm for new technologies and toward a critical understanding of AI as needing to be informed by a recognition of socio-economic

---

1.   For more information, see: https://aicbar.ca/.

inequalities. "Members of this network recognize that AI technologies are never neutral; rather, they are embedded within socio-technical frameworks and thereby bound by the limitations of their creators and the contexts within which they are deployed." (Montreal AI CBAR, 2022). Subsequently, the Montreal AI CBAR network began to meet on a bi-monthly basis to discuss the projects of its members and explore possible collaborations. This initially led to the creation of a book club on AI to be held at a local library, a co-authored piece on AI and its potential contributions toward a provincial rent registry, and a public talk held as part of a monthly Toronto urban design meetup.

A work in progress, the Montreal AI CBAR seeks to, first, create a forum for community members to propose AI-based projects such as the use of AI to investigate AI's role in gentrification and rising housing prices. In effect, the CBAR acts as a broker between members to develop AI-based research project. At the same time, a strong CBAR could act as a necessary passage point for AI projects to pass through the community. Rather than forming ad hoc consultations, the CBAR ideally serves as a standing, situated site of community expertise that guides AI development in communities.

The community-based research approach seeks to address the clear capacity issue with AIA. Specifically, a CBAR approach works toward:

1) Embedding expertise in the community;
2) Creating an ongoing community of practice and public culture; and
3) Ensuring the CBAR acts as an obligatory passage point for community research.

The Montreal AI CBAR network will continue to gradually expand, guided by its clear commitments to equity and relationality, and through the shared values of its affiliates who will continue to use this created space to forge an alternative narrative around the potential value of, and possible shortcomings of, AI, thus providing a central-ized forum for alternative voices and perspectives.

The CBAR approach, grounded locally in relationships of prox-imity and organizational common ground, has allowed for sustained engagement around issues requiring shared investment. The CBAR network has led to iterative explorations across professionalized spheres—ensuring a direct link between research imperatives, the community-based contexts likely to benefit from research and well positioned to inform it, and the local spaces and communities where this is applied. All this occurs publicly, thus leading to knowledge transfer opportunities in the area of explored reciprocity in applied technological initiatives stemming from research.

8.4. Enhancing the Security of Self with Community-Based AIA

Human-centric cybersecurity requires new innovations in helping people exercise their rights. Algorithmic or AI impact assessments have carried a lot of weight to advance these objectives, promising to ensure that impacts are considered in the design practice. Current best practices in Canada do not meet the human rights focus, but community-based AI research could complement or mitigate AIAs' downsides by building the capacity of affected communities, holding developers and vendors accountable, and widening the often-narrow corridors of participation and inclusion.

CBAR offers a novel improvement on the shortcomings of AIA. These recommendations take on an urgent matter as the TBS AIA was released as open source, allowing this approach to AIA to be translated to different contexts. At the time of writing, there have been some preliminary attempts to do so, notably by the Government of Uruguay, but none have been officially adopted.[2] In Canada, the tool has travelled beyond its use within the Government of Canada. Most notably, the Standards Council of Canada has integrated the TBS AIA into the pilot of its AI standards and accreditation pilot program. Our calls for action, firstly, demand major reforms to Canada's AIA to set standards of international best practice. The tool, simply put, cannot be just a risk-assessment tool and thereby requires a ground-up overhaul to address issues of enforcement, assessment, and consultation, as well as community redress. Without these reforms, AIA will not meet the needs of human-centric cybersecurity.

The deeper issue now is that the sudden turn toward general-purpose AI raises an existential issue for AIA and situated research. If a tool is for general purpose, how can it be assessed *in situ*? If general purpose AI, like OpenAI's ChatGPT, functions as anti-contextual, does that negate a more context-aware approach to AI development? Or, looking into the black box, could a general-purpose AI be able to

---

2.   For more on Uruguay's strategy, see: https://github.com/AGESIC-UY/aia-eia-js.

interpret its context without consultations or does the appeal of scale and utility imply another barrier to human-centric cybersecurity?

References

Balzacq, T., Léonard, S., & Ruzicka, J. (2015). "Securitization" revisited: Theory and cases. *International Relations, 30*(4), 494–531. https://doi.org/10.1177/0047117815596590

Bareis, J., & Katzenbach, C. (2021). Talking AI into being: The narratives and imaginaries of national AI strategies and their performative politics. *Science, Technology, & Human Values, 47*(5), 855–881. https://doi.org/10.1177/01622439211030007

Brandusescu, A., Jones, M., Linder, T., McKelvey, F., McPhail, B., Megelas, A., Rismani, S., Sengupta, U., & Sieber, R. (2022). *Response to Toronto Police Service's consultation on the draft governance for the acquisition and use of AI technology*. SSRN. https://doi.org/10.2139/ssrn.4366335

Cardoso, T., & Curry, B. (2021, February 7). National Defence skirted federal rules in using artificial intelligence, privacy commissioner says. *The Globe and Mail*. https://www.theglobeandmail.com/canada/article-national-defence-skirted-federal-rules-in-using-artificial/

CBAR Network in Parc-Extension. (2022, April). *Digital Divides—The impact of Montreal's AI ecosystems on Parc Extension: Housing, environment and access to services.* https://cbarparcex.ca/projects/digital-divides-the-impact-of-montreals-ai-ecosystems-on-parc-extension-housing-environment-and-access-to-services-april-2022/

Deibert, R. (2018). Toward a human-centric approach to cybersecurity. *Ethics & International Affairs, 32*(4), 411–424. https://doi.org/10.1017/S0892679418000618

Deibert, R. (2003). Black code: Censorship, surveillance, and the militarisation of cyberspace. *Millennium Journal of International Studies, 32*(3), 501–530. https://doi.org/10.1177/03058298030320030801

Gertler, N. (2023). *Hacking AI governance: Exploring the democratic potential of Canada's algorithmic impact assessment* [Master's thesis, Concordia University]. Spectrum Research Repository.

Jolivet, V., Guay, E., Vansintjan, A., Megelas, A., Renzi, A., Antoinette, R. R., Vukov, T., Darwish, A., & Reiser, C. (2020). *MIL façons de se faire évincer: L'Université de Montréal et la gentrification à Parc-Extension.*

Hadfield, G. K., & Clark, J. (2023). *Regulatory markets: The future of AI governance* (No. arXiv:2304.04914). arXiv. https://doi.org/10.48550/arXiv.2304.04914

Hansen, L., & Nissenbaum, H. (2009). Digital disaster, cyber security, and the Copenhagen School. *International Studies Quarterly, 53*(4), 1155–1175. https://doi.org/10.1111/j.1468-2478.2009.00572.x

Karanicolas, M. (2019). To err is human, to audit divine: A critical assessment of Canada's AI directive. *Journal of Parliamentary and Political Law, 14*(1). https://doi.org/10.2139/ssrn.3582143

Keung, N. (2023, June 2). How AI is helping Canada keep some people out of the country. And why there are those who say it's a problem. *Toronto Star.* https://www.thestar.com/news/canada/how-ai-is-helping-canada-keep-some-people-out-of-the-country-and-why-there/article_ea4dc715-debf-50e1-94c2-fda48a91dd09.html

Linder, T., Jones, M., & McKelvey, F. (2023, January 12). Toronto police consultation on AI lacks sufficient public engagement. *Toronto Star.* https://www.thestar.com/opinion/contributors/toronto-police-consultation-on-ai-lacks-sufficient-public-engagement/article_27eee104-9974-58aa-824e-d9002e273a50.html

Mathews, E. (2023, March 28). Microsoft introduces AI-powered cybersecurity assistant. *Reuters.* https://www.reuters.com/technology/microsoft-introduces-ai-powered-cybersecurity-assistant-2023-03-28/

McKelvey, F., & Macdonald, M. (2019). Artificial intelligence policy innovations at the Canadian federal government. *Canadian Journal of Communication, 44*(2), 43–50. https://doi.org/10.22230/cjc.2019v44n2a3509

Montreal AI CBAR. (2022, October 5). *Terms of engagement.* Montreal AI CBAR. Retrieved October 2, 2024, from https://aicbar.ca/

Moss, E., Watkins, E. A., Singh, R., Elish, M. C., & Metcalf, J. (2021). *Assembling accountability: Algorithmic impact assessment for the public interest.* Data & Society Research Institute.

Reilly, K., & Morales, E. (2023). Citizen data audits in the contemporary sensorium. *International Journal of Communication, 17,* 3582–3599. https://ijoc.org/index.php/ijoc/article/download/18832/4190

Reisman, D., Schultz, J., Crawford, K., & Whittaker, M. (2018). *Algorithmic impact assessments: A practical framework for public agency accountability.* AI Now Institute. https://ainowinstitute.org/aiareport2018.pdf

Scassa, T. (2020). Administrative law and the governance of automated decision-making: A critical look at Canada's directive on automated decision-making. *UBC Law Review, 54*(1). https://doi.org/10.2139/ssrn.3722192

Security Staff. (2023, August 29). *Study finds increase in cybersecurity attacks fueled by generative AI.* Security Magazine. https://www.securitymagazine.com/articles/99832-study-finds-increase-in-cybersecurity-attacks-fueled-by-generative-ai

Troppe, M. (1994). *Participatory action research: Merging the community and scholarly agenda.* Education Commission of the States.

Zeng, J. (2021). Securitization of artificial intelligence in China. *The Chinese Journal of International Politics, 14*(3), 417–445. https://doi.org/10.1093/cjip/poab005

CHAPTER 9

Securing Public Interest Cybersecurity Researchers in Canadian Universities

Adam Molnar

Abstract

Rooted in democratic ideals, public interest cybersecurity research is essential for understanding the complex relationship between cybersecurity, human rights, and social justice. Universities, with their long tradition of independent inquiry, provide a crucial space for challenging the dominant influence of private industry in shaping our understanding of cybersecurity. Researchers in these institutions are uniquely positioned to generate knowledge that goes beyond profit-driven narratives and encompasses a wider range of concerns, including those of civil society organizations, activists, journalists, and marginalized communities. However, researchers employing established computer security methods in public interest cybersecurity working at Canadian universities face their own crisis of the "security of self" due to substantial legal uncertainties surrounding the lawful permissibility of their research. These uncertainties not only threaten the personal and professional security of researchers, but also hinder their ability to contribute to a broader critical understanding of cybersecurity risks, ultimately limiting our collective "security of self" in the digital age. Building upon Deibert's (2018) call for a human-centric approach to cybersecurity that prioritizes digital security alongside public interest values, this chapter argues that the legal ambiguities surrounding cybersecurity research in Canadian universities threaten researchers' ability to conduct meaningful research in the public interest. It examines common methodological practices in this field and their interaction with legal considerations, exploring implications under criminal and copyright law, as well as civil issues like breach of contract and negligence. By scrutinizing potential interpretations of computer security methods under relevant law, the chapter highlights the need to protect researchers and foster an environment conducive to critical knowledge production in human-centred cybersecurity. Ultimately, it poses a series of recommendations for governments to strengthen legal safeguards for public interest cybersecurity research in Canadian universities.

D riven by a commitment to democratic principles and social justice, public interest cybersecurity research plays a vital role in examining the complex interplay between cybersecurity, human rights, and digital security. Universities, with their long tradition of critical independent inquiry, can serve as crucial sites for challenging the dominance of private industry in shaping imaginaries about "who" and "what" constitutes cybersecurity issues. University researchers are uniquely positioned to generate knowledge that diverges from market-driven trends, broadening the narrative of cybersecurity beyond commercial interests to encompass the threats faced by non-profit organizations, activists, journalists, and marginalized communities. This research prioritizes the often-overlooked human element of cybersecurity and privacy threats. However, the Canadian university environment presents significant challenges for researchers seeking to utilize established computer security methods in public interest cybersecurity research due to considerable legal uncertainty surrounding the permissibility of their work.

Building on Deibert's (2018) call for a "critical cybersecurity approach" that aligns digital security with the human-centric, this chapter argues that the legal ambiguities surrounding public interest cybersecurity research in Canadian universities pose a significant threat to researchers. This uncertainty can hinder the production of knowledge about cybersecurity risks that extend beyond narrowly defined commercial interests, ultimately limiting our understanding of the diverse threats faced by individuals and communities in the digital age.

This chapter offers an in-depth analysis of common methodological practices in public interest cybersecurity research and their legal implications. I examine these practices through the lens of relevant Canadian law, including the *Criminal Code*, the *Copyright Act*, and civil law considerations such as breach of contract and negligence. By scrutinizing the potential interpretations of computer security methods under existing statute and case law (where it exists), the chapter provides a thorough examination of the legal risks faced by researchers. Ultimately, I argue that protecting the "human security" of university researchers and fostering a robust environment for critical, independent, human-centred cybersecurity research requires the Canadian government to establish strong legal protections for this vital work.

Section 9.1 establishes the context for how the cybersecurity industrial complex shapes cybersecurity knowledge, emphasizing the unique contribution that university research can offer in understanding human-centred cybersecurity issues. Section 9.2 examines the potential threats to this critical research within universities. It introduces computer security methods commonly used in public interest cybersecurity research and analyzes how these methods can be opportunistically interpreted, leading to various legal liabilities for researchers in Canadian institutions, as discussed in Section 9.3. Section 9.4 proposes recommendations to protect the "human security" of cybersecurity and privacy researchers at Canadian universities. Overall, this chapter argues that strengthening these protections through robust statutory measures is essential for Canada to advance a comprehensive cybersecurity policy that harnesses the critical potential of university research.

9.1. The University as a Locus for Public Interest Cybersecurity Research

"Cybersecurity," as a body of knowledge and set of practices, is significantly influenced by both state and corporate interests. A primary source of information regarding cybersecurity and threats is derived from commercial threat reporting. Private cybersecurity organizations produce threat intelligence reports that gather and analyze data on cyber risks, ultimately guiding awareness and influencing strategies for securing communication infrastructure.

Commercial threat intelligence reports contain valuable details such as attacker techniques, information about vulnerabilities, and analyses of emerging threats and trends. However, these reports also serve a strategic purpose for the cybersecurity firms that produce them. As Maschmeyer et al. (2021) point out, an entrepreneurial strategy drives the production of these reports, designed to project expertise and bolster reputations to attract clients. This means that threat intelligence is carefully curated to align with profit-maximizing goals of cybersecurity firms, leading to distortions in the overall threat landscape presented.

Commercial threat intelligence reports are powerful cultural artifacts, serving as the primary, and often only, source of data on cyberconflict (Maschmeyer et al., 2021, p. 2). This gives them immense power to define the boundaries of what is known about cyberconflict, constructing narratives that highlight certain actors and trends while sidelining others. Their influence extends into the political sphere, where these reports, bolstered by perceptions of expertise, significantly shape the perspectives of government policy-makers, industry stakeholders, and even researchers.

Which versions of "cyberconflict" and "cybersecurity" actors, threats, and vulnerabilities are foregrounded, and which fade to the background or are made invisible altogether? First, according to Maschmeyer et al. (2021, p. 3) and Work (2021), commercial threat intelligence reports primarily focus on cybercrime, economic espionage, and sabotage of critical infrastructure. This focus systematically excludes the range of threats encountered by civil society organizations vital for democracy, such as human rights defenders, journalists, and environmental activists. As a result, these reports primarily reflect the specific security interests of "high-profile victims," such as government, military, and Fortune 500 companies.

Second, these reports often highlight "high-profile threat actors" often viewed as adversaries of Western/North American interests, like Russia, China, Iran, and North Korea, particularly since threat intelligence firms cater to a largely US audience. This emphasis can obscure the security vulnerabilities generated through US and European cyber operations and their supporting policies.

Third, within this narrow portrayal, producers of commercial threat intelligence reports often emphasize the "unique" or "spectacular," such as zero-day vulnerabilities or novel attack techniques. This focus on the dramatic can distract from the persistent digital threats faced by less prominent groups. Moreover, these reports tend to frame cyber risks primarily as technological vulnerabilities with technological solutions. This perspective neglects the human and socio-political dimensions of digital threats, overlooking risks that do not depend on sophisticated tools typically associated with well-resourced nation-state actors. Ultimately, this skewed representation of the threat landscape has real consequences. It influences decision-making, strategy, and resource allocation in cybersecurity, shaping what is, and is not, possible in the public interest.

Independent research, less entangled with profit-seeking motives, can more adequately embrace a human-centric approach to cybersecurity (Deibert, 2018). This approach, detached from the imperatives of capital accumulation, prioritizes principles such as fairness, justice, free expression, and freedom of association, enabling a critical examination of power dynamics and exploitation. It sheds light on the digital threats faced by marginalized groups such as civil society organizations, human rights advocates, Indigenous communities, and environmental defenders (Deibert, 2018). It also allows for exploration of the gendered dimensions of cyber risks (Harkin et al., 2020) and exposes how private corporations often fail to protect vulnerable groups, focusing instead on product-based solutions (Harkin & Molnar, 2021). Moreover, it can critically examine how the pursuit of "cybersecurity" itself can be used to undermine freedoms and facilitate social control (Deibert et al., 2017).

Universities are vital hubs for pursuing human-centric cybersecurity research in the public interest. While the pervasive influence of neoliberalism within academia often prioritizes applied research, technology transfer, and industry partnerships with an overriding focus on commercial viability, universities still offer a crucial space for conducting research that aligns with broader societal needs and democratic values.

The Citizen Lab at the Munk School of Global Affairs and Public Policy at the University of Toronto provides a compelling example of public interest cybersecurity research. They have a long track record of investigating digital threats targeting civil society organizations, journalists, and political refugees (Citizen Lab, 2023). Employing a multidisciplinary approach, they combine techniques from network measurement, information security, law, and social sciences to expose threats to digital security, human rights, and democracy. For instance, their research into the cybersecurity risks of mercenary spyware has led to the discovery of multiple vulnerabilities in Apple iOS. In another notable project, they investigated information communication technologies used for content filtering, revealing how vendors sell computer networking devices, commonly known as "middleboxes," to authoritarian governments to censor content, including material related to LGTBQ+ issues (Dalek et al., 2021).

In the context of corporate accountability research, a key objective is to identify security and privacy risks associated with specific technologies and their impact on democratic freedoms and human rights. This research often involves using established computer science methods to analyze the technical capabilities and data-sharing practices of vendors and their technologies. While these forensic methods are central to building an independent human-centric approach to cybersecurity research, and addressing critical information gaps within the cybersecurity field more broadly, their use is shrouded in legal uncertainty.

To explore this tension further, this chapter will now delve into two common techniques used in this research: reverse engineering and network traffic analysis. By examining these techniques as case studies, we can gain a deeper understanding of the legal challenges faced by researchers working in the public interest. This analysis will encompass the ethical protocols followed when these methods uncover technical vulnerabilities and how these practices intersect with the current legal landscape governing such research, ultimately highlighting the risks posed to researchers.

9.2. The Ubiquitous Use of Computer Security Methods

Computer security and other technical methods often involve observing and analyzing software applications and information communications systems. These techniques are widely used by computer security researchers at universities worldwide to understand how computer systems operate, identify security vulnerabilities, and ultimately improve the security of computer systems and networks. In the context of a public interest and human-centred approach to cybersecurity, these methods can be used to defend vulnerable communities, protect civil liberties, and promote transparency and accountability.

One common technique is reverse engineering (RE), which involves deconstructing a product or technology to learn more about its design, functionality, and underlying code. For digital technologies and computer systems, RE typically involves disassembling or decompiling machine-readable binary code into a more human-readable format, such as a programming language. This allows researchers to analyze software for security flaws, vulnerabilities, or other design and operational features. Researchers often acquire the technology by obtaining a licence from the vendor, which may involve agreeing to terms of service.

Another common technique is network traffic analysis, which involves monitoring and analyzing network traffic data to identify anomalies. This technique has various applications in cybersecurity research (and digital research more broadly), such as conducting security audits to determine if an application uses encryption, learning about the server infrastructure of a product or service (including its geographical location), and detecting malware and botnets by identifying abnormal traffic patterns.

Researchers at Canadian universities use these methods to uncover and report vulnerabilities, leading to security updates for major tech companies like Apple and Google (among others), ultimately enhancing the privacy and data security of billions of devices and users worldwide. These researchers adhere to robust ethical obligations, including obtaining approval from university research ethics boards (REBs) that enforce the Tri-Council Policy Statement (TCPS 2, 2018), where required. Furthermore, researchers also follow rigorous procedural standards, such as coordinated vulnerability disclosure (CVD) programs, which govern the responsible reporting of information about software vulnerabilities discovered during research. To fully assess the legal implications of these computer security and technical methods and understand the risks researchers face, it is essential to first examine the ethical frameworks that guide this research and how those frameworks are embodied in CVD protocols.

9.3. Coordinated Vulnerability Reporting

Public interest cybersecurity research often employs a CVD policy, a framework for responsibly and promptly reporting security flaws. When researchers acting in good faith discover a software vulnerability, they initiate the CVD process to mitigate potential harm. This typically involves reporting the vulnerability to the software vendor, either directly or through a neutral coordinating party. The vendor then assesses the severity and risk and typically has a thirty- to sixty-day window to develop and issue a patch.

However, responsible disclosure extends beyond simply reporting the vulnerability in a carefully managed way. Ethical CVD practices also emphasize minimizing the collection, use, and disclosure of copyrighted material during the course of the research process, limiting what is strictly necessary for proof of concept, as highlighted in cases like *Proctorio v. Linkletter* (2022, para. 83; 2023, para. 32). Once the vendor has addressed the vulnerability, researchers may choose to disclose their findings more broadly. This may include reporting to the Canadian Centre for Cyber Security, which plays a similar role in Canada to CERT/CC in the United States, particularly if the vulnerability has broader implications for Canadian Internet infrastructure. At this final stage, researchers may choose to disseminate their findings through various channels, such as publishing in scholarly journals, presenting at conferences, or contributing to public awareness initiatives.

CVD is a framework designed to minimize harm by fostering collaboration and transparency between security researchers and vendors. It encourages prompt remediation of vulnerabilities and promotes trust by establishing clear communication channels and timelines. Ideally, CVDs incentivize vendors to enhance the security of their products and services, and ensure researchers adhere to established best-practice standards for vulnerability reporting (Householder et al., 2017).

However, the practical reality of vulnerability disclosure is often more complicated. While CVDs provide ethical research protocols, they do not always guarantee legal protection for researchers. Vendors may favour their own vulnerability disclosure policies (VDPs), which can be unilaterally imposed and vary significantly in their terms and scope. This can create legal uncertainty for researchers, even when adhering to CVD best practices. Some vendors might exploit proactive disclosure by security researchers, using the CVD process as an opportunity to threaten or intimidate them with legal action to prevent or delay public disclosure, often due to concerns about potential liabilities or reputational risk associated with the vulnerability.

Where poorly formulated VDPs can exacerbate legal uncertainty; well-formulated VDPs can mitigate risk by providing explicit and irrevocable authorization for security research. A well-crafted VDP would take careful steps to clarify legal boundaries within various regimes (e.g., criminal, copyright, contract, etc.). Notably, there are multiple efforts currently being made to promote the standardization and adoption of "researcher-friendly" VDPs, including from the National Institute of Standards and Technology (NIST) in the United States, the European Union Agency for Cybersecurity (ENISA), the Canadian government's aim to formulate a government-wide CVD, and commercial efforts like HackerOne's VDP map and Bugcrowd's dislcose.io platform. These initiatives, alongside ongoing advocacy for responsible disclosure practices, are essential for fostering a legal environment that supports public interest cybersecurity research.

Despite the crucial role of CVDs in promoting responsible disclosure, security researchers in Canadian universities often navigate these processes without the support of institutional policies. While researchers generally adhere to ethical guidelines, Canadian universities have largely overlooked the establishment of internal CVD policies to guide research, despite the potential public benefit. This lack of formal guidance could leave researchers more vulnerable to the inconsistencies of externally imposed VDPs, which may offer inadequate protection or impose overly restrictive terms. Even when researchers closely follow CVD protocols and adhere to responsible disclosure practices, they may still face a raft of legal risks stemming from the ambiguous legal landscape surrounding public interest cybersecurity research in Canada.

9.4. Assessing the Legal Risk

9.4.1. Criminal Code

Regarding the *Criminal Code*, if research is conducted within an ethical and controlled environment, the risk of criminal violation should be minimal. Specifically, ss. 342.1(1)(a) and (b) of the *Criminal Code* prohibit, respectively, fraudulently and without colour of right, obtaining any computer service and intercepting any function of a computer system. These arcane terms are further defined in s. 342.1(2) to mean using any data processing or retrieval functions or observing any functions of a computer program without authorization. The term "colour of right" refers to an honest belief in a legal right to possess or access something, even if that belief is mistaken. While the requirement for fraudulently seems to suggest a subjective element of dishonest intent, Canadian courts have interpreted the *mens rea* requirement to be that the computer was "used intentionally, without mistake, with subjective knowledge that the use is unauthorized" (*R. v McNish*,

2020, para 58; see also *R. v Parent*, 2012, paras 50; *Manning v Canada*, 2022, paras 53–61). In short, the accused does not have to subjectively believe their use is blameworthy (*R. v McNish*, para 59). Given broad interpretations of unauthorized computer use in Canada under *R. v Parent*, *R. v McNish*, and *R. v Manning*, where the objective standard has largely focused on intentional access with knowledge that it is unauthorized, there is further ambiguity for interpreting university research, even if the intent of the researcher is to responsibly disclose any vulnerabilities discovered.

This is in contrast to the legal landscape in the United States, where the *Computer Fraud and Abuse Act* has been interpreted narrowly by the US Supreme Court in *van Buren v United States* (2021). The Court held that the crime of exceeding authorized access to a computer does not apply to everyday violations of computer use policies. In this case, a police officer was found to have not exceeded his authorized access when he used a police database to look up a licence plate number for unofficial purposes in exchange for money (see Mackey & Opsahl, 2021). A vendor VDP, if properly formulated, could clarify the requisite authorization. In any case, provisions under the Canadian *Criminal Code* lack explicit exemptions for independent public interest computer security research. The absence of such exclusions means that authorities possess broad discretion in interpreting certain forms of independent security research, potentially leaving researchers vulnerable due to this ambiguity.

9.4.2. Copyright Act

The *Copyright Act* is often regarded as a delicate balance, aiming to provide protections to copyright owners while simultaneously fostering the creative generation and exchange of ideas and information deemed crucial for a healthy democratic society (*Théberge v Galerie d'Art du Petit Champlain Inc.*, 2002, at para 30). While this Act grants copyright owners exclusive rights to control their protected works, it also grants general rights to users and exceptions for specific groups, including educators, journalists, and public interest researchers. Concerning public interest cybersecurity researchers, certain forms of RE methods may potentially constitute infringing activities. Specifically, these methods may involve making copies of vendors' software programs and bypassing technological protection measures to access software. However, these methods may also fall under certain "user rights" exceptions. User rights, particularly relevant to RE methods, are delineated in sections related to encryption research (s. 30.62), security (s. 30.63), and fair dealing (ss. 29 and 29.1).

The exception for conducting encryption research is complex. It applies when it is necessary to make a copy of a computer program to conduct the research (s. 30.62 1a), as long as the program was lawfully obtained (s. 30.62.1b) and the researcher notified the owner of the copyrighted material about their intention to conduct the research (s. 30.62.1c). However, the obligation for cybersecurity researchers to inform vendors of their research intentions has exceptions. Notification may be exempted if "the public interest in making the vulnerability or security flaw public without prior notice outweighs the owner's interest in receiving that notice" (s. 30.62[3]). Due to the limited requirement for advanced notification, it is conceivable that vendors could take legal action to impede the research. For public interest cybersecurity researchers, this notification requirement could potentially hinder the meaningful execution and dissemination of independent critical research.

The *Copyright Act* offers a similar exception to copyright infringement for researchers regarding the reproduction of software for security research: "It is not an infringement of copyright for a person to reproduce a work or other subject matter for the sole purpose, with the consent of the owner or administrator of a computer, computer system or computer network, of assessing the vulnerability of the computer, system or network or of correcting any security flaws" (s. 30.63[1]). Similar to encryption research, if security researchers want to make public a security vulnerability, they must notify the copyright owner, except if the public interest outweighs giving this notice (s. 30.63[3]). While it appears that researchers making copies of software for public interest cybersecurity research enjoy exceptions under the Act, there is currently no case law that could provide further clarification regarding the definitions and boundaries of "encryption" or "security research."

Sections 30.62 and 30.63 solely exempt the act of reproducing a work—and courts have yet to clarify the scope of the provision. However, the *Copyright Act* also prohibits the circumvention of technological protection measures (TPMs) that "control[] access to a work" (s. 41). Circumventing TPMs might encompass activities such as "descrambling a scrambled work or decrypting an encrypted work" (s. 41) or other actions like "bypassing, removing, deactivating, or impairing the technological protection measure" (s.41). In the context of RE, it remains unclear whether circumventing a TPM violates copyright unless authorized by the copyright owner (s. 41.1). However, it is important to note that exceptions to the TPM prohibition, such as those for encryption or security research, may be relevant to RE activities.

For instance, the circumvention of TPMs does not apply to a person conducting encryption research if "it would not be practical to carry out the research without circumventing the technological protection measure" (s. 41.13[1][a]), provided "the person has lawfully obtained the work" (s. 41.13[1][b]) and "the person has informed the owner of the copyright in the work" (s. 41.13[1][c]). Likewise, the prohibition on the circumvention of TPMs does not apply to a person conducting security research, granted it is done "with the consent of the owner or administrator of a computer, computer system, or computer network," where the sole purpose is "assessing the vulnerability of the computer, system, or network or correcting any security flaws" (s. 41.15[1]). These exceptions to anti-circumvention provisions, while vital for guiding security research, introduce authorization requirements that can complicate the conduct of free and fair public interest security research.

Fair dealing exceptions also exist for the purpose of research and education (s. 29). The Supreme Court has established six factors that guide the fair dealing analysis: 1) the purpose of the dealing, 2) the character of the dealing, 3) the quantity or amount of the dealing, 4) whether alternatives to the dealing existed, 5) the nature of the work, and 6) the effect of the dealing on the market for the work (*CCH Canadian Ltd. v Law Society of Upper Canada*, 2004, at para 53). In the context of university security researchers, the strength of fair dealing exceptions as a defence remains unclear. However, it is crucial to recognize that conducting encryption or security research often involves circumventing some form of TPM. Fair dealing remains a complex area of law characterized by the absence of clear bright-line rules, particularly in the realm of public interest cybersecurity research. Given this legal ambiguity, it is a matter of subjective interpretation regarding what constitutes fair dealing in the context of public interest cybersecurity research. Again, while not a reliable solution, a vendor's VDP, if properly formulated, could streamline requirements relating to copyright and fair dealing by providing clear guidance on what types of research are permitted and what conditions must be met.

9.4.3. Contract Law

Terms of service (ToS) agreements are another source of tension for university researchers using computer security methods. Acquiring access to software for analysis often requires agreeing to a ToS or end-user licence agreement (EULA). ToS agreements set out the legal rights, responsibilities, and restrictions between the service provider and end users. While some provisions of ToS have been declared unenforceable, they are binding contracts in Canada. ToS set out the scope of activities relating to what the end user is allowed to do with the software, for example, whether the software can be installed on one or multiple devices or whether the end user is able to make copies of the software. VPD conditions can be incorporated by reference through a ToS or EULA, imposing restrictions on the conditions of disclosure. It is an open question, however, whether these (or other ToS/EULAs) are ultimately enforceable against security researchers entering into a contract of adhesion as a customer (see, e.g., *Century 21 Canada Limited Partnership v Rogers Communications Inc.*, 2011, paras 120, 122).

In any case, regarding RE activities to conduct security research, ToS may not expressly mention using the software to undertake RE activities, though in some cases they may even expressly prohibit making copies of software for the purposes of RE. Overall, given the often narrowly defined usage restrictions found in ToS agreements, they introduce legal ambiguity into the production of public interest cybersecurity research. Despite this ambiguity, however, a major limitation is that any software vendor seeking to threaten or intimidate public interest cybersecurity researchers with contract violation must demonstrate damages—which can be challenging—and non-pecuniary damages for harm to their reputation from disclosure of the security vulnerability are rarely awarded. Adhering to coordinated vulnerability disclosure practices can significantly reduce the likelihood of a successful breach of contract claim. This is because vendors typically need to prove they suffered economic damages due to the researcher's actions. By following responsible disclosure practices, researchers can demonstrate they acted in good faith to minimize any potential harm. While not a guarantee against legal action, this can make it more difficult for vendors to prove they suffered damages, especially when the researcher's actions are aligned with established best practices. Currently, there are no known cases in Canada where a software company has successfully sued a "good faith" cybersecurity researcher for breach of contract related to RE for security vulnerability analysis. However, further research should attempt to inquire into the status of unreported cases, settled lawsuits, or documented threats that highlight the potential risks researchers face.

9.4.4. Anti-SLAPP Motions

If good-faith cybersecurity researchers find themselves on the receiving end of litigation that seeks to threaten or intimidate public interest work, potential recourse is available through anti-SLAPP (Strategic Lawsuits Against Public Participation) laws. These laws provide defendants with expedited summary processes for a swift dismissal of a lawsuit. Anti-SLAPP laws vary in application across provinces in Canada. They are currently in force in Ontario, British Columbia, Quebec, and Prince Edward Island. Other provinces, including Alberta, Saskatchewan, Manitoba, New Brunswick, Nova Scotia, and Newfoundland and Labrador, do not yet have anti-SLAPP legislation.

In Ontario, under section 137.1(3) of the *Courts of Justice Act*, the defendant must present a compelling argument to secure a dismissal of the proceeding. Specifically, they must demonstrate that the litigation targets their research as a form of expression connected to the public interest. This includes any form of expression, not just defamation. The plaintiff must also demonstrate that the proceeding has merit, that the defendant lacks a valid defence, and that any resulting harm is a consequence of the expression (s 137.1[4][a] and [b]). A crucial element in the judge's decision is the assessment of the harm inflicted, which must reach a level of severity such that allowing the proceeding to continue outweighs the societal interest in safeguarding the specific expression in question (s 137.1[4][b]). In practical terms, this means that the judge must consider whether the societal value of public interest cybersecurity research, aimed at discovering and mitigating security and privacy risks, outweighs the interests of private sector organizations in being shielded from independent assessment. It is worth noting that, in Canada, anti-SLAPP legislation has not been applied in the context of cybersecurity research. Nevertheless, it is essential to recognize that anti-SLAPP motions have been successful in protecting various legal claims related to the defendant's expressions. Overall, the effectiveness of anti-SLAPP motions as a viable avenue for legal protection in the practice of public interest cybersecurity research remains an open question.

9.5. Securing Research

By shifting the focus from the external cybersecurity landscape affecting the "security of self" to the conditions governing knowledge production, this chapter underscores the importance of safeguarding researchers who strive to understand and address cyber risks and digital accountability from a human-centred and justice-oriented perspective. These researchers challenge the prevailing information environment on cyber risks, often dominated by narrow economic considerations, and offer crucial insights into the complex interplay between cybersecurity, human rights, and social justice. However, the legal uncertainties surrounding such critical work casts a shadow on the ability to conduct critical research, jeopardizing both current and future efforts to advance knowledge in the public interest. To mitigate these challenges, the chapter proposes the following recommendations:

> 1) **Establish clear legal protections:** As an interim measure, the Minister of Justice and Attorney General of Canada should immediately issue a non-prosecution directive concerning ss. 342.1 and 430(1.1) of the *Criminal Code* in relation to good-faith security research. This directive would provide immediate relief for researchers facing legal threats or prosecution, aligning with the US Department of Justice's policy on charging cases under the *Computer Fraud and Abuse Act* (2022), which explicitly discourages prosecution of good-faith security research. In the longer term, the government should enact comprehensive legislation that explicitly protects cybersecurity and digital accountability researchers engaged in public interest work. This legislation should clearly define permissible research activities, establish a safe harbour for responsible vulnerability disclosure, and shield researchers from legal threats and repercussions. This could be achieved through a public interest exception in the *Criminal Code* under s. 342.1 (and s. 430[1.1]), and a model security research shield law adopted by provinces to protect responsible security researchers from civil litigation.

2) **Formalize coordinated vulnerability disclosure (CVD) frameworks:** Promote the widespread adoption of CVD frameworks within Canadian universities as well as the broader cybersecurity community. These frameworks should provide clear guidelines that allow researchers to report vulnerabilities responsibly and without fear of legal repercussion. Further, efforts should be made to standardize VDPs across the industry, potentially through collaboration with standards organizations, to ensure they adequately protect responsible security research.

3) **Enhance security-related exceptions in the *Copyright Act*:** Clarify and strengthen the security research exceptions within the *Copyright Act* to better accommodate the needs of cybersecurity researchers. Ensure these exceptions explicitly cover activities related to vulnerability analysis, including the circumvention of technological protection measures when necessary for security research. To further support these exceptions, policy-makers should explore the possibility of expressly prohibiting private sector vendors from using terms of service to contractually override statutory provisions in the Act that allow fair use exceptions to undertake public interest security research.

4) **Strengthen anti-SLAPP legislation:** Expand and enhance anti-SLAPP legislation in all Canadian provinces to offer stronger and more tailored protection for public interest cybersecurity researchers. These laws should provide a robust defence against legal actions designed to intimidate researchers and suppress public interest research.

5) **Support public interest cybersecurity research:** Increase funding, grants, and other incentives for public interest cybersecurity research programs in Canadian universities. Encourage partnerships between academia, industry, government, and advocacy groups to support research that prioritizes human-centred and justice-oriented approaches to cybersecurity challenges.

Failure to make progress in these areas will undermine the university's essential role in fostering a public interest and human-centred approach to cybersecurity—one that prioritizes human values and justice over the influence of powerful corporate actors and a legal system that can be wielded to serve their interests.

Acknowledgements

This chapter draws on research supported by the Social Sciences and Humanities Research Council. The author would like to thank Tamir Israel for feedback on parts of an earlier draft of the proposal and an anonymous reviewer for their constructive comments. Any errors or omissions remain the responsibility of the author.

References

Canadian Institutes of Health Research, Natural Sciences and Engineering Research Council of Canada, Social Sciences and Humanities Research Council. (2018). *TCPS2. Tri-council policy statement: Ethical conduct for research involving humans.* https://ethics.gc.ca/eng/documents/tcps2-2018-en-interactive-final.pdf

CCH Canadian Ltd. v Law Society of Upper Canada, 2004 SCC 13, [2004] 1 SCR 339.

Century 21 Canada Limited Partnership v Rogers Communications Inc., 2011 BCSC1196.

Citizen Lab. (2023). *Citizen lab research.* https://citizenlab.ca/category/research/

Computer Fraud and Abuse Act, 18 USC § 1030 (2002). https://www.justice.gov/jm/jm-9-48000-computer-fraud

Copyright Act, RSC 1985, c C-42.

Courts of Justice Act, RSO 1990, c C.43.

Criminal Code, RSC 1985, c C-46.Dalek, J., Dumlao, N., Kenyon, M., Poetranto, I., Senft, A., Wesley, C., Filastò, A., Xynou, M., & Bishop, A. (2021). *No access: LGBTIQ website censorship in six countries.* The Citizen Lab, OutRight Action International, and OONI. https://citizenlab.ca/2021/08/no-access-lgbtiq-website-censorship-in-six-countries/Deibert, R. J. (2018). Toward a human-centric approach to cybersecurity. *Ethics & International Affairs,* 32(4), 411–424. http://dx.doi.org/10.1017/S0892679418000618

Deibert, R. J., Gill, L., Israel, T., Legge, C., Poetranto, I., & Singh, A. (2017). *Submission of the Citizen Lab (Munk School of Global Affairs, University of Toronto) to the United Nations Special Rapporteur on violence against women, its causes and consequences, Ms. Dubravka Šimonović.* The Citizen Lab, Munk School of Global Affairs, University of Toronto. https://citizenlab.ca/wp-content/uploads/2017/11/Final-UNSRVAG-CitizenLab.pdf

Harkin, D., Molnar, A., & Vowles, E. (2020). The commodification of mobile phone surveillance: An analysis of the consumer spyware industry. *Crime, media, culture,* 16(1), 33–60. http://dx.doi.org/10.1177/1741659018820562

Harkin, D., & Molnar, A. (2021). Operating-system design and its implications for victims of family violence: The comparative threat of smart phone spyware for Android versus iPhone users. *Violence against women,* 27(6–7), 851–875. DOI: http://dx.doi.org/10.1177/1077801220923731

Householder, A. D., Wassermann, G., Manion, A., & King, C. (2017). *The CERT guide to coordinated vulnerability disclosure.* Software Engineering Institute. https://doi.org/10.1184/R1/12367340.v1

Mackey, A. & Opsahl, K. (2021, June 3). Van Buren is a victory against over-broad interpretations of the CFAA, and protects security researchers. *Electronic Frontier Foundation: Deeplinks Blog.* https://www.eff.org/deep-links/2021/06/van-buren-victory-against-overbroad-interpretations-cfaa-protects-security

Manning v Canada, 2022 File No 0018-C1-00135-01, (CA IRB).

Maschmeyer, L., Deibert, R. J., & Lindsay, J. R. (2021). A tale of two cybers — how threat reporting by cybersecurity firms systematically underrepresents threats to civil society. *Journal of Information Technology & Politics, 18*(1), 1–20. http://dx.doi.org/10.1080/19331681.2020.1776658

Proctorio v Linkletter, 2022 BCSC 400.

Proctorio v Linkletter, 2023 BCCA 160.*R v McNish*, 2020 ABCA 249.*R v Parent*, 2012 QCCA 1653.

Théberge v Galerie d'Art du Petit Champlain Inc., 2002 SCC 34.

van Buren v United States, 593 US 374 (2021).

Work, J. D. (2020). Evaluating commercial cyber intelligence activity. *International Journal of Intelligence and CounterIntelligence, 33*(2), 278–308. https://doi.org/10.1080/08850607.2019.1690877

CHAPTER 10

The Online Mutual Help Practices of Romance Fraud Victims

Pascale-Marie Cantin, Fyscillia Ream,
and Benoît Dupont

Abstract

Online services have become integral to modern human interactions, making life and work much more efficient for individuals and businesses. However, they also bring a broad range of new harms, including a steep rise in online scams, which now represent the main category of crimes experienced by Canadians. As online scams have become a major source of digital, financial, and psychological insecurity for a significant share of the population, it is essential to include this type of harm in the "security of self" research agenda to craft more effective mitigation and prevention policies, including intervention strategies that are community-driven and rely on a human-centric approach rather than on a national cybersecurity mindset. This chapter examines one such community-driven approach: how romance fraud victims leverage online platforms to help each other. To this end, we analyzed the content of three online discussion forums focusing on romance fraud to study the mutual help practices adopted by victims in the aftermath of their experiences. The results show that a significant proportion of victims use these forums to tell their stories, find assistance and receive advice, and also to support and provide guidance to other potential victims who have doubts about their online relationships. Moreover, these platforms are used to expose cybercriminals by sharing identifying information, photographs, and modus operandi linked to romance scammers. Finally, victims also use these mutual help forums to raise awareness among general Internet users about these schemes and to provide the names of institutions and organizations to contact if they are ever confronted with a possible romance scam. This chapter highlights how the "security of self" can emerge from bottom-up practices when state institutions are unable to fulfill the needs of online scam victims.

The emergence of digital communication tools and platforms has profoundly altered how people interact, offering many societal benefits but also generating new criminal opportunities that are notoriously under-policed (Dupont, 2019). A particular form of online fraud, the romance scam, has proved particularly lucrative for cyber-offenders and devastating for its victims. In the context of this research, a romance scam refers to a scheme whereby a scammer pretends to be a potential partner for a user registered on a dating site or application, to create a relationship of trust in order to extract money from the victim later on. Typically, scammers play on the victims' emotional motivations, resulting in serious psychological and financial harms. As people increasingly use online dating sites to locate new romantic partners within a much larger pool of potential matches, related scams have spiked to the point where they are considered the second most financially damaging type of fraud, behind investment scams (Canadian Anti-Fraud Centre, 2022).

This trend is unfolding in a context where 80 percent of Canadians who use the Internet are concerned about the negative impact of malware and scams, while more than half are concerned about privacy violations through social media platforms or mobile devices (CIRA, 2019). These concerns reflect actual risks and harms: It is estimated that cybercrime now constitutes almost half of all property crimes in Organisation for Economic Co-operation and Development (OECD) economies (Levi, 2017: Anderson et al., 2019). In the United Kingdom, citizens are ten times more likely to be defrauded online than to fall victim to traditional theft (Whitty, 2019). Comparable data has not been collected in Canada. The impact of these online harms on victims is not only financial but can also generate profound emotional, psychological, and even physiological distress (Modic and Anderson, 2015; Cross, 2017; Zhang-Kennedy et al., 2018). This impact is also highly differentiated and affects vulnerable groups disproportionately (Virtanen, 2017). Moreover, individual cybercrime victims have specific needs rarely met by law enforcement agencies and conventional victim support institutions (Leukfeldt et al., 2020). So online scams have now become a major source of digital, financial, and psychological insecurity for a significant share of Canadians, requiring us to incorporate these types of harms into the "security of self" research agenda to craft more effective mitigation and prevention policies, including intervention strategies that are community-driven and rely on a human-centric approach rather than on a national cybersecurity mindset.

To date, minimal research has been conducted in Canada and beyond to understand romance fraud. Most publications deal with the structure of romance fraud networks and the consequences of this specific crime for victims. So far, no research has focused on the post-incident experiences of romance fraud victims and how they leverage online mutual help strategies to mitigate the harm suffered and rebuild their lives. Most of the existing literature on online mutual help focuses on public health and education. Still, this chapter identifies a new domain of application: cybercrime prevention and support services. The underlying assumption is that individuals experiencing similar incidents are not trapped in the helpless status of "crime victim" but can regain agency by seeking and providing help to their peers on discussion forums dedicated to their problems. By doing so, they contribute to a bottom-up "security of self" that emerges when state institutions are unable to fulfill the needs of online scam victims.

This chapter explores the types of mutual help practices that take place on three large discussion forums focused on various types of online scams. It starts with a quick overview of the online mutual help literature and why this particular form of peer support can prove helpful for cybercrime victims. Section 10.2 briefly discusses the data sources and how the analysis was conducted. In the following three sections, study findings are presented and discussed. Section 10.3 examines how mutual help forums help romance fraud victims share their stories, enabling them to break their isolation and regain control of the narrative. Section 10.4 describes how mutual help forums provide a repository of digital traces collected by victims during their interactions with prolific scammers, whose detailed modes of operation can then be shared with a broad audience. Finally, Section 10.5 explains how victims use online mutual help forums as *ad hoc* prevention and awareness platforms that can warn potential victims before they transfer money to the scammer or help new victims orient themselves in the maze of public and private institutions that can assist them in their recovery. Section 10.6 distills the insights gained from this research into actionable policy recommendations that could be adopted to increase the quality of support offered to romance fraud victims.

10.1. Online Mutual Help

Most criminological studies focusing on victims' experiences have adopted a passive perspective, primarily examining online fraud victims' profiles and susceptibility factors (Buchanan & Whitty, 2014; Whitty, 2017, 2019; Lazarus et al., 2023). The negative impacts of romance scams are not limited to financial losses, as victims suffer the double emotional trauma of losing money and a relationship they valued, developing feelings of shock, shame, anger, loss of trust in people, or mourning for the relationship that vanished (Coluccia et al., 2020). Few studies have focused on the agency of victims, meaning the types of responses and actions they take to overcome the negative impacts of the incidents they have experienced. In addition, the cybercrime literature has focused mainly on how offenders help each other online, particularly through underground discussion forums. Few studies have examined how victim communities mobilize these same communication tools to their own ends. Moreover, qualitative studies have shown that many cybercrime victims do not share their experiences with their loved ones (Cross et al., 2016; De Kimpe et al., 2020). From a resilience and victim support perspective, it seems essential to study how victims help each other online to manage the consequences of their victimization.

To date, studies on the use of online mutual help as a support tool have primarily originated from the fields of public health (see, e.g., Pistrang et al., 2008; Smith-Merry et al., 2019; Berthelot-Guiet & Charbonneaux, 2020) and education (see, e.g., Puustinen et al., 2015). A study by Berthelot-Guiet and Charbonneaux (2020) examined intergenerational digital mutual help on discussion forums for patients with glioblastoma, a rare form of cancerous brain tumour. Their research showed that patients and their families used forums to share their "narratives" by providing descriptions of the extraordinary experiences and challenges associated with the disease. These users also produced experiential knowledge and claimed a discrete form of expertise. Greiner et al. (2017) have shown that members of cannabis discussion forums post messages that reflect two forms of support: emotional support and support aimed at providing information. In their study of individuals suffering from mental health problems, Smith-Merry et al. (2019) suggested that online discussion forums enabled them to develop social relationships missing from their daily lives, as well as seek and provide practical advice. One of the main findings from online mutual help studies show that many individuals facing an important problem turn to discussion forums to share their experience, receive support, and/or find or provide relevant information in a positive and accepting environment (Salem et al., 1998). Very few evaluations of mutual help groups have been conducted to date, but a systematic review in the field of mental health suggests positive outcomes for more than half of the studies surveyed, neutral outcomes for the remaining studies, and no cases of adverse effects (Pistrang et al., 2008). These encouraging results point toward a cost-efficient and grassroots alternative to costly professional interventions. However, few, if any, empirical studies have focused on online mutual help among crime victims, and we do not know whether these victims can derive the same benefits from these practices, such as those medical patients and students receive. The current study focuses on this concern, assessing how victims of romance scams help each other online in response to their experience.

10.2. Data and Methods

To better understand how victims of online romance fraud leverage mutual help practices, this study relies on a hybrid methodology, blending the systematic collection of large datasets on public discussion forums through automated tools with qualitative analysis techniques. Three forums were selected for this project: ScamWarners,[1] ScamSurvivors,[2] and Signal-Arnaques.[3] They were chosen primarily because of the abundance and relevance of their content. The data extracted from these forums consisted of messages with the following

1. ScamWarners. (n.d.). ScamWarners. Retrieved on May 3, 2025, from https://www.scamwarners.com/.
2. ScamSurvivors. (n.d.). ScamSurvivors. Retrieved on May 3, 2025, from https://scamsurvivors.com/.
3. Signal-Arnaques. (n.d.). Retrieved on May 3, 2025, from https://www.signal-arnaques.com/.

features: title, message content, publication date, number of views, number of replies, telephone numbers provided by the scammer (if available), scammer's email address (if available), and pseudonyms of the scammer and the author of the publication. For this purpose, a customized Python script developed by Quentin Rossy was used. Given the number of posts returned by the crawling bot, the sample of conversations had to be limited to perform an in-depth qualitative analysis. Therefore, one thousand conversations (335 in each discussion forum) were selected for content analysis. These threads were selected based on the length of the original post and the number of views and responses, also called interactions, it elicited. The selected conversations were then transferred into the QDA Miner coding software to facilitate content analysis. An inductive approach was then used to generate codes based on the observed data, enabling for three main themes (supporting victims, identifying fraudulent profiles, and raising awareness) to be derived that explain how romance scam victims leverage mutual help to recover.

10.3. Supporting Victims by Helping them Regain a Voice, Overcome Isolation, and Access Personal Advice

This first theme describes the various types of support mutual help discussion forums provide to victims of online fraud. The first kind of support enables victims to free themselves from their traumatic experience through written testimony, activating public expressions of peer encouragement. The second kind of support stems from their realization that many other victims can be found on these forums, breaking their sense of isolation. The third kind of support results from the personalized advice new victims receive from "survivors." In this context, survivors are often past victims characterized by their resilience, knowledge of romance scams, and role in providing support. They participate differently in exchanges, depending on how far they have advanced in the victimization process.

Many posts on the three discussion forums studied take the form of written testimonials describing victims' experiences. Many victims turn to these platforms to share their stories and talk about the emotional and financial consequences generated by the scam. Following the publication of these stories, several forum members generally offer support and praise the victim's courage. In this form of support, forum members are less inclined to exchange information with one another, instead focusing on the original publication and its author. Sharing written testimonials on discussion forums helps victims "release" themselves from the traumatic experience they just suffered and the state of despair the romance scam has submitted them to. These testimonials frequently feature sequences of confidence and emotional statements. Telling one's story becomes a tool of empowerment where the author regains control over her life and can thrive again. Testifying about one's experience thus becomes a way of recognizing and accepting fraud. The rebuilding process is facilitated by the encouragement and moral support of peers who have gone through the same ordeal. The following excerpt illustrates this kind of moral support: "I hope you'll be relieved to have had the courage to confide in me even after such a long time and I know that despite your serious health problems that your partner supports you" (excerpt from Signal-Arnaques; our translation).

Moreover, the fact that victims can share their stories anonymously through a pseudonym limits exposure to others' judgment, which some victims might fear. Written testimonials are reminiscent of traditional support groups' benefits, helping people cope better with a fraudulent experience and manage its aftermath by connecting them with peers able to provide moral support.

This analysis also highlighted how identifying with peers is an important support mechanism for victims seeking to break the isolation they frequently feel following a scam. Being involved in discussions with other individuals who have undergone similar experiences allows the victim to dispel the impression that they are alone in facing such a situation. Some victims are reluctant to share their experiences with their loved ones, fearing being misunderstood, taken for a fool, or even scolded by them. In other cases, victims do not wish to share their experiences since they were cheating on their spouse, as expressed in the following passage:

> I don't know what to do as he has some not very indecent photos of me and I wouldn't like him to publish them on the web as I think this is possible, I'm afraid of what will happen next. Should I block him or should I tell him I've discovered the scam? My husband doesn't know of course and I don't want him to find out about my stupidity. If I don't answer, will he get angry? What can I do? Thank you for your feedback and help. (Excerpt from Signal-Arnaques; our translation)

Discussion forums enable individuals experiencing the same adverse events to talk about their situation and share a common understanding of the issues they are facing. It should be noted that a romance scam involves a particular form of victimization, first because the police generally do not have the resources or the means to arrest a perpetrator abroad, and second, because it is virtually impossible to recover the money lost. As a result, it can be difficult for victims to move on. Realizing that other people are experiencing the same consequences can help victims break the sense of isolation that might invade them, share their experiences, which non-victims often misunderstand, and gradually come to terms with the fraud's aftermath. This particular form of support can be indirect, as many victims read testimonies without responding to them or contributing to follow-up conversations. They still can find comfort in discovering they are not alone.

Finally, this analysis also revealed a third type of support based on personal advice. Obviously, joining a discussion forum, whatever the subject, is often motivated by a will to help other members requiring some form of support. For romance scam victims, this means using the lessons learned from one's own negative experience to advise others. This implies that victims accept the outcome of their experience and are ready to support others by acting as mentors and advisors. Being familiar with the scammers' operation modes and manipulation strategies, victims can contribute positively to conversations and speak with authority. To do so, they must overcome the financial and emotional consequences of their own victimization and assign a new meaning to their fraudulent experience. Providing helpful advice to actual and potential victims enables them to demonstrate resilience and shift their status from a victim to that of a survivor. With this new role comes the responsibilities of preventing scams and supporting those who have fallen victim to them. This mutual help practice suggests several stages of victimization, with two main types of victims populating discussion forums. First, there are "novice" victims, characterized by their unfamiliarity with romance scams and their candour toward scammers. Second, there are "experienced" victims, now referred to as "surviving victims," characterized by their resilience, knowledge of the internal dynamics of romance fraud, and role as supportive contributors. The following passage explores this idea:

> Closure. You want closure? To do this, you must change your
> own mind from that of a victim to that of a survivor. This helps

you remove him from your life and also helps other victims of the same scammer, who has many more hooked at that moment. You must realize that you are not the only victim of him at that point in time or in the future and that posting his details can and does save others from falling to the same scammer. Your posts here can and do save real lives. (Excerpt from ScamSurvivor)

10.4. Identifying Fraudulent Profiles

One of the main ways people help each other on online discussion forums is by reporting malicious profiles from various dating sites or social network platforms. This practice was observed on the three forums under study. On the ScamWarners and ScamSurvivors forums, members created posts whose titles provided identifying information about scammers' profiles. The content of the messages varied, but generally included a cut-and-paste of the fraudster's exchanges with the victim, as well as various digital traces (such as pseudonyms, telephone numbers, email addresses, stolen photographs, etc.) that can be used to report individuals with malicious intent. The French-language site Signal-Arnaques has a dedicated reporting platform, which means that a significant proportion of the publications shared in the forum are intended to deal with other issues, mainly testimonials. The reporting tool provides access to an abundance of digital traces that can be useful in establishing links between fraudulent profiles, as is the case for English-language forums. This tool is reminiscent of indicators of compromise (IOCs) that cybersecurity professionals share with each other to provide information about the attacks they have experienced so that other organizations being targeted can detect them much more quickly. Reporting platforms can thus serve the same purpose as the IOC framework and be useful for general Internet users and cyber-crime investigators. Sharing fake profiles is a mutual help mechanism designed to combat romance scams by aggregating information about suspicious profiles that can then be discovered easily through search engines such as Google, thus restricting scammers' criminal opportunities. This practice enables victims to take an active role in the fight against romance fraud and warn potential victims.

Similarly, many victims share the content of conversations they have had with scammers to illustrate their *modus operandi*, particularly regarding the technological tools they favour. For example, social networks can be ranked to see how fraudsters contact potential victims or the email service providers most frequently used by fake profiles. This information enables identification of platforms most at risk of hosting fraudulent profiles and the companies that could implement effective measures to prevent malicious users from exploiting their services. This analysis showed that, based on testimonies on ScamWarners between 2012 and 2021, Facebook is the platform most used by romance scammers (50 percent), followed by—the now discontinued—Skype (29 percent). Scammers also use other platforms such as Instagram, WhatsApp, LinkedIn, and Tinder, but to a much lesser extent. Since 2021, new platforms have gained in popularity, and this ranking may now differ slightly. Concerning email providers, the data collected on ScamSurvivors between 2013 and 2021 show that Yahoo (42%) and Gmail (36%) are the most attractive services for scammers impersonating potential lovers, with Yandex (9%) and Hotmail (7%) coming in as a distant third and fourth choice. It may be worth investigating what protective factors adopted by some email service providers limit the creation of fake accounts.

Although these data analyses are limited within the scope of this chapter, the reporting and sharing of fraudulent profiles is a form of mutual help that can be used as a source of open-source intelligence to support the prevention and even the investigation of romance scams. Since many victims never file a formal complaint with their local police agency, discussion forums and reporting platforms can help cybercrime investigators identify emerging trends.

10.5. Raising Awareness

Finally, discussion forums help victims raise awareness about romance scams. This data shows that many members actively share tips and general information designed to educate other users about the risks of online dating and what to do if faced with a potential scam. The first mutual help practice linked to this awareness function is sharing tips to expose a romance scam:

> Usually, the main reasons for money requests are: medical bills for an illness of the scammers' child he cannot deal with, while, due to being abroad for business; unexpected costs due to a new contract signed by the scammer abroad or partnership in a recent business developed by the scammer abroad that should bring him huge revenues; accidents affecting the scammer such as robbery

leaving him without money and documents [...]. (Excerpt from ScamSurvivors)

When a publication reports a situation in which a new user questions the intentions of their virtual lover, some members will provide tips to convince the author that they are indeed facing a fraud attempt. These interventions are frequently made by "survivor" victims. This mutual-help practice aims to prevent a suspected scam from succeeding and the potential victim from being deceived. In addition, most forums contain advice pages written by administrators and moderators that list common red flags for romance scams and can alert potential victims to the scammers' most frequent tricks. Anti-scam discussion forums operate as preventative tools that enable the general population to learn about real and concrete fraud configurations and how to avoid them.

Victims of romance scams also help each other by sharing tips on how to cut off contact with a fraudster. Since these scams are often characterized by repeat victimization, such as blackmail, victims must understand what steps they can take to cut off all contact with their abuser to remove the power and control they hold over them. This mutual-help practice also comforts the victim, reassuring them that they are not alone and that fraudsters rarely follow through on their threats. Cutting ties with the fraudster is the best way to end an ongoing scam. Many forum members are indirect victims of scams through their spouses or other family members. As a result, they especially value advice on how to uncover fraud and put a stop to it:

> Hello, we've just found out that my 72-year-old mother is (probably) a victim of fraud and we're distraught. We're also worried about her safety. My mother lives alone and (relatively) socially isolated, outside the family. She recently decided to look for someone to meet (it's only getting better), but seems to have fallen into a sentimental scam trap [...] She has had telephone communication with someone (she says she realized that this person did not speak the way they wrote, but nothing more) and has (probably) sent money [...] She remains defensive, despite our attempts to find out a little more, or to try and warn her. For the rest, she's in denial. (Excerpt from Signal-Arnaques, our translation)

In addition, users and victims on discussion forums share information about reporting scams to authorities. This aims to inform and raise awareness. However, this analysis revealed many victims are reluctant to contact the police. With low chances of recouping lost money and feelings of shame and humiliation from being victimized, few report being scammed. Still, many want support and help from organizations to rebuild their lives after the fraud. So, forum members exchange details on available victim support services and how to connect with them. Distrust of institutions may partly explain the under-reporting of romance scams. Mutual help forums provide an alternative to study the scope of romance fraud beyond police data. They offer users awareness and support while informing researchers about emerging romance scam trends and issues.

10.6. Incentivizing and Regulating Mutual Help

As shown in this chapter, the security of self is not only an outcome delivered by state institutions. It can also result from the bottom-up practices of individual victims who find a community online and develop supportive mutual help strategies. Even after experiencing online fraud, many victims still value online interactions and platforms for the social benefits and sense of community they can provide. Victims helping each other on dedicated forums create a safe space where they can express themselves and find support without fear of being judged. Through their mutual help practices, they reclaim power online. Sometimes, romance scam victims suffer irreparable harm, but they can also use the same tools to fight back and build a support community that does not exist offline.

The three intertwined mutual help practices outlined in this chapter (supporting victims, identifying fraudulent profiles, and raising awareness) have the same goal: preventing new victims from being defrauded. Some posts share experiences, others expose criminals, and more raise awareness. Even the majority of forum visitors who read posts without engaging further, known as "lurkers," benefit and can gain first-hand insights on how to identify, prevent, or recover from romance fraud. However, very little research exists on mutual help practices related to online fraud and their efficacy. Criminologists, sociologists, legal scholars, and psychologists should systematically and rigorously assess the benefits and shortcomings of these practices. This would be an essential first step to gauge whether this approach could be leveraged on a larger scale to enhance the cyber-resilience of Internet users, consumers, and online fraud victims. Academics could also extend their investigations to other platforms where online mutual help practices thrive organically, such as popular social media sites.

If early assessments demonstrate promise, government agencies could engage more deeply with mutual help forums covering their jurisdiction. For instance, they could promote mutual help forums for victims through public service announcements. Or they could provide financial backing to forum administrators, enabling sustainability and growth, and letting them hire additional staff to handle potential abuses such as libellous posts. There is also a risk that these mutual help platforms jeopardize the privacy of those who use them, and governments should ensure that they abide by commonly accepted security and privacy standards. Agencies could also monitor discussions to gather intelligence on romance scam trends and identify prolific scammers. This would help prioritize investigative resources. Essentially, governments have many opportunities to collaborate with and reinforce these online mutual help communities, which provide information and support that are not accessible through conventional institutions such as police or victim services.

Acknowledgements

Financial support was provided by the Université de Montréal Research Chair in the Prevention of Cybercrime and the Social Sciences and Humanities Research Council of Canada.

References

Anderson, R., Barton, C., Boehme, R., Clayton, R., Ganan, C., Grasso, T., Levi, M., Moore, T., & Vasek, M. (2019). Measuring the changing cost of cybercrime. *The 18th Annual Workshop on the Economics of Information Security*. https://doi.org/10.17863/CAM.41598

Berthelot-Guiet, K., & Charbonneaux, J. (2020). Vers une entraide numérique intergénérationnelle ? Le cas du Glioblastome sur les forums de discussion en ligne. *Revue française des sciences de l'information et de la communication, 19*, 1–15. http://dx.doi.org/10.4000/rfsic.8642

Buchanan, T., & Whitty, M. (2014). The online dating romance scam: Causes and consequences of victimhood. *Psychology, Crime, and Law, 20*(3), 261–283. http://dx.doi.org/10.1080/1068316X.2013.772180

Canadian Anti-Fraud Centre. (2022). *Canadian anti-fraud centre annual report 2021*. Royal Canadian Mounted Police. https://www.publications.gc.ca/site/eng/9.917185/publication.html

CIRA. (2019). *Canada's Internet factbook*. Canadian Internet Registration Authority. https://cira.ca/resources/corporate/factbook/canadas-internet-factbook

Coluccia, A., Pozza, A., Ferretti, F., Carabellese, F., Masti, A., & Gualtieri, G. (2020). Online romance scams: Relational dynamics and psychological characteristics of the victims and scammers. A scoping review. *Clinical Practice and Epidemiology in Mental Health, 16*(1), 24–35. http://dx.doi.org/10.2174/1745017902016010024

Cross, C. (2017). I've lost some sleep over it: Secondary trauma and the provision of support to older fraud victims. *Canadian Journal of Criminology and Criminal Justice, 59*(2), 168–197. DOI: https://doi.org/10.3138/cjccj.2016.E11

Cross, C., Richards, K., & Smith, R. (2016). The reporting experiences and support needs of victims of online fraud. *Trends & Issues in Crime and Criminal Justice, 518*, 1–14. https://www.aic.gov.au/publications/tandi/tandi518

De Kimpe, L., Ponnet, K., Walrave, M., Snaphaan, T., & Pauwels, L. (2020). Help, I need somebody: Examining the antecedents of social support seeking among cybercrime victims. *Computers in Human Behavior, 108*(3), 1–11. http://dx.doi.org/10.1016/j.chb.2020.106310

Dupont, B. (2019). Enhancing the effectiveness of cybercrime prevention through policy monitoring. *Journal of Crime and Justice, 42*(5), 500–515. http://dx.doi.org/10.1080/0735648X.2019.1691855

Greiner, C., Chatton, A., & Khazaal, Y. (2017). Online self-help forums on cannabis: A content assessment. *Patient Education and Counseling, 100*(10), 1943–1950. https://doi.org/10.1016/j.pec.2017.06.001

Lazarus, S., Whittaker, J., McGuire, M., & Platt, L. (2023). What do we know about online romance fraud studies? A systematic review of the empirical literature (2000–2021). *Journal of Economic Criminology, 2*, 1–17. https://philpapers.org/archive/LAZWDW.pdf

Leukfeldt, R., Notté, R. J., & Malsch, M. (2020). Exploring the needs of victims of cyber-dependent and cyber-enabled crimes. *Victims & Offenders, 15*(1), 60–77. https://doi.org/10.1080/15564886.2019.1672229

Levi, M. (2017). Assessing the trends, scale and nature of economic cybercrimes: Overview and issues. *Crime, Law and Social Change, 67*(1), 3–20. https://doi.org/10.1007/s10611-016-9645-3

Modic, D., & Anderson, R. (2015). It's all over but the crying: The emotional and financial impact of Internet fraud. *IEEE Security & Privacy, 13*(5), 99–103. https://doi.org/10.1109/MSP.2015.107

Pistrang, N., Barker, C., & Humphreys, K. (2008). Mutual help groups for mental health problems: A review of effectiveness study. *American Journal of Community Psychology*, 42(1–2), 110–121. http://dx.doi.org/10.1007/s10464-008-9181-0

Puustinen, M., Bernicot, J., Volckaert-Legrier, O., & Baker, M. (2015). Naturally occurring help-seeking exchanges on a homework help forum. *Computers & Education*, *81*, 89–101. http://dx.doi.org/10.1016/j.compedu.2014.09.010

Salem, D. A., Bogat, A., & Reid, C. (1998). Mutual help goes online. *Journal of Community Psychology*, 25(2), 189–207. https://doi.org/10.1002/(SICI)1520-6629(199703)25:2%3C189::AID-JCOP7%3E3.0.CO;2-T

Smith-Merry, J., Goggin, G., Campbell, A., McKenzie, K., Ridout, B., & Baylosis, C. (2019). Social connection and online engagement: Insights from interviews with users of a mental health online forum. *JMIR Mental Health*, 6(3), 1–13. https://doi.org/10.2196/11084

Virtanen, S. (2017). Fear of cybercrime in Europe: Examining the effects of victimization and vulnerabilities. *Psychiatry, Psychology and Law*, 24(3), 323–338. https://doi.org/10.1080/13218719.2017.1315785

Whitty, M. T. (2017). Do you love me? Psychological characteristics of romance scam victims. *Cyberpsychology, Behavior, and Social Networking*, 21(2), 105–109. http://dx.doi.org/10.1089/cyber.2016.0729

Whitty, M. T. (2019). Predicting susceptibility to cyber-fraud victimhood. *Journal of Financial Crime*, 26(2), 277–292. http://dx.doi.org/10.1108/JFC-10-2017-0095

Zhang-Kennedy, L., Assal, H., Rocheleau, J., Mohamed, R., Baig, K., & Chiasson, S. (2018, August 12–17). The aftermath of a crypto-ransomware attack at a large academic institution. In W. Enck & A. Porter Felt (Eds.), *SEC'18: Proceedings of the 27th USENIX Security Symposium* (pp. 1061–1078). USENIX Association.

CHAPTER 11

When Victims Strike Back: Online Fraud Victims' Response to their Victimization

Fyscillia Ream, Akim Laniel-Lanani, and Benoît Dupont

Abstract

Research on cybercrime victimization consistently concludes that victims experience similar impacts, such as negative financial, psychological, and emotional effects, and have the same needs as victims of traditional crime. However, these needs, such as social support, financial assistance, legal aid, and technical support, are often unmet, explaining why reporting rates of online fraud are low. As a result, victims and potential victims often turn to online forums and social networks to seek justice. Over the past forty years, crime prevention and control rhetoric have lowered community expectations about the state's ability to contain crime, leading citizens to take responsibility for protecting themselves and their property. This includes incorporating cybersecurity practices into daily routines and engaging in online vigilantism, or "digilantism." This informal justice-seeking movement can provide a sense of safety and self-confidence. This chapter examines how victims of online fraud leverage social media networks to seek justice. The results show that victims can mobilize against online fraud through digital vigilantism. Beyond simply reporting fraud, users turn to social media to expose fraudsters, seek retribution, and inform and raise awareness of online fraud. However, this chapter also reveals several challenges, such as distinguishing fraud and unethical practices, and discriminatory bias toward fraudsters. While this study highlights the attractions for digilantism practices, it also notes that Canada has a strong need for developing prevention and intervention strategies, as well as services offering emotional, psychological, and informational aid throughout the victimization journey.

The COVID-19 pandemic has accelerated individuals' reliance on online services and platforms to access essential goods and services (Ma & McKinnon, 2020). This reliance on online services offers new opportunities for fraudsters (Button & Cross, 2017; Cross et al., 2016a, 2016b). Despite its scale, severity of impact on victims, and issues with victim reporting, fraud, and more specifically cyberfraud, is one of the least studied crimes by researchers today (see, among others, Button et al., 2014; Cross et al., 2016a, 2016b). These issues are becoming more important considering that, in Canada, only an estimated 5 percent of fraud cases are reported (Canadian Anti-Fraud Centre [CAFC], 2022). This comes as no surprise, as scientific literature has consistently shown over several years that cybercrime victims report their experiences at a significantly lower rate than victims of traditional crimes, even though reporting rates for the latter are already relatively low (Yar & Steinmetz, 2019).

The increased victimization responses frequently accompanying online fraud and the absence of action from law enforcement and politicians exacerbate such harms. The apparent inability of the police to effectively combat online fraud and cybercrime has motivated certain individuals to take matters into their own hands and proactively address these issues. Digital vigilantism, or digilantism (Trottier, 2017), involves individuals collectively taking action against the crimes committed by others and responding through coordinated reprisals in digital domains, encompassing mobile devices and social media. Digilantism's behaviours include "scambaiting," the public exposure of criminal acts or breaches of social norms, as well as revenge-seeking, "naming and shaming" acts, "hacktivism," and more. This is by no means a new phenomenon; it is primarily attributable to the advancement of technology, which has the potential to facilitate and/or amplify certain types of criminality (Button & Cross, 2017). Social networking platforms, Web 2.0, and all other applications allow the Internet to offer various online interactions between people (Prins, 2010). As such, cybercrime victims have leveraged social media to find support and some form of justice through digilantism.

The chapter proceeds as follows: First, online fraud victimization is situated within the broader context of cybercrime. The discussion then examines in more detail how victim blaming and *responsibilization* are directed toward victims of online fraud. The chapter further explores how some victims are challenging such biases by developing resilience through digilantism and revenge-seeking initiatives.

11.1. Overview of Online Fraud Victimization

11.1.1. Cyberfraud Victimization Impacts

Cyber frauds are generally defined as all frauds "that exploit mass communication technologies" (Whitty, 2015, p. 84) such as email, instant messaging, or social networking platforms. This implies that victimization specific to this type of offending could be defined as: "The experience of a person who has responded, via the Internet, to a dishonest invitation, request, notification or offer by providing personal information or money, resulting in financial or non-financial loss or impact of some kind" (Cross et al., 2016a, p. 2).

This definition makes it possible to include victims who have not suffered financial loss but feel just as victimized as those who have lost money and may suffer psychological impacts just as severe (Whitty & Buchanan, 2016).

Studies on cybercrime victimization have all made the same finding: Victims experience the same impacts and have the same needs as victims of traditional crime (Button & Cross, 2017; Notté et al., 2021). Financial consequences tend to be one of the most significant impacts to victims. Depending on the victim, losses can range from tens to hundreds of thousands of dollars. In Canada, in 2021, the financial losses related to fraud amounted to nearly $379 million, an increase of 120 percent compared to 2020 (CAFC, 2022). The financial impact is not always proportional to the amount of money lost; participants who have lost considerable amounts of money may report minimal harm, whereas for those with smaller losses but living in economic insecurity, the consequences can be disastrous (Button et al., 2014; Cross et al., 2016a, 2016b). The financial loss victims suffer can also lead to indirect economic consequences, such as partial or total loss of their retirement pension, savings, and home.

(Button et al., 2009a, 2009b; Cross et al., 2016a; Notté et al., 2021; Titus et al., 1995.)

Cyber fraud has other negative effects on victims. In a study conducted by Button et al. (2014), 36.7 percent of participants rated their psychological and emotional impacts as severe or serious. According to several studies, victims describe a wide variety of psychological and emotional reactions following the fraud, including embarrassment, shame, guilt, sadness, anger, shock, hatred, anxiety, loss of self-esteem and self-confidence, loneliness, fear, depression and, post-traumatic stress (Notté et al., 2021). In addition, in the most severe cases across all frauds, many victims were exposed to suicidal thoughts and even acted on the impulse (Button et al., 2009b, 2014; Cross et al., 2016a; Whitty & Buchanan, 2016).

Finally, several studies also point to negative impacts on victims' relationships with their loved ones. For example, Button et al. (2009b) found that fraud against an individual resulted in serious relationship problems with their partner, family, and friends because financial losses may create severe tensions with those around them. Victims may also feel isolated from their families and loved ones due to the stigma they face (Cross, 2015).

11.1.2. Victims' Needs and the Reporting Experience

Regarding victims' needs, several authors have sought to better understand the needs and expectations of victims following the reporting of fraud to various institutions and organizations. Regarding emotional and psychological needs and expectations, most victims are generally concerned with being received with courtesy, dignity, and respect (Button et al. 2009b; Cross et al., 2016a; Leukfeldt et al., 2020). They also aspire to obtain a sympathetic and non-judgmental response, have their victimization acknowledged, and expect to be able to tell their story and be listened to (Button et al., 2009b; Cross et al., 2016a; Leukfeldt et al., 2020). In addition, regarding needs and expectations related to the criminal process, victims generally value receiving follow-up contact with authorities/officials, and being kept up-to-date and informed on the details of their case and any associated legal developments. In terms of financial needs and expectations, victims place a high value on being able to receive restitution or compensation for the money they have lost (Button et al., 2009b; Cross et al., 2016a; Leukfeldt et al., 2020). Finally, victims also expressed needs and expectations related to information sharing: Victims need to get a clear initial response from the organization about what they can expect regarding their case and how it will be handled, even if the response falls short of their expectations (Button et al., 2009b; Cross et al., 2016a; Leukfeldt et al., 2020). However, their experiences often indicate that the vast majority of them have been disappointed, frustrated, and angry with the police, felt the police had not met their needs and expectations, and often perceive this as an injustice (Cross, 2019; Cross & Blackshaw, 2015; Cross & Kelly, 2016; Leukfeldt et al., 2020). In addition to the police, victims of online fraud also turn to their financial institutions or credit bureaus to report their victimization, sometimes more frequently than to the police (Reynolds, 2022). Similarly to their experiences with the police, victims have expressed frustration when reporting to these other institutions, particularly due to the lack of assistance and information (Reynolds, 2024).

While similar to "traditional" crime, the needs and expectations of cybercrime victims are rarely met because victims are often never recognized as such, their complaints are often not addressed, and investigations are seldom initiated (Leukfeldt et al., 2020). This failure of agencies to adequately address the needs and expectations of cyber fraud victims can thus contribute to additional trauma, anger, and frustration (Cross, 2018). However, victims also overestimate the powers, resources, and capabilities of the agencies they turn to (Cross, 2018).

Finally, studies on the victimization experience of cybercrime victims showed that very few victims share their experiences with friends or family. When it comes to cybercrime, victims are often blamed for their own victimization, which affects their ability to share their experiences. In an offline context, support-seeking is a very effective way to successfully manage victimization. It helps to counteract negative emotional and psychological effects, and can provide victims with helpful information to prevent future incidents (De Kimpe et al., 2020). Before seeking support, victims must first go through three steps. First, they must recognize themselves as victims. Then, they must assess the seriousness of the crime. After these two steps, victims report their victimization to appropriate authorities or discuss the incident informally, such as within a support group (De Kimpe et al., 2020). Receiving more support helps to manage the aftermath of victimization, while maintaining or increasing self-esteem. In their study, Cross et al. (2016a, 2016b) show that victims of online fraud who sought professional support felt it was beneficial to receive help, advice, and reassurance.

11.2. Vigilantism, Digilantism, and Online Victimization

11.2.1. The Responsibilization Policy

The victimization experience explains why some victims turn to online communities to share their stories and seek recognition of the wrongdoing done to them (Powell et al., 2018; see also Cantin et al., 2024). For example, in cases of victims of domestic violence, Powell et al. (2018) argue that victims might use the Internet to share their experiences in private or semi-private forums. These virtual spaces allow victims to meet their personal needs, whether therapeutic or justice-seeking. One reason for communication via closed forums is because the criminal justice system is often perceived as failing victims of interpersonal violence. Similarly, victims of cybercrime feel that law enforcement agencies are not equipped to combat cybercrime and do not prosecute criminals. As a result, victims and potentially victimized individuals can take matters into their own hands using online forums and social networks (Prins, 2010). Another element is that they may also be motivated by what they see as a failure of online regulation (Button & Whittaker, 2021). For example, Button & Whittaker (2021) highlighted the failure of Internet governance such as the ICANN Registrar Accreditation Agreement, which requires domain registrars to address reports of abuse. The authors noted that Internet users argued that registrars are neglecting their duties by inadequately policing registrant data and refusing to take down fraudulent websites (Button & Whittaker, 2021).

According to Evans (2003), this phenomenon must be understood within the contemporary politics of active citizenship and "responsibilization." The rhetoric of crime prevention and control over the past forty years has sought to reduce community expectations about the ability of the state and its agents to contain crime and, conversely, has rendered citizens responsible for protecting themselves and their property (Garland, 1996). The responsibilization of citizens for crime prevention and control reflects a broader neoliberal turn in which states seek to shift responsibility to the private sector, communities, and individuals to provide solutions to problems previously thought to be the exclusive responsibility of central authorities (Monahan, 2009; Powell et al., 2018). Indeed, Whitson and Haggerty (2008) showed that this responsibilization policy is reflected in various entities' treatment of identity theft victims. One such initiative focuses specifically on encouraging citizens to change their routines to reduce the risk of victimization. Cybersecurity awareness efforts are thus, by extension, included in these types of accountability initiatives. For Whitson and Haggerty (2008), these policies lead to empowered and individualized forms of risk management. Such practices aim to establish forms of care for one's virtual self in which citizens are expected to incorporate security practices into their daily routines.

An underlying problem regarding this perspective of responsibilization is that judgment and responsibility are intertwined, and blame is a result affecting how victims are viewed (Sugiura & Smith, 2020). As such, when it comes to online fraud, there is a perpetual message that it is an individual's responsibility to avoid being scammed, rather than the responsibility of the perpetrator not to scam. Indeed, scammers and cybercriminals, in general, are often depicted as smart and resourceful, while victims are considered naive and greedy, and hence blamed for their own victimization (Cross, 2018).

11.2.2. From Vigilantism to Digilantism

When state institutions fail to address social issues or crime effectively, individuals may feel compelled to take matters into their own hands and assume a vigilante role to enforce what they perceive as justice. This phenomenon highlights the potential unintended consequences of overreliance on responsibilization policies in addressing complex societal problems. Vigilantism, according to Johnston (1996), includes six characteristics: 1) it involves planning and premeditation on the part of the actors involved; 2) its participants are private citizens whose engagement in vigilantism is voluntary and whose actions are not being supported by governmental bodies; 3) it is a form of autonomous citizenship and thus constitutes a social movement; 4) it uses, or threatens to use, violence; 5) it occurs when the established order is threatened with transgression or potential transgression; 6) it has the goal of controlling crime or other social offences by providing assurance or guarantees of safety to participants and others. For Moncada (2017), another important author on vigilantism, this phenomenon can be described as "the use or threat of use of extralegal violence in response to an alleged criminal act" (p. 408). Thus, for Moncada (2017), vigilantism is a collective action that involves violence, or the threat of violence, and takes place in response to an alleged crime that the state should have punished. Although Johnston's (1996) definition excludes individuals acting alone (which can be understood as revenge), it also excludes non-violent forms of response (such as naming and shaming). Moreover, the definition does not consider harms outside of state-bound territory or not legislated as a crime (Powell et al., 2018).

Scholars are engaged in a debate regarding the semantic parameters of vigilantism. Although this chapter does not seek to resolve this academic debate, it is worth noting that Silva (2018) emphasizes vigilantism as a reactionary response following social disruptions, rather than a preventive measure. Vigilantes, in this perspective, do not function as crime controllers. Consistent with the viewpoint presented by Haas (2010), Silva (2018) contends that the concept of vigilantism should be confined to reactions aimed at perceived criminal acts. Extending the definition of vigilantism to responses against non-criminal behaviours, such as the "#manspreading" movement on social media, it could potentially encompass anti-social actions that infringe upon essential rights. Both Haas (2010) and Silva (2018) assert that determining societal norms and socially acceptable behaviour cannot be the sole prerogative of a limited group of citizens.

The proliferation of web technologies has allowed vigilantism to expand into the online space, where the development of social media platforms has increased the visibility of certain types of misbehaviour (Dunsby & Howes, 2019). Vigilantism appears to be facilitated by various characteristics of the Internet, such as its interconnectedness and lack of institutional control mechanisms. Several concepts have emerged to discuss the phenomenon of online vigilantism. Smallridge et al. (2016) expanded upon Johnston's (1996) notion and introduced the concept of cyber vigilantism, stating that cyber vigilantism often involves widespread retaliation and collaborative endeavours, grouping individuals who react to perceived criminal acts recursively. The application of force in this context is rarely physical but, instead, takes the form of digital retaliation inflicted on the alleged wrongdoer's online identity and reputation.

Silva (2018) focused on restoring cybersecurity and trust in digital realms by proposing the term "cybersecurity vigilantism." This refers to a "social movement composed of individuals or groups who employ technical means to counter perceived criminal actions against Internet security and information systems" (p. 24). However, this definition primarily refers to individuals possessing the technical capability to respond, which overlooks avenues more accessible to the general populace. For Silva (2018), cybersecurity vigilantes primarily consist of adept individuals who utilize their technical expertise in computer science and engineering to retaliate against crimes targeting information systems and to rectify cybersecurity breaches. Huey et al. (2012) introduced the term "civilian policing" to describe "forms of collaborative online action aimed at pooling resources to investigate cybercrimes and furnish information to law enforcement" (p. 83), and focused solely on online community initiatives that actively support public law enforcement efforts.

Considering these perspectives, the concept of "digilantism" formulated by Trottier (2017) gains prominence. This process involves citizens collectively taking offence at the actions of fellow citizens and responding through coordinated reprisals in digital domains, encompassing platforms like mobile devices and social media. The transgressions that trigger these reactions range from minor breaches of social norms to more severe acts like terrorism and participation in riots. Importantly, these offensive actions typically do not seek extensive recognition on a large scale. With digilantism, citizen vigilantes seek a form of informal justice and recognition outside the formal justice system operated by governments (Powell et al., 2018; Trottier, 2017). Interesting records of digilantism can be found in citizen initiatives for victims of crime that aim to establish a sense of safety and self-confidence or a kind of "eye-for-an-eye" revenge (Prins, 2010). Actors in digilantism may be more or less coordinated and quickly emerge as a group or be highly organized and collectively maintained (Powell et al., 2018). Some practices may be spontaneous, such as capturing or uploading content, and commenting or sharing content. Other actions require deliberate planning, such as managing a digital presence, creating private pages or groups on social media, or coordinating a whistleblowing operation (Trottier, 2017). Digilantism refers to collaborative practices but can also arise from individual initiatives. It can also occur in collaboration with legitimate authorities or, on the contrary, replace them in some instances, such as for surveillance (Loveluck, 2016).

11.3. Fighting Cyberfraud on Facebook

11.3.1. Digitalism and Online Fraud

At the time of writing, very few studies on digilantism and cybercrime seem to have been conducted, with only a few of these studies focused on scambaiting (Button, 2020; Cross & Mayers, 2021; Sorell, 2019). According to Sorell (2019), scambaiting is one of the many forms of digilantism and has mainly been used to denounce and arrest pedophiles online. In those cases, the scambaiter poses as a child and initiates a dialogue with pedophiles to coerce them into arranging a meeting with the putative child, with whom they believe to be in communication (Sorell, 2019). In regard to online fraud, scambaiting has been widely used to uncover 419 scams[1] and there are several online forums dedicated to this pursuit (Button & Whittaker, 2021; Byrne, 2013; Sorell, 2019).[2]

Unlike scambaiting, digilantism initiatives against online fraud do not seek to interact with fraudsters but rather seek to expose, raise awareness, report, and educate individuals against online fraud (Button & Whittaker, 2021). A French study (Benbouzid & Paucellier, 2016) focused on victims of online fraud and how online forums allow for a space to voice their emotions. It showed that victims of fraudulent business practices, such as online shopping websites, were angrier and more vocal in demanding justice and reparation. In contrast, victims of scams such as advance-fee fraud or romance scams were more measured as they were looking for recognition of their victimization and to demonstrate the absence of responsibility for what happened to them. Similarly, Cantin et al. (2024) showed that victims of romance scams leveraged online communities to support one another, share their experiences, and offer guidance to fellow victims. In neither study did the victims aspire to pursue the scammers themselves or seek revenge.

Numerous studies have explored the use of social media by victims of cybercrime, especially in cases of sexual offences and misogyny (Powell et al., 2018; Sugiura & Smith, 2020). Victims leverage these platforms predominantly to share personal experiences,

---

1.   "419 scam," also known as advance-fee scam, involves persuading a victim to pay a sum of money with the false promise of receiving a much larger amount later. Its name comes from the article in the Nigerian Criminal Code that prohibits obtaining property through false pretenses (Kapersky IT Encyclopedia, n.d.).

2.   See 419eater.com for additional information.

publicly shame offenders, and seek some semblance of justice. Several groups have emerged to discuss the problems with online fraud. The rise of online sites dedicated to exposing fraudsters can be seen as a grassroots response to the increasing prevalence of fraudulent activities in today's digital age. These activities encompass a wide range of issues, including online scams, financial fraud, and unethical practices, and can be found by anyone on social media through a keyword search. Some pages or groups focus on general scams, while others focus on more specialized or particular forms of fraud. Some pages or groups are "public" (open to everyone), "closed" (the site's moderators must approve you to join), or "private" (only available to members and not available to view without an invitation). These forums function as a form of digilantism and empower users to not only report fraud, but also to act against alleged wrongdoers. The inclination of online fraud victims to resort to social media platforms is unsurprising, and this tendency is supported by research. Van de Wijer et al. (2020) conducted a hypothetical study that revealed participants were more inclined to report offences to organizations rather than the police, except in cases of identity theft. These findings align with the earlier discussion of barriers victims face when reporting cybercrime. As individuals and consumers encounter these challenges daily, they often find themselves searching for ways to protect themselves and others from falling victim to such scams.

11.3.2. Leveraging Facebook Against Cyberfraud

The focus of this study is on francophone Facebook pages (n=30) and public and private groups (n=66) dedicated to exposing fraudsters. A series of keywords were listed (such as *arnaque* [scam], *escroquerie* [scam], *fraude* [fraud], and more) to identify relevant pages and groups on the platform. Since several pages were created more than ten years ago and are still active, the period of focus is March 2020, the point in time when the World Health Organization officially declared COVID-19 a pandemic. This period of time was selected as rates of online fraud have grown exponentially with the pandemic (Buil-Gil et al., 2020; Kemp et al., 2021). Posts and comments were collected through a Facebook scraper using the Python software language, and qualitative content was analyzed with NVivo to identify themes. Data collection ended on October 31, 2022.

This research reveals several noteworthy findings that will be elaborated on below. First, these pages align with forms of digilantism aimed at exposing fraudsters and seeking retribution. Second, these pages also inform and raise awareness among their members about various types of fraud, methods used by fraudsters, and their persuasion strategies. Third, analysis of different pages highlights the challenge of distinguishing between fraud and unethical practices. Finally, the results also indicate a distinct discriminatory bias toward fraudsters by assuming they originate from sub-Saharan African countries.

11.3.2.1. Exposing Scammers and Revenge Seeking

Due to the prominent nature of these denunciation platforms, they align more closely with Trottier's digilantism concept (2017). This involves activities such as gathering information about the scammer, publicly naming and shaming alleged culprits, and attempting to thwart their actions through tactics like scambaiting. Such an example can be seen in Figure 11.1, representing a picture of an alleged scammer impersonating an Italian businessman. In this instance, vigilantes revealed the scammer's identity behind the fake profile. In some other cases, several Facebook pages and groups were found that specifically aimed at scambaiting (e.g., "Les chasseurs de brouteurs" group).[3]

Ultimately, these groups seek a sense of justice that they perceive as lacking from formal authorities. In the context of these pages, users adopt roles similar to vigilantes by independently investigating and publicizing alleged fraudulent activities. In this case, a deep sense of moral outrage and desire for justice are powerful motivators.

11.3.2.2. Inform and Raise Awareness

While these groups are established with the intention to expose scammers, an analysis of user posts and comments reveals that their underlying goal is often to seek advice for reimbursement or assistance. Many victims still feel powerless against scammers, even when

---

3.   Translation: "Scammer hunters." *Brouteur* is an Ivorian French term to designate a scammer. The word refers to a sheep that feeds effortlessly and to the expression *couper l'herbe sous le pied* (pull the rug out from under you), which means to steal or to deceive.

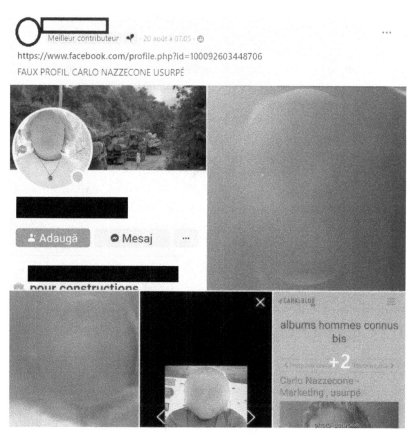

Figure 11.1. Screenshot of a post from a member showing the scammer's identity and the fake profile used.
Source: Facebook.

receiving support from other users. As such, these dedicated pages serve as virtual forums where users share information about fraudulent activities. Users post detailed accounts of their encounters with alleged fraudsters, providing insights into the tactics and methods used by these wrongdoers. They also share evidence, such as screenshots, transaction records, and correspondence, to substantiate their claims. Users believe that sharing their experiences and evidence can help others recognize and avoid falling prey to scams or unethical practices. This collective awareness-raising effort empowers individuals to make more informed decisions and protect themselves in an increasingly complex digital landscape.

11.3.2.3. Cyberfraud and Unethical Practices: A Blurred Line

One of the significant challenges associated with Facebook pages that expose fraudsters is the blurred line between actual fraud and unethical practices. Users often confuse questionable business practices with outright fraud, leading to potentially false accusations. This challenge stems from a lack of understanding or differentiation between fraudulent activities and practices that may be considered unethical, but not necessarily illegal. Fraud is a legally defined term encompassing a broad range of deceptive activities intended to secure an unfair or unlawful financial gain. It often involves misrepresentation, concealment of information, or the abuse of trust.

Le mariage gris : La fraude aux sentiments

Figure 11.2. The *Mariage gris* group likens marriage fraud to romance scam.
Source : Facebook.

However, unethical practices can involve business matters, such as aggressive marketing tactics or poor customer service, or judicial matters, such as *mariage gris* (marriage fraud), among others.[4] Regarding unethical business practices, several pages and groups were created to denounce poor customer service, which users considered fraudulent (e.g., groups "Arnaque Evollis-Samsung"[5] and "Cdiscount Arnaque et escroquerie").[6] For example, users would complain about a lack of communication from companies or no exchange policies. As for marriage fraud, users tend to liken it to romance fraud, or *mariage gris* (see Figure 11.2). While both

---

4.   "Romance fraud" involves exploiting the appearance of a genuine relationship to deceive an individual for financial gain (Cross, 2022). Victims of romance fraud are usually not aware of the scam. In contrast, "marriage fraud" is the act of entering into a marriage to circumvent immigration laws to gain benefits, such as obtaining citizenship, permanent residency, or a visa in a particular country (Government of Canada, 2023). This can involve both parties knowingly agreeing to the arrangement or one party deceiving the other.

5.   Evollis is a company associated with Samsung in France that offers phone trade-ins in exchange for a sum of money. Many customers have expressed dissatisfaction with the service, claiming they were deceived when sending their phones and receiving a trade-in value lower than expected.

6.   Cdiscount is an online shop.

types of fraud involve a partner with hidden intentions, in the case of romance fraud, scammers hide their identity, and they are not interested in immigrating to the country of their "significant other."

One of the primary reasons users struggle to differentiate between fraud and unethical practices is the subjective nature of the assessment. What one person considers an unethical practice may be perceived by another as standard industry behaviour. This subjectivity can lead to inconsistencies in identifying and denouncing fraudulent activities online. Users of these pages may inadvertently accuse individuals or businesses of fraudulent behaviour when, in reality, they are only guilty of unethical commercial practices.

11.3.2.4. Reinforcing Stereotypes and Discriminatory Biases

Finally, another concerning aspect of some of these Facebook pages is the tendency to target specific regions, such as Africa, when exposing fraudsters. Posts and comments on these pages sometimes perpetuate harmful stereotypes and generalize entire regions or communities as hotbeds of fraudulent activity. Such generalizations not only fuel misinformation but also contribute to prejudice and discrimination. It reflects a bias that assumes fraudulent activities are more prevalent in certain areas than others without sufficient evidence to support such claims. Users on these pages portray certain areas as inherently dishonest or prone to fraudulent activities. For instance, several of these pages use the pejorative term *brouteur* as a label, referring to sub-Saharan African scammers to generalize the fraudsters mentioned on this page as originating from this region. A clear example is the social media page in Figure 11.3.

Such generalizations perpetuate misleading stereotypes about the origins of scammers. The tendency to focus on specific regions can lead to confirmation bias, where users seek information confirming their preconceived notions about fraud. This confirmation bias can result in the disproportionate exposure of cases from targeted regions while overlooking fraud occurring elsewhere. This is not uncommon in digilantism practices, where the wrong individual can be identified and wrongly accused of misconduct (Nhan et al. 2017). Moreover, several recent studies on cybercrime have shown that fraudsters operate within local markets and can often successfully target local victims (Lusthaus, 2018). Montreal, for example, is known to be a thriving hub for online fraudsters in Quebec and Canada (Holt et al., 2016; Joncas, 2022).

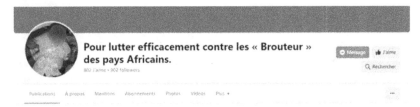

Figure 11.3. Social media page targeting African scammers.[7]
Source: Facebook.

11.4. From Victim Blaming to Victim Empowerment

The responsibilization policy plays a significant role in driving victims toward online communities as a means to unmask scammers. In response, digilantism emerges as an effective remedy. Not only does it shed light on the blame attributed to victims through responsibilization policies, but it also empowers them to take matters into their own hands, essentially strengthening existing forms of vigilantism. While traditional forms of vigilantism persist, they have been ineffective in crime control and prevention. In the digital sphere, these online platforms manifest as a form of digital vigilantism against fraudulent activities, underscoring the influence of collective action in our interconnected world. However, similar challenges associated with vigilantism extend to the digital domain. There is a potential risk for proliferation of false accusations and misinformation, necessitating user caution to ensure the accuracy and well-documented nature of the information they share to prevent harm to innocent parties. Additionally, there are regulatory concerns surrounding these platforms, including the tampering of evidence that could be pertinent to a police or judicial case. Lastly, as evidenced in this study, despite users' good intentions, biases and discrimination, including racial discrimination, can surface and reinforce stereotypes and biases.

Addressing online fraud victimization demands a comprehensive strategy that places victim support, public education, and digital safety at the forefront. It is imperative to initiate public awareness campaigns that empower victims to report cybercrimes without fear of blame or culpability, while emphasizing the essential provision of dedicated support services. Such services already exist for victims of traditional criminal acts, such as the Centre d'aide aux victimes d'actes

---

7.   Translation: "To fight effectively against scammers from African countries."

criminel (CAVAC) in Quebec, but these organizations do not have sufficient resources to develop services for victims of cybercrime. Canada urgently needs services offering emotional, psychological, and informational aid throughout the victimization journey. Concurrently, law enforcement agencies must undergo comprehensive training to enhance their understanding of cybercrime dynamics and the unique challenges faced by victims. Ensuring transparency regarding law enforcement's capacity to investigate cybercrime is vital in managing victim expectations and needs effectively. Finally, one of the main attractions explaining the rise of digilantism practices is the offering of agency to Internet users and victims who may feel helpless against well-organized scammers. Government agencies should consider developing prevention and intervention strategies that could harness this untapped resource and manage it appropriately. For instance, they could promote fraud and cybersecurity awareness on platforms where digilantism occurs, directly targeting these users. This holistic approach is instrumental in effectively combatting the escalating problem of online fraud while providing necessary support and justice to victims, thus mitigating their reliance on unregulated online communities.

References

Benbouzid, B., & Paucellier, S. (2016). L'escroquerie sur Internet: La plainte et la prise de parole publique des victimes. *Réseaux, 197–198*, 137–171. https://doi.org/10.3917/res.197.0137

Buil-Gil, D., Miró-Llinares, F., Moneva, A., Kemp, S., & Díaz-Castaño, N. (2020). Cybercrime and shifts in opportunities during COVID-19: A preliminary analysis in the UK. *European Societies, 23*(1), S47–S59. http://dx.doi.org/10.1080/14616696.2020.1804973

Button, M. (2020). The "new" private security industry, the private policing of cyberspace and the regulatory questions. *Journal of Contemporary Criminal Justice, 36*(1), 39–55. https://doi.org/10.1177/1043986219890194

Button, M., & Cross, C. (2017). Technology and fraud: The "fraudogenic" consequences of the Internet revolution. In M. R. McGuire & T. Holt (Eds.), *The Routledge handbook of technology, crime and justice* (pp. 78–95). Routledge International Handbooks.

Button, M., Lewis, C., & Tapley, J. (2009a). *Fraud typologies and the victims of fraud literature review*. National Fraud Authority. http://www2.port.ac.uk/media/contacts-and-departments/icjs/ccfs/Fraud-typologies-andvictims.pdf

Button, M., Lewis, C., & Tapley, J. (2009b). *A better deal for fraud victims: Research into victims' needs and experiences*. National Fraud Authority. https://researchportal.port.ac.uk/portal/files/1924328/NFA_Report_1_15.12.09.pdf

Button, M., Lewis, C., & Tapley, J. (2014). Not a victimless crime: The impact of fraud on individual victims and their families. *Security Journal, 27*(1), 36–54. https://doi.org/10.1057/sj.2012.11

Button, M., & Whittaker, J. (2021). Exploring the voluntary response to cyber-fraud: From vigilantism to responsibilisation. *International Journal of Law, Crime and Justice, 66*(3), 100482. https://doi.org/10.1016/j.ijlcj.2021.100482

Byrne, D. N. (2013). 419 digilantes and the frontier of radical justice online. *Radical History Review, 117*, 70–82. http://dx.doi.org/10.1215/01636545-2210464

Canadian Anti-Fraud Centre. (2022). *Annual report 2021*. https://www.antifraudcentre-centreantifraude.ca/annual-reports-2021-rapports-annuels-en.htm

Cross, C. (2015). No laughing matter: Blaming the victim of online fraud. *International Review of Victimology, 21*(2), 187–204. https://doi.org/10.1177/0269758015571471

Cross, C. (2018). Expectations vs reality: Responding to online fraud across the fraud justice network. *International Journal of Law, Crime and Justice, 55*, 1–12. . https://doi.org/10.1016/j.ijlcj.2018.08.001

Cross, C. (2019). "Oh we can't actually do anything about that": The problematic nature of jurisdiction for online fraud victims. *Criminology & Criminal Justice, 20*(3), 358–375. https://doi.org/10.1177/1748895819835910

Cross, C. (2022). A guide to understanding romance fraud. *QUT Centre for Justice Briefing Papers, 22*. https://doi.org/10.5204/book.eprints.233966

Cross, C., & Blackshaw, D. (2015). Improving the police response to online fraud. *Policing, 9*(2), 119–128. https://doi.org/10.1093/police/pau044

Cross, C., & Kelly, M. (2016). The problem of "white noise": Examining current prevention approaches to online fraud. *Journal of Financial Crime, 23*(4), 806–818. https://doi.org/10.1108/JFC-12-2015-0069

Cross, C., & Mayers, D. (2021). Scambaiter narratives of victims and offenders and their influence on the policing of fraud. *Policing, 15*(4), 2148–2164. https://doi.org/10.1093/police/paaa050

Cross, C., Richards, K., & Smith, R. G. (2016a). The reporting experiences and support needs of victims of online fraud. *Trends and Issues in Crime and Criminal Justice, 518*, 1–14. https://aic.gov.au/publications/tandi/tandi518

Cross, C., Richards, K., & Smith, R. G. (2016b). *Improving the response to online fraud: An examination of reporting and support: Final Report*. Criminology Research Grant, Australian Institute of Criminology. http://www.crg.aic.gov.au/reports/1617/29-1314-FinalReport.pdf

De Kimpe, L., Ponnet, K., Walrave, M., Snaphaan, T., Pauwels, L., & Hardyns, W. (2020). Help, I need somebody: Examining the antecedents of social support seeking among cybercrime victims. *Computers in Human Behavior, 108*(3), 106310. https://doi.org/10.1016/j.chb.2020.106310

Dunsby, R. M., & Howes, L. M. (2019). The NEW adventures of the digital vigilante! Facebook users' views on online naming and shaming. *Australian & New Zealand Journal of Criminology, 52*(4), 41–59. http://dx.doi.org/10.1177/0004865818778736

Evans, J. (2003). Vigilance and vigilantes: Thinking psychoanalytically about anti-pedophile action. *Theoretical Criminology, 7*(2), 163–189. http://dx.doi.org/10.1177/1362480603007002416

Garland, D. (1996). The limits of the sovereign state: Strategies of crime control in contemporary society. *British Journal of Criminology, 36*(4), 445–471. https://doi.org/10.1093/oxfordjournals.bjc.a014105

Goverment of Canada. (2023). Immigration marriage fraud. Retrieved from https://www.canada.ca/en/immigration-refugees-citizenship/services/protect-fraud/marriage-fraud.html

Haas, N. E. (2010). *Public support for vigilantism* [Doctoral dissertation]. Universiteit Leiden: Netherlands Institute for the Study of Crime and Law Enforcement (NSCR).

Holt, T. J., Smirnova, O., & Hutchings, A. (2016). Examining signals of trust in criminal markets online. *Journal of Cybersecurity, 2*(2), 137–145. https://doi.org/10.1093/cybsec/ty

Huey, L., Nhan, J., & Broll, R. (2012). "Uppity civilians" and "cyber-vigilantes": The role of the general public in policing cyber-crime. *Criminology & Criminal Justice, 13*(1), 81–97. http://dx.doi.org/10.1177/1748895812448086

Johnston, L. (1996). What is vigilantism? *British Journal of Criminology, 36*(2), 220–236. https://doi.org/10.1093/oxfordjournals.bjc.a014083

Joncas, H. (2022, March 16). Montréal au cœur de l'écosystème de la fraude en ligne. *La Presse.* https://www.lapresse.ca/affaires/2022-03-16/cybersecurite/montreal-au-coeur-de-l-ecosysteme-de-la-fraude-en-ligne.php#

Kapersky IT Encyclopedia. (n.d). 419 Scam. Retrieved August 22, 2022 from https://encyclopedia.kaspersky.com/glossary/419-scam/

Kemp, S., Buil-Gil, D., Moneva, A., Miró-Llinares, F., & Díaz-Castaño. (2021). Empty streets, busy Internet. A time series analysis of cybercrime and fraud trends during COVID-19. *Journal of Contemporary Criminal Justice, 37*(4), 480–501. https://doi.org/10.1177/10439862211027986

Leukfeldt, E. R., Notté, R. J., & Malsch, M. (2020). Exploring the needs of victims of cyber-dependent and cyber-enabled crimes. *Victims & Offenders, 15*(1), 60–77. https://doi.org/10.1080/15564886.2019.1672229

Loveluck, B. (2016). Le vigilantisme numérique, entre dénonciation et sanction : Auto-justice en ligne et agencements de la visibilité. *Politix, 115*(3), 127–153. http://dx.doi.org/10.3917/pox.115.0127

Lusthaus, J. (2018). *Industry of anonymity: Inside the business of cybercrime.* Harvard University Press. https://doi.org/10.4159/9780674989047

Ma, K. W. F., & McKinnon, T. (2020). COVID-19 and cyber fraud: Emerging threats during the pandemic. *Journal of Financial Crime, 29*(2), 433–446. http://dx.doi.org/10.2139/ssrn.3718845

Monahan, T. (2009). Identity theft vulnerability: Neoliberal governance through crime construction. *Theoretical Criminology, 13*(2), 155–176. http://dx.doi.org/10.1177/1362480609102877

Moncada, E. (2017). Varieties of vigilantism: Conceptual discord, meaning and strategies. *Global Crime, 18*(4), 403–423 http://dx.doi.org/10.1080/1 7440572.2017.1374183

Nhan, J., Huey, L., & Broll, R. (2017). Digilantism: An Analysis of Crowdsourcing and the Boston Marathon Bombings. *The British Journal of Criminology, 57*(2), 341–361, https://doi.org/10.1093/bjc/azv118

Notté, R., Leukfelt, E. R., & Malsch, M. (2021). Double, triple or quadruple hits? Exploring the impact of cybercrime on victims in the Netherlands. *International Review of Victimology, 27*(8), 272–294. https://doi.org/10. 1177/0269758021101069

Powell, A., Stratton, G., & Cameron, R. (2018). *Digital criminology: Crime and justice in digital society.* Routledge.

Prins, C. (2010). The online dimension of recognized victims' rights. *Computer Law & Security Review, 26*(2), 219–221. http://dx.doi.org/10.1016/j.clsr.2010. 01.005

Reynolds, D. (2022). Decisions, decisions: An analysis of identity theft victims' reporting to police, financial institutions, and credit bureaus. *Victims & Offenders, 18*(7), 1373–1400. https://doi.org/10.1080/15564886.2022.21281 29

Reynolds, D. (2024). "Screaming into the void": Canadians' experiences reporting identity theft. *Canadian Journal of Criminology and Criminal Justice, 66*(1), 87–106. https://muse.jhu.edu/article/935667

Silva, E. K. K. (2018). Vigilantism and cooperative criminal justice: Is there a place for cybersecurity vigilantes in cybercrime fighting? *International Review of Law, Computers & Technology, 32*(1), 21–36. http://dx.doi.org/10 .1080/13600869.2018.1418142

Smallridge, J., Wagner, P., Crowl, J. N. (2016). Understanding cyber-vigilantism: A conceptual framework. *Journal of Theoretical & Philosophical Criminology,* 8(1), 57–70. http://www.jtpcrim.org/2016February/Smallridge.pdf

Sorell, T. (2019). Scambaiting on the spectrum of digilantism. *Criminal Justice Ethics, 38*(2), 153–175. http://dx.doi.org/10.1080/0731129X.2019.1681132

Sugiura, L., & Smith, A. (2020). Victim blaming, responsibilization and resilience in online sexual abuse and harassment. In J. Tapley & P. Davies (Eds.), *Victimology: research, policy and activism* (pp. 45–79). Palgrave Macmillan. http://dx.doi.org/10.1007/978-3-030-42288-2_3

Titus, R. M., Heinzelmann, F., & Boyle, J. M. (1995). Victimization of persons by fraud. *Crime & Delinquency*, *41*(1), 54–72. https://doi.org/10.1177/0011128795041001004

Trottier, D. (2017). Digital vigilantism as weaponisation of visibility. *Philosophy & Technology*, *30*(1), 55–72. https://link.springer.com/article/10.1007/s13347-016-0216-4

Van de Weijer, S. G. A., Leukfeldt, E. R., & Van der Zee, S. (2020). Reporting cybercrime victimization: Determinants, motives, and previous experiences. *Policing: An International Journal*, *43*(1), 17–34. https://doi.org/10.1108/PIJPSM-07-2019-0122

Whitson, J., & Haggerty, K. D. (2008). Identity theft and the care of the virtual self. *Economy and Society*, *37*(4), 572–594. http://dx.doi.org/10.1080/03085140802357950

Whitty, M. T. (2015). Mass-marketing fraud: A growing concern. *IEEE Security & Privacy*, *13*(4), 84–87. https://doi.org/10.1109/MSP.2015.85

Whitty, M. T., & Buchanan, T. (2016). The online dating romance scam: The psychological impact on victims—both financial and non-financial. *Criminology & Criminal Justice*, *16*(2), 176–194. https://doi.org/10.1177/1748895815603773

Yar, M., & Steinmetz, K. F. (2019*). Cybercrime and society (3rd edition)*. SAGE Publications.

Biographies

Editors

Emily B. Laidlaw is the Canada Research Chair in Cybersecurity Law and an Associate Professor in the Faculty of Law at the University of Calgary. She is also a Senior Fellow at the Centre for International Governance Innovation, an Associate Member of the University of Ottawa's Centre for Law, Technology and Society and a Fellow of the Centre for Military, Security and Strategic Studies. Her research centres on technology regulation, cybersecurity, and human rights, with particular emphasis on platform regulation, privacy, online harms, freedom of expression, and corporate governance.

Florian Martin-Bariteau is the University Research Chair in Technology and Society and an Associate Professor in the Faculty of Law, Common Law Section at the University of Ottawa, where he is the director of the Centre for Law, Technology and Society. He is co-investigator of the Human-Centric Cybersecurity Partnership where he leads the "Transparency and Accountability" stream and also a Faculty Associate of the Berkman-Klein Center for Internet and Society at Harvard University.

Contributors

Amarnath Amarasingam is an Assistant Professor in the School of Religion, and is cross-appointed to the Department of Political Studies, at Queen's University. He is also Senior Fellow at the International Centre for the Study of Radicalisation. His research interests are terrorism, radicalization and extremism, online communities, diaspora politics, post-war reconstruction, and the sociology of religion.

Jane Bailey is a Full Professor in the Faculty of Law, Common Law Section, at the University of Ottawa, where she teaches Cyberfeminism, Technoprudence, and Contracts. She co-leads the eQuality Project, a seven-year SSHRC-funded partnership grant focused on young people's experiences in digitally networked environments and is a working group co-leader on the Autonomy Through Cyberjustice Technologies Project, a four-year SSHRC-funded partnership grant focused on the use of technology to improve access to justice. Her research focuses on TFV, particularly as perpetrated through algorithmic profiling and other practices of technology corporations and governments. She co-edited *The Emerald International Handbook on Technology-Facilitated Violence and Abuse*, an open access publication.

Jacquelyn Burkell is a Full Professor in the Faculty of Information and Media Studies at the University of Western Ontario. Her research focuses on the social implications of technology, with particular reference to privacy and equality impacts. She is a co-investigator on two SSHRC Partnership grants focused on the implications of technology: the eQuality Project, co-led by Jane Bailey and Valerie Steeves, and the Autonomy Through Cyberjustice Project, where she co-leads a working group with Jane Bailey. Her research focuses on the social implications of technology, with particular attention to issues of privacy and autonomy.

Matthew Bush is a master's student at Toronto Metropolitan University studying computer science. He also has a background in business technology management, which provides him with a unique perspective to bridge the gap between technology and people. His current research is focused on adjusting state-of-the-art organizational cybersecurity practices to the unique needs of consumer IoT environments. This includes creating access control schemes for smart homes that give individual users more control over their own data. His other research interests include secure and privacy-preserving AI, zero-trust architecture, and privacy-preserving technologies.

Pascale-Marie Cantin holds a master's degree in Criminology, with a specialization in forensics and information, from the Université de Montréal, and a certificate in Cyberinvestigation from École Polytechnique. During her studies, she was particularly interested in economic crime and the dynamics between human beings and technology. Having graduated in 2021, she is currently a stock market crime investigator.

Benoît Dupont is a Professor of Criminology at the Université de Montreal, where he holds the Canada Research Chair in Cyber-Resilience and the Endowed Research Chair for the Prevention of Cybercrime. He is the Scientific Director of the Human-Centric Cybersecurity Partnership, an interdisciplinary network of academic, government, and industry partners.

Sébastien Gambs is the Canada Research Chair in Privacy and Ethical Analysis of Massive Data and a Professor in the Department of Computer Science at the Université du Québec à Montréal. His main research theme is privacy in the digital world. He is also interested in solving long-term scientific questions such as the existing tensions between massive data analysis and privacy as well as ethical issues such as fairness, transparency, and algorithmic accountability raised by personalized systems.

Nick Gertler is a master's student in Media Studies at Concordia University.

Akim Laniel-Lanani is Director and Cofounder of the Cybercriminology Clinic (*Clinique de cyber-criminologie*), where he is in charge of the everyday activities and the supervision of the student volunteer team. With a bachelor's degree in security and police studies from the School of Criminology at the Université de Montréal, he is also a candidate for the Certified Financial Crime Specialist certification.

Jordan Loewen-Colón is the former AI, Ethics, and Data Justice Fellow at Queen's University and teaches AI and policy at the Smith

2

20 THE SECURITY OF SELF

School of Business. His research looks at philosophy, religion, and digital technology such as virtual reality and artificial intelligence to answer questions about what it means to be and feel like a human in the twenty-first century.

Atefeh Mashatan is the Canada Research Chair in Quality of Security (QoS) Framework and an Associate Professor at the Ted Rogers School of Information Technology Management and Founder and Director of the Cybersecurity Research Lab at Toronto Metropolitan University (formerly Ryerson University). Her research is focused on the development of novel cybersecurity designs based on emerging technologies. She investigates challenges and opportunities brought forward by these new technologies and how they change the threat landscape of cybersecurity. Her expertise at the frontlines of the global cybersecurity field was recognized by SC Magazine in 2019, when she was named one of the top five Women of Influence in Security globally.

Fenwick McKelvey is an Associate Professor of Information and Communication Technology Policy in the Department of Communication Studies at Concordia University. He is Associate Director of the Milieux Institute and former Co-Director of the Applied AI Institute.

Alex Megelas is Manager, Research Innovation and Business Development at the Applied AI Institute at Concordia University.

Adam Molnar is an Assistant Professor of Sociology and Legal Studies and a member of the Cybersecurity and Privacy Institute at the University of Waterloo. His research involves a multidisciplinary approach, using theoretical approaches and methods from social theory, computer science, law, and socio-legal studies. At present, he is principal investigator of a multi-year, SSHRC-funded project on employee monitoring applications and the regulation of workplace surveillance and privacy in Canada.

Sharday Mosurinjohn is Associate Professor of Contemporary Religious Context at Queen's University. She studies the discursive construction of spirituality and religion as well as concepts of nonreligion and secularity; specific interests include the study of "new religious movements," ritual, and religion and/as media. Her broad interest in the material turn touches on contexts of contemporary (especially conceptual) art, museums, everyday aesthetics, digital contexts (e.g., social media and surveillance cultures), and affect.

Jonathon Penney is a legal scholar and social scientist with expertise at the intersection of law, technology, and human rights. He is an Associate Professor at Osgoode Hall Law School, ork Research Chair in Artificial Intelligence, Data Governance, and the Law, Faculty Associate at Harvard's Berkman Klein Center for Internet & Society, and Research Fellow at the Citizen Lab based at the University of Toronto's Munk School of Global Affairs and Public Policy. His work on privacy, security, and technology law and policy has received national and international coverage, including in CBC, *The Globe and Mail*, *The Washington Post*, *Reuters*, *The New York Times*, WIRED, *The Guardian*, and *Le Monde*, among others.

Fyscillia Ream is a PhD candidate in Criminology at the Université de Montreal. She is also the Scientific Coordinator at the Research Chair in Cybercrime Prevention and Cofounder of the Cyberminology Clinic (*Clinique de cyber-criminologie*). While her dissertation lies at the intersection of organizational deviance and insider threat, she has developed expertise in cybercrime victimization.

Teresa Scassa is the Canada Research Chair in Information Law and Policy and a Full Professor in the Faculty of Law, Common Law Section at the University of Ottawa, where she is a member of the Centre for Law, Technology and Society. Her research addresses digital and data governance issues. She has written widely in the areas of privacy law, data governance, intellectual property law, law and technology, artificial intelligence, and smart cities. She is co-editor of the books *AI and the Law in Canada* (2021), *Law and the Sharing Economy* (2017), and *The Future of Open Data* (2022), and co-author of *Digital Commerce in Canada* (2020) and *Canadian Intellectual Property Law* (2022).

Chris Tenove is the Assistant Director of the Centre for the Study of Democratic Institutions and a researcher and instructor in the School of Public Policy & Global Affairs at the University of British Columbia. He writes on the challenges that digital media pose to democracy and human rights, focusing on topics such as electoral disinformation, social media regulation, and online harassment of politicians and health communicators. He has published policy reports, book chapters, and peer-reviewed articles in journals including *Political Communication, Political Research Quarterly,* and *International Journal of Press/Politics.*

Kristen Thomasen is an Associate Professor and Senior Chair of Law, Robotics and Society at the University of Windsor's Faculty of Law. Her research and teaching focus on the regulation of automated technologies, privacy, and tort law. She recently served as a member of the RISE Women's Legal Center Board, the LEAF Tech-Facilitated Violence Sub-Committee, and the BC Law Institute Tort Law and AI Committee. She previously served as law clerk to the Honourable Madam Justice Rosalie Abella at the Supreme Court of Canada.

Heidi Tworek is the Director of the Centre for the Study of Democratic Institutions and a Canada Research Chair (Tier II) and Professor of Public Policy and History at the University of British Columbia. She has published the award-winning *News from Germany: The Competition to Control World Communications, 1900–1945* (Harvard University Press, 2019) and co-edited several volumes. She has published over fifty journal articles and book chapters as well as many policy reports on the history and policy of communications and media. She is Senior Fellow at the Centre for International Governance Innovation and a non-resident Fellow at the German Marshall Fund of the United States and the Canadian Global Affairs Institute.

Law, Technology, and Media

Series editor: Michael Geist

The *Law, Technology, and Media* series explores emerging technology law issues with an emphasis on a Canadian perspective. It is the first University of Ottawa Press series to be fully published under an open access licence.

Previous titles in *Law, Technology, and Media* Series

Yan Campagnolo, ed., *Artificial Intelligence's Impact on Legal: Challenges and Opportunities for the Ottawa Law Review*, 2025.

Pamela Robinson and Teresa Scassa, eds., *The Future of Open Data*, 2022.

Elizabeth Dubois and Florian Martin-Bariteau, eds., *Citizenship in a Connected Canada: A Research and Policy Agenda*, 2020.

Alana Maurushat, *Ethical Hacking*, 2019.

Derek McKee, Finn Makela, and Teresa Scassa, eds., *Law and the "Sharing Economy": Regulating Online Market Platforms*, 2018.

Karim Benyekhlef, Jane Bailey, Jacquelyn Burkell, and Fabie Gélinas, eds., *eAccess to Justice*, 2016.

Michael Geist, *Law, Privacy and Surveillance in Canada in the Post-Snowden Era*, 2015.

Jane Bailey and Valerie Steeves, *eGirls, eCitizens*, 2015.

Lucie Thibault and Jean Harvey, *Sport Policy in Canada*, 2013.

For a complete list of our titles, please visit:
www.Press.uOttawa.ca

www.ingramcontent.com/pod-product-compliance
Lightning Source LLC
Chambersburg PA
CBHW070942050326
40689CB00014B/3302